Global Issues in Tort Law

By

Julie A. Davies
Professor of Law
University of the Pacific,
McGeorge School of Law

Paul T. Hayden
Professor of Law and
Jacob J. Becker Fellow
Loyola Law School, Los Angeles

AMERICAN CASEBOOK SERIES®

Mat #40451381

610 Opperman Drive
St. Paul, MN 55123
1–800–313–9378

Printed in the United States of America

ISBN: 978–0–314–16759–0

To Tom, Rachel, and Daniel

J.A.D.

To Diane, always.

P.T.H.

Preface

This book is primarily intended for use as a supplement in domestic torts courses, but may also be used as the foundation for a stand-alone course in Global Issues in Tort Law.

We see at least three distinct facets of tort law that fit squarely within the "global issues" framework: (1) tort laws of other countries, which can be compared to the law in the United States; (2) domestic U.S. statutes that authorize tort claims in American courts either *by* aliens when international norms have been violated (such as the Alien Tort Statute), or *against* aliens or foreign governments (such as the Anti-Terrorism Act and the Foreign Sovereign Immunities Act); and (3) international treaties, such as the Warsaw Convention governing injuries aboard international air flights, to which the United States adheres.

Apart from the specifics of tort law, a focus on other legal systems provides a medium by which one can gain a window on different conceptions of law, the role of courts, both national and supranational, and of the role of important agreements among nations, such as the European Convention on Human Rights, that have profoundly affected domestic tort law. This rich selection of materials adds depth and perspective to our views of the U.S. tort system and the larger legal world.

Several chapters in this book, beginning with the comparative overview in Chapter 1, look at various aspects of the tort law of other countries. Why engage in such an inquiry with students who are focused, quite correctly, on learning the tort law of the United States? There are several reasons, beyond the fact that for many of us, it is simply interesting and important for its own sake to become more conversant in world affairs. First, looking at the way another legal system addresses a particular problem enlarges our own view of what is conceivable, what is perhaps feasible, as we struggle to reform and improve our own law. Second, a study of other nations' tort law leads to a deeper understanding of our own tort law, both in terms of its scope and in terms of the policy choices it reflects. By seeing many of the same issues in a completely different context, we are able to step outside of ourselves in a way that is not possible when we are limited to comparing approaches among the fifty U.S. states. Finally, developing even a passing familiarity with the major systems of tort law outside one's own can "facilitate communication on behalf of clients with one's counterparts and with officials in other countries, and enhance one's ability to be persuasive in international contexts." MARY ANN GLENDON, MICHAEL WALLACE GORDON & CHRISTOPHER OSAKWE, COMPARATIVE LEGAL TRADITIONS 9 (2d Ed. 1994). On this final point it should be noted that an American who is injured while working or vacationing in a foreign country may well be subject to the tort law of the foreign country – the site of the injury – rather than being able to sue under the tort law of the United States. *See, e.g., Sosa v. Alvarez-Machain*, 542 U.S. 692, 124 S.Ct. 2739, 159 L.Ed.2d 718 (2004) (citing cases, and noting that under traditional choice-of-law rules, a court adjudicating such a claim would "apply foreign law to determine the tortfeasor's liability").

We should stress that our goal in this modest endeavor is not to turn American law students into experts in foreign tort law. It takes more than one thin volume, and part of one law school course, to do that. But one can profit from the comparison with other countries' laws even without reaching the same level of expertise one attains with respect to one's own domestic law.

Of course, even a brief look at the global issues in today's tort law is incomplete without giving some attention to some topics beyond comparative law. As our coverage in this book reflects, we believe that several domestic legal structures are worth more than a passing glance for any 21st century lawyer-in-training. First, a series of U.S. statutes, some very old (such as the Alien Tort Statute, which dates to 1789) and some much newer (such as the Foreign Sovereign Immunities Act (1976), the Torture Victim Protection Act (1991), and the Anti-Terrorism Act (1991)), set forth substantive rules for suits involving alien plaintiffs suing to enforce customary international tort law, and suits against alien defendants, including foreign governments, for torts committed against Americans. Some of these laws authorize suits even where the acts took place outside the borders of the United States. This is domestic U.S. tort law, but with a distinctly international component.

Further, we spend a chapter on the Warsaw Convention, an international treaty promulgated in 1929 and ratified by this country five years later, that establishes substantive rules that provide the exclusive remedy for persons who are injured during international air travel. As you will see in Chapter 6, the Warsaw

Convention contains its own elements and damages restrictions that have been held by the U.S. Supreme Court to displace domestic tort law in this particular factual context. This, then, is international tort law that will be applied by any American lawyer handling cases for either plaintiffs or defendants that involve injuries in connection with international air transit.

We have ordered the chapters in this book to parallel the order of the presentation of issues found in many domestic torts casebooks. After the comparative overview in Chapter 1, the next three chapters (Chapters 2 though 4) relate most closely to intentional torts. Chapters 5 and 6 tie in most closely to the prima facie case of negligence, especially the elements of duty and breach. Chapters 7 through 10 parallel domestic issues about special or limited duties in negligence law. Chapter 11, on defective products, is of course connected to that subject in American law. Chapters 12 and 13 are on privacy and defamation torts. Chapter 14 is a bookend to Chapter 1, making some explicit connections between substantive tort law and procedural rules.

That being said, we have tried to design this book for maximum flexibility. You need not cover the entire book, or study chapters at any particular point in a domestic torts course, to enhance your learning experience.

The world is getting ever smaller. More and more professors and students are interested in looking outside our national borders for guidance and perspective as we think of ways to improve our own legal structures. And more and more lawyers are faced with issues that cross national borders, simply because their clients are no longer confined to this country.

We hope you profit from this broadened perspective, as we have.

Acknowledgments

We would like to thank the many people who have helped us with this book. Series editor Franklin Gevurtz conceived the Global Issues concept. We benefitted greatly from the insights of our colleagues in Torts who attended the Pacific McGeorge Workshop on Globalizing the Law School Curriculum: Rogelio Lasso, Lawrence Levine, Mathias Reimann, Anthony Sebok, Ernest Weinreb, and Ellen Wertheimer. Louis Higgins and Roxy Birkel, from Thomson West, demonstrated patience and support at every turn. We received help with translations from Clemence George (French) and Sabine Schlemmer-Schulte (German). Sharleen Jackson,Pacific McGeorge, provided invaluable secretarial help.

Julie would like to thank her research assistants Brad Farrar, Matt Carlson, Charmaine Lee, Andrew McClelland, Andalyn Pace, and James Sunkenberg, who researched areas of foreign law with enthusiasm and dedication. Thanks also to Librarians Dragomir Cosanici and Jack Schroeder, and to Library Assistants Sandra Burdi and Deborah Waggershauser for an unending stream of books and technical support. I appreciate the support of Deans Elizabeth Rinsdkopf Parker and Christine Manolakas. In addition, I have benefitted from discussion and correspondence with Robert Leflar, Larry Levine, Thomas Main, Ángel Oquendo, John Sims, and Kojo Yelpaala.

Paul would like to thank Dan Dobbs, Ellen Bublick and David Glazier for helpful suggestions on topics and materials. Thanks also to attendees at a workshop I conducted on these materials at Loyola Law School, Los Angeles. Special thanks to my friends in Italy, most notably Chiara Giovannucci Orlandi (University of Bologna) and Domenico Borghese (University of Modena), and my colleague Edith Friedler, who are most responsible for sparking and maintaining my interest in comparative and international law. I have benefitted from several years' worth of good feedback and good feelings from my students in comparative tort law in the Loyola-Brooklyn summer program at the University of Bologna. Thanks to my dean, David W. Burcham, for his consistent support for my work. And last but not least, I am always indebted to my wife Diane and to my daughters, without whose support and understanding I would get nothing done.

Portions of the following copyrighted works are reprinted by permission:

Modibo Ocran, Justice, The Clash of Legal Cultures: The Treatment of Indigenous Law in Colonial and Post-Colonial Africa, 39 Akron L. Rev. 465 (2006).

Martin Shapiro, Courts, A Comparative and Political Analysis (1981). © 1981 by the University of Chicago.

Miguel Martín-Casals, Cass. Ass. Pleniere, 13 deciembre 2002, Bull. Civ.AP, No.3, J.C.P.G2003 II, 10010: Parental Liability for the Acts of Their Children, 12 Eur.Rev. of Private L. 691 (2004). Reprinted with the permission of Kluwer Law International.

Christian Von Bar, The Common European Law of Torts (2000). Reprinted with permission of Oxford University Press.

Willem H. van Boom, Children as Tortfeasors Under Dutch Law, in Children in Tort Law, Part I: Children as Tortfeasors 293 (Miguel Martín Casals, ed., 2006). Reprinted with permission of Springer-Verlag/Wien.

Robert B Leflar, Informed Consent and Patients' Rights in Japan, 33 Hous. L. Rev. 1 (1996).

Edward A. Tomlinson, The French Experience with Duty to Rescue: A Dubious Case for Criminal Enforcement, 20 N.Y.L.Sch. J. Int'l & Comp. L. 451 (2000).

Alberto Cadoppi, Failure to Rescue and the Continental Criminal Law, in The Duty to Rescue: The Jurisprudence of Aid (Michael A. Menlowe & Alex McCall Smith, eds., 1993).

John Henry Merryman & Rogelio Pérez-Perdomo, The Civil Law Tradition, An Introduction to the Legal Systems of Europe and Latin America (3d ed. 2007). Copyright © 2007 by the Board of Trustees of the Leland Stanford Jr. University.

James E. Pfander, Government Accountability in Europe: A Comparative Assessment, 35 Geo. Wash. Int'l L. Rev. 611 (2003). © 2003 The George Washington International Law Review.

Claudio Grossman, Suing the Sovereign from the Latin American Perspective, 35 Geo. Wash. Int'l L. Rev. 653 (2003). © 2003 The George Washington International Law Review.

Ángel R. Oquendo, Latin American Law (2006). Reprinted with permission of Foundation Press.

Mathias Reimann, Liability for Defective Products at the Beginning of the Twenty-First Century: Emergence of a Worldwide Standard?, 51 Am. J. Comp. L. 751 (2003).

Hans Claudius Taschner, Harmonization of Products Liability Law in the European Community, 34 Tex. Int'l L. J. 21 (1999). As originally published in the Texas International Law Journal. Reprinted with permission of the author.

James A. Henderson and Aaron D. Twerski, What Europe, Japan, and other Countries Can Learn From the New American Restatement of Products Liability, 34 Tex. Int'l L. J. 1 (1999). As originally published in the Texas International Law Journal. Reprinted with permission of the authors.

Jane Stapleton, Products Liability in the United Kingdom: The Myths of Reform, 34 Tex. Int'l L. J. 45 (1999). As originally published in the Texas International Law Journal. Reprinted with permission of the author.

Walter van Gerven, Jeremy Lever & Pierre Larouche, Cases, Materials and Text on National, Supranational and International Tort Law (2000). Reprinted with permission of Hart Publishing Co.

Geraint Howells and Thomas Wilhelmsson, EC and US Approaches to Consumer Protection – Should the Gap Be Bridged?, 17 Yearbook of European Law 207 (1997). Reprinted with permission of Oxford University Press.

Robert L. Rabin, Keynote Paper: Reassessing Regulatory Compliance in Symposium, Regulatory Compliance as a Defense to Product Liability, 88 Geo. L. J. 1 (2001). Reprinted with permission of the publisher, Georgetown Law Journal © 2000.

Klaus Vieweg, The Law of Torts in Introduction to German Law (Werner F. Ebke & Matthew W. Finken, eds., 1996). Reprinted with permission of Kluwer Law International.

Guy Vassall-Adams, A Resounding Victory for Newspapers, Times Online, October 11, 2006. www.timesonline.CO.UK/td/comment/article668356.ece. Reprinted with permission of the author.

Heather Maly, Publish at Your Own Risk or Don't Publish at All: Forum Shopping Trends in Libel Litigation Leave the First Amendment Un-Guaranteed, 14 J.L.& Pol'y 883 (2006).

Esther Chang, Fitting a Square Peg Into a Round Hole? Imposing Informed Consent and Post-Trial Obligations on United States Sponsored Clinical Trials in Developing Countries, 11 S.Cal. Interdisc. L.J.339 (2001-2002).

Global Issues Series

Series Editor, Franklin A. Gevurtz

Titles Available Now

Global Issues in Civil Procedure by Thomas Main, University of the Pacific, McGeorge School of Law
ISBN 978–0–314–15978–6

Global Issues in Constitutional Law by Brian K. Landsberg, University of the Pacific, McGeorge School of Law and Leslie Gielow Jacobs, University of the Pacific, McGeorge School of Law
ISBN 978–0–314–17608–0

Global Issues in Contract Law by John A. Spanogle, Jr., George Washington University, Michael P. Malloy, University of the Pacific, McGeorge School of Law, Louis F. Del Duca, Pennsylvania State University, Keith A. Rowley, University of Nevada, Las Vegas, and Andrea K. Bjorklund, University of California, Davis
ISBN 978–0–314–16755–2

Global Issues in Corporate Law by Franklin A. Gevurtz, University of the Pacific, McGeorge School of Law
ISBN 978–0–314–15977–9

Global Issues in Criminal Law by Linda Carter, University of the Pacific, McGeorge School of Law, Christopher L. Blakesley, University of Nevada, Las Vegas and Peter Henning, Wayne State University
ISBN 978–0–314–15997–7

Global Issues in Employment Discrimination Law by Samuel Estreicher, New York University School of Law and Brian K. Landsberg, University of the Pacific, McGeorge School of Law
ISBN 978–0–314–17607–3

Global Issues in Employment Law by Samuel Estreicher, New York University School of Law and Miriam A. Cherry, University of the Pacific, McGeorge School of Law
ISBN 978–0–314–17952–4

Global Issues in Family Law by Ann Laquer Estin, University of Iowa College of Law and Barbara Stark, Hofstra University School of Law
ISBN 978–0–314–17954–8

Global Issues in Labor Law by Samuel Estreicher, New York University School of Law
ISBN 978–0–314–17163–4

Global Issues in Legal Ethics by James E. Moliterno, College of William & Mary, Marshall-Wythe School of Law and George Harris, University of the Pacific, McGeorge School of Law
ISBN 978–0–314–16935–8

Global Issues in Property Law by John G. Sprankling, University of the Pacific, McGeorge School of Law, Raymond R. Coletta, University of the Pacific, McGeorge School of Law, and M.C. Mirow, Florida International University College of Law
ISBN 978–0–314–16729–3

Global Issues in Tort Law by Julie A. Davies, University of the Pacific, McGeorge School of Law and Paul T. Hayden, Loyola Law School, Los Angeles
ISBN 978–0–314–16759–0

Summary of Contents

*

Table of Contents

Page

Page

*

Table of Cases

The principal cases are in bold type. Cases cited or discussed in the text are roman type. References are to pages. Cases cited in principal cases and within other quoted materials are not included.

Global Issues in Tort Law

*

Chapter 1

GLOBAL TORTS: COMPARING THE MAJOR SYSTEMS

Tort law deals with "conduct that amounts to a legal wrong and that causes harm for which courts will impose civil liability. . . . The essence of tort is the defendant's potential for civil liability to the victim for harmful wrongdoing and correspondingly the victim's potential for compensation or other relief." 1 DAN B. DOBBS, THE LAW OF TORTS § 1, at 1 (2001).

This succinct definition is true not only in the United States, but in other countries as well, although other legal systems may use different terminology to cover the same ground. In particular, civil law countries most often use the term *delict* rather than *tort*. The word *tort* comes from the Latin *tortus*, meaning twisted or tortuous. It entered our lexicon from medieval *Law-French*, the language that was spoken for centuries in English courts. The word *delict* comes from the Latin *delictum*, meaning a lapse, a mistake, or an offense. As a leading comparativist scholar has pointed out after noting this history, "There is no practical reason why current English legal terminology calls this field the law of torts or tort law, and not the 'law of delict.'" 1 CHRISTIAN VON BAR, THE COMMON EUROPEAN LAW OF TORTS 7 (1998). The law of *delict* is itself a part of a larger civil-code legal framework generally called the *law of obligations*, which includes contract law as well. For the sake of simplicity, in this book we will typically use the English and American terminology and speak of *torts* and *tort law*.

There are many ways to compare how the major world legal systems address torts. Perhaps the most useful, and usual, is to compare *common law* systems (those based on case law, derived from English law, and followed in the old English commonwealth countries, including the United States, Canada, New Zealand, India, Singapore, Australia, Israel, Nigeria, Tanzania, and Kenya, among others) and *civil law* systems (those based on Codes, and followed in continental Europe, South and Central America and much of Asia and Africa). We can also draw a finer distinction, between common law systems and the two major civil law tort schemes, that of Germany and that of France, on which most other civil-law countries (with some notable exceptions, such as the Nordic countries and some Islamic countries) base their substantive tort law. Yet another useful comparison for us is to compare the United States with the rest of the world.

In several upcoming chapters in this book, we compare particular substantive tort law doctrines along one or more of these matrices. As we will see, sometimes various national approaches are quite similar substantively; at other times we see rather stark differences.

In this Chapter, we present a simplified introductory overview of the world's most important tort law systems, looking broadly at both the substantive law itself and the procedural systems and social contexts in which that law resides.

The substantive tort law of the United States is largely state common law, which means that one cannot really speak of "American" tort law at all – there are potentially as many different current doctrinal approaches to some particular legal problem as there are states. But setting that very real caveat aside, we can say that the general substantive tort law applied in the United States bears a close resemblance to the tort law applied in other common-law countries.

Tort law has never been viewed by common law courts as a truly "unified" area of law, conceptually or doctrinally, leading many scholars to refer to our common-law scheme somewhat pejoratively as a "pigeonhole" approach. This means that rather than having a law of *tort* we perhaps more properly have a law of *torts* – a number of distinct causes of action, each with its own elements. This is most obviously seen in the intentional torts (battery, assault, false imprisonment, trespass, and so on). The closest we come to a "unified" general tort claim is in negligence, but even there our courts have created particularized negligence-based torts (such as negligent infliction of emotional distress and negligent misrepresentation, for example) that have special elements beyond the familiar duty, breach, causation, scope of risk, and damage requirements.

Nations outside the common-law world view tort law very differently. While each country has its own unique approach, of course, in broad brush the two most important models for the world's substantive tort law have come from France, with its 1803-vintage Code Napoleon, and Germany, whose 1900 Civil Code has proved equally, if not more, influential on the rest of the world. In part the influence of these two systems may be explained by colonialism; colonizers often impose their legal systems on the colonized, and even after colonies gain independence they frequently maintain a good deal of the former colonizer's law. Common language is also part of the explanation – other German-speaking countries, for example, have often derived their substantive tort law code provisions in significant part from the German Civil Code. And finally, these two great civil-law codes have been influential in other countries simply because they represent well-thought-out, theoretically-sound legal structures, a phenomenon that may explain how Japan's tort law came to based on the German code. Few nations have adopted *in toto* a substantive set of rules from another country, of course; most have adapted portions of one scheme or another (or portions of *each* scheme) into a unique set of tort code provisions. But it remains true that the three foundational building blocks of substantive tort law are England, for the common-law world, and Germany and France for the civil-law world. See, e.g., WALTER VAN GERVEN, JEREMY LEVER & PIERRE LAROUCHE, CASES, MATERIALS AND TEXT ON NATIONAL, SUPRANATIONAL AND INTERNATIONAL TORT LAW 3-8 (2000).

The French Civil Code contains just five articles covering tort law. The first general clause, Article 1382, states simply:

> Any person's act which causes damage to another requires the one by whose fault it occurred to compensate for the damage.[1]

Article 1383 further amplifies that rather simple and brief formulation:

---

[1]Translated by Clemence George.

> Everyone is responsible for the damage he causes not only by his intentional act, but also by his negligent conduct or by his imprudence.[2]

As interpreted by courts over the last two centuries, these two general tort clauses create a basic, three-element claim: The plaintiff must prove that the plaintiff suffered **damage** (*dommage*), **caused by** defendant's **fault** (*faute*).

A third key provision in the French Civil Code is Article 1384(1), which provides:

> A person is liable not only for the damages he causes by his own act, but also for that which is caused by the acts of persons for whom he is responsible, or by things which are in his custody.[3]

While not facially evident, this Article has been interpreted by courts since 1930 to authorize a *strict liability* claim – one not based on fault at all – against someone who is the *gardien* of either a person or a thing who has caused the plaintiff's injury. We see this peculiar provision in more detail in Chapter 5.

The German Civil Code reflects a very different theoretical approach. Rather than beginning from the presumption that any faulty act that causes damage should be actionable, the German tort law begins by defining particular interests that the law protects against invasion. To this end, the German Civil Code sets out three general *heads* or *headings* of tort liability, augmented by a number of specific Code provisions (usually called paragraphs) that address particular issues, ranging from the wrongfulness of fraudulently inducing a woman to agree to unlawful cohabitation (para. 825), to the liability of joint tortfeasors (para. 830), to the duty to compensate a person for damage done by an animal under one's control (paras. 833-34), to the liability of children and those who have a duty to supervise them (paras. 828-29 & 832). In total there are 30 tort provisions in the German Civil Code. The code also contains a number of provisions of general application, which may be applicable to a tort action. For example, paragraph 249 states the rule that a person who is bound to make compensation under the code "must restore the situation which would exist if

---

[2]Translated in Legifrance (trans. Georges Rouhette & Anne Barton).

[3]Id.

the circumstance making him liable to compensate had not occurred."

Civil Code paragraph 823(1) is the logical starting point. It provides:

> A person who, intentionally or negligently, and unlawfully injures the life, body, health, liberty, ownership or any other right of another person is bound to compensate him for any damage arising therefrom.[4]

This key provision thus delimits the interests that tort law will protect: life, body, health, liberty (sometimes translated as "freedom," and ownership (or "property") – plus the flexible "any other right," which has been construed by the courts to apply only to "absolute" rights, those which may apply to anyone and against anyone. The Code itself does not define the coverage of these protected interests; this is left to court adjudication. If an asserted interest is found not to be among those listed, then there is no recovery under section 823. As interpreted by courts, paragraph 823(1) requires proof of four elements: (1) that the defendant **invaded a listed, protected interest** of the plaintiff, (2) acted with **fault** (either willfulness or negligence), and (3) **caused** (4) **harm**.

Paragraph 823(2) sets forth the second head of liability under German tort law, relating to violating a statute – analogous to the common law of "negligence per se." That section provides:

> The same obligation attaches to a person who violates a statutory provision aimed at the protection of others. If according to the substance of the statute violation is possible even without fault, the duty to make compensation accrues only if some fault may be imputed to the wrongdoer.[5]

Note that this section also requires fault for liability to attach where the tortfeasor's act violates an applicable statute.

---

[4]Translated in Klaus Vieweg, *The Law of Torts*, in INTRODUCTION TO GERMAN LAW (Werner F. Ebke & Matthew W. Finkin eds., 1996).

[5]Translated by Sabine Schlemmer- Schulte.

Finally, the third and final general head of liability under German tort law appears in paragraph 826, which states:

> A person who intentionally causes injury to another in a manner *contra bonos mores* is under an obligation to compensate the other for the damage.[6]

The Latin phrase *contra bonos mores* translates into English as "against good morals." As with other operative terms in the German Civil Code, it is not defined in the code itself. Courts have interpreted it consistently to mean "the sense of propriety of all good and right-thinking members of society." BASIL S. MARKESINIS & HANS UNBERATH, THE GERMAN LAW OF TORTS: A COMPARATIVE TREATISE 890 (4th Ed. 2002). Because it is an independent ground of liability, intentional acts that harm others in this "immoral" way may be actionable even without reference to whether one of the protected interests listed in Code paragraph 823(1) was invaded, or whether a statutory provision under paragraph 823(2) was violated. Paragraph 826, then, requires a plaintiff to prove that: (1) the defendant acted **intentionally** (2) in a manner that can be said to be ***contra bonos mores*** and which (3) **caused** (4) **harm**.

Many scholars have opined that substantively speaking, the common law approach and the German approach to torts have the most in common, whereas the French seems most different. Both the common law and German systems apply significant limitations on recovery – the common law nations through both the "pigeonhole" elements approach and the negligence elements of duty and scope of risk (more commonly called "*proximate cause*"), the Germans primarily through the list of protected interests found in Civil Code paragraph 823(1). France, by comparison, has no "pigeonhole" torts, no limitations based on duty, no developed proximate cause concept, and no *a priori* set of protected interests.

The role of case law. As must be clear even from this brief overview, case law – the body of judicial opinions – plays a crucial role in all systems. In the common law, case law *is* law. Lower courts are bound to follow the precedents set by higher courts. In tort law particularly, such things as the required elements of tort claims and defenses are usually set forth *only* in case law. Civil law countries view the *code provisions* as the operative law, but

---

[6]Translated by Sabine Schlemmer- Schulte.

case law is needed to interpret these provisions and to fill in any gaps in the code in order to decide concrete cases. Quite obviously, courts have much work to do in any country whose tort law is based on the French Civil Code, since that code is so general and open-ended. But even in Germany and the countries that follow its more detailed code approach, courts play an indispensable role in defining operative terms and deciding when particular provisions can apply. While it is true that in civil law countries, courts are not legally bound to follow precedent, in practice courts are aware of prior opinions and value consistency. As a leading treatise puts it, "In practice a judgment of the [French] Court of Cassation or of the Bundesgerichtshof [high court] in Germany today can count on being followed by lower courts just as much as a judgment of an appeal court in England or in the United States." KONRAD ZWEIGERT & HEIN KOTZ, AN INTRODUCTION TO COMPARATIVE LAW 262 (Tony Weir trans., 3d Ed. 1998).

This raises the issue of the style of judicial opinions, a topic worth raising here if only as a way to explain what appears (and does not appear) in subsequent chapters of this book. American law students are familiar with the usual style of U.S. court opinions. Much like their English counterparts, American judges often write lengthy, detailed opinions that contain long explanations of the applicable facts and copious citations to case law. One would expect no less from courts in common law systems, where the case decisions make up part – often a large part – of the law itself. French courts provide the most dramatic contrasts to this Anglo-American style. French judicial opinions are very short, often containing the briefest summary of the facts and only citations to the applicable Code provision – no citation at all to prior judicial opinions, even if the advocates and the court had utilized those opinions prior to the final decision's publication. This renders the reasoning of particular judicial opinions elusive at best. German judicial opinions fall somewhere in between the detail of the common law courts and the generality of the French. German opinions tend to be succinct, often summarizing facts in a rather cursory way, but the judges do cite and discuss, albeit rather abstractly, prior case law and scholarly writings to interpret the applicable Code paragraphs. Indeed, German judges place much more reliance on scholarly academic writing than do judges in the U.S. or England.

In short, then, while case law is important in understanding what tort law is, and means, in virtually all countries of the world, the very style of opinion writing may make case law from other countries – especially France and its followers – difficult to understand and less useful to American students than it would be if it were written in the more familiar Anglo-American style.

Interplay with criminal law. Another important distinction between civil law and common law tort schemes is in the former's more expanded view of the role of criminal law as a compensation method for personal injuries. As one scholar puts it, "the force of criminal law as an indicator of wrongful behaviour is much stronger in the rather general law of delict than in the common law of torts with its array of intentional wrongs." Gerhard Wagner, *Comparative Tort Law*, in THE OXFORD HANDBOOK OF COMPARATIVE LAW 1010 (Mathias Reimann & Reinhard Zimmerman eds., 2006). We can see this phenomenon reflected in the fact that more kinds of conduct that Americans would treat only as torts being treated as crimes in other countries – such as the duty to rescue described in Chapter 7. We also see that in many civil law countries (especially France) that a different structure of criminal law and procedure may obviate the need for a separate tort claim. Differences exist here between American courts and other common-law countries, as well. English criminal courts have had the power for decades to award compensatory damages for injuries caused by the defendant's criminal act. *Id.* at 1011.

The most dramatic blurring of the distinction between criminal and tort liability occurs in France and its sister systems, where the criminal procedure law allows an injured crime victim to join a criminal prosecution of the defendant/tortfeasor as a so-called *partie civile*, for the purpose of obtaining damages in the criminal proceeding. See RAYMOND YOUNGS, ENGLISH, FRENCH & GERMAN COMPARATIVE LAW 219 (1998). "For all practical purposes, the crimes of the *Code penal* are thereby converted into delicts. As such, they provide firm bases for the claims of victims." Wagner, *supra*, at 1011. Indeed, where the tort is also a crime the civil court is barred from proceeding until the criminal court has settled the issues pertaining to the tortfeasor's legal responsibilities. Since, as noted above, more acts are considered crimes in these countries than in the United States, this means that tort liability is often adjudicated by *criminal* courts in other countries. *Id.* at 1012.

Procedural differences. One cannot understand tort law without some grasp of the procedural schemes in which it sits. In common law countries, the centerpiece of litigation is the trial, a somewhat theatrical end-point at which all the live witnesses appear, documents are introduced into evidence, and the lawyers make arguments in open court. Civil law countries do not have such a centerpiece. Instead, litigation takes the form of a series of often-short hearings at which witnesses testify and documents are introduced. This "no trial" difference either reflects or produces (depending on your point of view) a rather stark difference in the way the common-law and civil-law systems define the role of lawyers and judges. In common-law systems, lawyers take the main role in determining which witnesses to call, which questions to ask, and what documentary evidence to place before the trier of fact. Judges in this system act more as referees or umpires than active participants in evidence-gathering and presentation. In civil-law countries, the judges take a far more active role, lessening the role of counsel. Judges, not lawyers, make the decision about which witnesses to hear, and often do the questioning themselves after receiving suggestions from counsel. The scope of appellate review is yet another distinction. In common-law countries the appeals process is circumscribed by the need to give deference to the fact-finding that occurred during the trial, but no such need – and thus no such limitation – is found in the civil law. Thus in civil-law countries appellate courts are free to re-examine many matters, including facts, *de novo*.

Judges in common-law countries are typically drawn from the ranks of practicing lawyers. In civil-law countries, by contrast, judges are usually educated for that particular role and often lack any experience in practice.

Perhaps the starkest procedural distinctions are found between the United States and the rest of the world, including the rest of the common-law world. The number one difference, without a doubt, is that only the United States uses juries in civil cases – as guaranteed to litigants in federal court by the Seventh Amendment to the Constitution and to those in state court by each state Constitution. In all other countries, the judge is the sole trier of fact and decisionmaker, with only a few narrow exceptions (such as for defamation cases in England). This unique feature of American litigation has a ripple effect on a number of other procedural features. See, e.g., Oscar G. Chase, *American "Exceptionalism" and Comparative Procedure*, 50 AM. J. COMP. L. 277 (2002). Litigation in the U.S. is said to be more adversarial than in other countries; specifically "the American version of the adversary system generally affords the advocates far more latitude in the form and style of the case's presentation than in other common-law systems." Geoffrey C. Hazard Jr., *From Whom No Secrets Are Hid*, 76 TEX. L. REV. 1665, 1674 (1998). American pre-trial discovery is also far more liberal than any other common-law country, and of course far more so than in civil-law countries where the judges closely control information gathering. *Id.* Rules of evidence for American courts are far more detailed and important, given the potential presence of a lay jury, than in any other country.

Who pays for litigation. In the United States, we follow what is grandly called the *American Rule*, pursuant to which each party pays its own lawyer's fees, win or lose. It is true that federal and state statutes may provide for a fee recovery by the prevailing plaintiff in many situations, most notably in civil rights cases. But where statutory authorization for fee-shifting does not exist, as it will not in most common-law tort cases, the American rule means that the prevailing defendant will not be able to recover his fees from the losing plaintiff in our country – and even the prevailing plaintiff will have to bear his or her own attorney's fees and litigation costs. By contrast, the rest of the world follows the *English Rule*, under which the loser must pay the winner's costs and attorney's fees. This is a two-way fee-shifting rule, meaning that a prevailing defendant can obtain its attorney's fees from the losing plaintiff. While certain exceptions exist in a number of countries, there can be little doubt that this difference in who pays for litigation produces a different set of incentives for litigants and their lawyers.

How can personal-injury plaintiffs afford to pay for their lawyers under the American Rule? The usual answer is the contingency fee, which is usually a combination of a true contingent fee (payment of any fee being contingent on obtaining a settlement or a judgment) and a percentage fee (the lawyer taking as payment a percentage of the recovery, usually one-third). The contingency fee is not allowed in most other countries. It is considered an unethical and improper professional practice that places the lawyer's interests in conflict with those of the client. See W. Kent Davis, *The International View of Attorney Fees in Civil Suits*, 16 ARIZ. J. INT'L & COMP. L. 361 (1999).

At first glance, both the English "loser pays" rule and the restriction or outright ban on contingency fees could create a substantial access-to-courts problem. Countries outside the United States have developed various measures to address this, such as government legal aid for low-income persons (used extensively in both England and in many civil law countries), widespread availability of legal expense insurance, and mandatory pro bono work by lawyers. *Id.*; see also Virginia G.

Maurer, *Attorney Fee Arrangements: The U.S. and Western European Perspectives*, 19 NW. J. INT'L L. & BUS. 272 (1999).

Damages. While all countries see the proper measure of compensatory damages as that amount of money that will put the plaintiff back into the position he or she would have been in but for the injury, we can identify a number of differences in the way damages are determined and paid, and in the kind of damages that may be awarded in a torts suit. In the United States, England and the other common-law countries, a litigant who proves a tort claim may recover past and future damages that can be shown to flow from the defendant's tortious conduct. These sums are typically paid out as a single lump sum; that is, the winning plaintiff gets a judgment from the court at the end of the trial that orders the defendant to pay the plaintiff a particular sum, representing both past and future damages as proved at trial. An English statute, the Damages Act of 1996, now allows a court to award damages in the form of periodic payments rather than as a lump sum, if all parties consent.

While lump-sum payments are probably the most common kind even in civil law countries, courts in many of those countries routinely award damages in the form of periodic payments (also called "annunities" or "rent"), especially where the plaintiff has suffered a permanent, continuing injury. See ULRICH MAGNUS (ED.), UNIFICATION OF TORT LAW: DAMAGES 204 (2001). France and the Netherlands allow judges the discretion to award damages as periodic payments in any torts case. *Id.* A periodic-payment scheme allows for the adjustment of the plaintiff's damages up or down, depending on actual experience – for example, where the plaintiff's injury gets worse than was predicted, the defendant might be ordered to pay additional money. BASIL MARKESINIS, MICHAEL COESTER, GUIDO ALPA & AUGUSTUS ULLSTEIN, COMPENSATION FOR PERSONAL INJURY IN ENGLISH, GERMAN AND ITALIAN LAW 37-38 (2005).

For the most part the classes of damages available in tort actions for personal injury are similar from nation to nation, although for reasons explored more fully below, the size of damages awards tends to be larger in the U.S. than in other countries. All countries view lost wages and earning capacity, and medical expenses (to the extent they are not compensated through non-tort social security systems) as compensable damages in a tort suit. And all countries allow recovery for some form of pain and suffering, which is often called "non-material" damage. In Germany such damage is specifically authorized by Civil Code paragraph 847(1). France divides this non-material measure of damages (called *dommage moral*) into three categories: compensation for physical suffering; compensation for "aesthetic prejudice," which is the emotional distress the plaintiff suffers from being disfigured; and compensation for "loss of amenity," which is a diminution of the quality of life due to an inability to do certain kinds of activities. YOUNGS, *supra*, at 329. Italian law also allows for compensation for pain and suffering awards, called *danno morale*, or damage to the moral sphere, although under a strict interpretation of its Civil Code, it may be awarded only where the defendant's act violates a criminal provision. MARKESINIS, ET AL., COMPENSATION FOR PERSONAL INJURY, *supra*, at 91-92.

But we see a major difference between nations on one particular class of damages: punitive or exemplary damages. In the common law countries, where the defendant's conduct is proved to be willful or wanton the plaintiff may also be entitled to an award of such damages, which are not designed to compensate, but rather to punish. By contrast, virtually all civil law countries disallow punitive damages in tort cases, seeing such damages as more suited to criminal processes.

Yet another difference is in how damages are computed. In the United States, the computation of damages is left to the jury's discretion in light of the evidence. The jury is given very little (if any) guidance on what kinds of damages have been awarded in similar cases. When a judge is determining the damages, as will be true in the rest of the world, the judge can of course look to similar cases in setting the amount of damages. See, e.g., *Ward v. James*, [1966] Q.B. 273 (C.A.) (setting forth the need for judges to do just that, in the case that effectively sounded the death knell for civil jury trials in England). In England, the level of tort damages awards is now set by guidelines determined by the Court of Appeal. MARKESINIS, ET AL., COMPENSATION FOR PERSONAL INJURY, *supra*, at 16. German courts find explicit guidance in non-statutory compilations of similar damages awards, and rely heavily on prior similar cases in computing damages. *Id.* at 18, 67; see also ANDREW MCCLURG, ADEM KOYUNCU & LUIS EDUARDO SPROVIERI, PRACTICAL GLOBAL TORT LITIGATION 178 (2007). A number of jurisdictions, both common law (New South Wales, Australia, for example) and civil law (such as France and Italy) have gone a step further and have developed specific "schedules" or "point systems" for determining the proper amount of damages for particular kinds of injuries, or classes of injuries. See, e.g., Stephen D. Sugarman, *A Comparative Law Look at Pain and*

Suffering Awards, 55 DEPAUL L. REV. 399, 423 (2006) (discussing Australia); Anthony J. Sebok, *Translating the Immeasurable: Thinking About Pain and Suffering Comparatively*, 55 DEPAUL L. REV. 379, 389 (2006) (discussing France and Italy, among others).

Role of tort law. In closing, perhaps the greatest difference between the tort law of the United States and that of other industrialized nations is the very role of tort law itself in the wider scheme of compensation for injuries.

While any brief synopsis on this point is surely over-simplified, the short story is this: injured plaintiffs in the U.S. have fewer government-supported options for compensation for injuries than exist in most other industrialized countries. For example, the United States does not provide any national health insurance for injured persons, or any general law directing employers to continue to pay the wages of injured workers, unless they are injured on the job within the scope of their employment (and thus covered under workers' compensation). This necessarily means that many injured persons in the United States will *need* to use tort law to gain compensation from a defendant for such basic things as lost wages and medical care.

The contrast with the rest of the industrialized world (including the rest of the common law world) could hardly be more stark. Virtually all other countries have extensive "social security" systems that provide medical care at very low, or no, cost. And many other countries have laws that compel employers to continue to pay the wages of workers who are injured, even where the injury is unconnected to the job. In many countries the national health insurer and the employer are given the right to sue the tortfeasor directly to recoup these expenditures. But the injured person either may not need to sue to pay for these expenses, or may not be allowed to sue, on the theory that they have not actually been incurred by the injured person at all. To the extent that any medical or lost-earning-capacity losses are not compensated by the government (or by an insurer) or by the employer, the plaintiff can collect them directly from the tortfeasor in a tort suit. In Germany, for example, a person unable to work due to an injury, even not job-related, is entitled by law to have his wages fully paid by the employer for the first six weeks that he cannot work. The employer is granted the option to sue the tortfeasor to recover this money. MARKESINIS, ET AL., COMPENSATION FOR PERSONAL INJURY, *supra*, at 35. In Italy, if an injury is treatable in a domestic hospital – which treatment is fully paid for by the national health service – the injured person cannot claim any medical expenses from the tortfeasor who caused the injury, since the plaintiff in fact has suffered no loss. *Id.* at 170. In France, all people "living lawfully" there "enjoy some social protection against consequences of personal injury and illness"; any publicly-funded agency that provides treatment to an injured person may recoup its costs from the tortfeasor. Suzanne Carval, *The Impact of Social Security Law on Tort Law in France*, in THE IMPACT OF SOCIAL SECURITY LAW ON TORT LAW 74, 76, 79 (Ulrich Magnus ed., 2003).

While these social security payments do not by all accounts *fully* compensate injured persons (for example, pain and suffering is not paid by any social security system), it is clear that tort law does not have the primary role in compensating injured plaintiffs in other countries that it does in the United States. In Germany, for example, "the development of social security systems and diverse forms of private insurance has led to a situation in which victims are less dependent on tort law for the compaensation of pecuniary loss due to personal injury." Jorg Fedtke & Ulrich Magnus, *The Impact of Social Security Law on Tort Law in Germany*, in THE IMPACT OF SOCIAL SECURITY LAW ON TORT LAW 90 (Ulrich Magnus ed., 2003). Even in our own sister nation, England, the amount of money paid to accident victims by the social security system "greatly exceeds the total damages paid by the tort system. Tort is very much the junior partner of the social security system." Richard Lewis, *The Impact of Social Security Law on Private Tort Law in England and Wales*, in THE IMPACT OF SOCIAL SECURITY LAW ON TORT LAW 67 (Ulrich Magnus ed., 2003).

With this perspective in mind, we must remain cautious about calling for the adoption of some particular foreign legal doctrine, whether it be "loser pays," the elimination of punitive damages, or wholesale restrictions on contingency fees, since such foreign laws exist in an entirely different social and economic context than we have here.

Still, we can learn a great deal from how other countries deal with the problem of personal injuries through their tort doctrines. Broadening our perspective beyond our national borders helps us both to understand more deeply our own law, and to formulate ideas for reform and improvement.

REFERENCES

Several books describe and compare the major systems in greater detail than space has allowed us here. Noteworthy sources include the following:

MARY ANN GLENDON, MICHAEL WALLACE GORDON & CHRISTOPHER OSAKWE, COMPARATIVE LEGAL TRADITIONS (2d Ed. 1994).

H. PATRICK GLENN, LEGAL TRADITIONS OF THE WORLD (2000).

BASIL S. MARKESINIS, MICHAEL COESTER, GUIDO ALPA & AUGUSTUS ULLSTEIN, COMPENSATION FOR PERSONAL INJURY IN ENGLISH, GERMAN AND ITALIAN LAW: A COMPARATIVE OUTLINE (2005).

BASIL S. MARKESINIS & HANNES UNBERATH, THE GERMAN LAW OF TORTS: A COMPARATIVE TREATISE (4th Ed. 2002).

WALTER VAN GERVEN, JEREMY LEVER & PIERRE LAROUCHE, CASES, MATERIALS AND TEXT ON NATIONAL, SUPRANATIONAL AND INTERNATIONAL TORT LAW (2000).

CHRISTIAN VON BAR, THE COMMON EUROPEAN LAW OF TORTS (1998) (two-volume treatise).

Gerhard Wagner, *Comparative Tort Law*, in THE OXFORD HANDBOOK OF COMPARATIVE LAW 1003, 1013-34 (Mathias Reimann & Reinhard Zimmerman eds., 2006).

RAYMOND YOUNGS, ENGLISH, FRENCH & GERMAN COMPARATIVE LAW (1998).

KONRAD ZWEIGERT & HEIN KOTZ, AN INTRODUCTION TO COMPARATIVE LAW (Tony Weir trans., 3d Ed. 1998).

Chapter 2

TORT LIABILITY FOR VERBAL INSULTS

One benefit of understanding the law of other countries is that it provides an opportunity to take a fresh look at the assumptions that underlie our own law. An overarching question in torts is what conduct ought to be deemed actionable. The answer to this question depends on our goals in imposing tort liability and our decisions reflect many of our most deeply held beliefs and values. This Chapter provides an occasion to reconsider an area of U.S. law that is considered well-settled. In the United States, there is remarkable agreement among state courts that offensive comments or insults without more do not lead to tort liability. Although courts routinely recognize claims for intentional or negligent infliction of emotional distress, these actions require pleading and proof hurdles that are difficult to surmount. For example, liability for intentional infliction of emotional distress requires proof of "extreme and outrageous" conduct on the part of the defendant, which courts have interpreted as conduct beyond the bounds tolerable in a civilized society. Courts consistently state that mere insults are trivialities that do not rise to the level of extreme and outrageous conduct. Even racial insults rarely suffice to meet this element, leading critics to suggest that the U.S. legal establishment is blind to the extraordinary damage such insults cause. In addition, the plaintiff must suffer *severe* emotional distress. This does not necessarily require physical symptoms, but courts require that the plaintiff plead and prove an emotional injury that is truly debilitating rather than a source of fleeting discomfort.

Because the law is so restrictive, a better strategy for redress in the U.S. is to utilize a different cause of action if its requirements can be met. Thus, battery could be pleaded if the insult was accompanied by a harmful or offensive touching or assault if the insult and accompanying acts created imminent apprehension of a contact. Depending on the content of the insulting comment and its factual falsity, the tort of defamation might apply, but that could also carry with it the requirement that the plaintiff establish a resulting pecuniary loss. In addition, of course, there is constitutional protection of speech that applies to the defamation claims of large numbers of plaintiffs. Federal or state antidiscrimination statutes may also offer redress for certain plaintiffs, if, for example, the comment may be characterized as sexual or racial harassment. In essence, then, success really depends on re-casting the offending conduct to de-emphasize the insult.

Some other cultures are not nearly so sanguine about insults. One interesting contrast for us here is not with the civil law systems based on French or German law, but rather on the customary law of a nation once occupied by both common-law and civil-law colonizers.

Chapter 1 provided an introduction to the major systems of tort law, with a focus on the common law (originating in England) and the two major civil law models (Germany and France). As described there briefly, these three models of tort law have influenced much of the rest of the world, for various reasons. One such reason is, of course, colonial expansion. But in many colonies and former colonies, the traditional law that was in place before the colonizers appeared still exerts some sway, and indeed may compete with the colonizer's law for dominance in particular areas. See Michael Graziadei, *Comparative Law as the Study of Transplants and Receptions, in* THE OXFORD HANDBOOK OF COMPARATIVE LAW 442-55 (Mathias Reimann & Reinhard Zimmermann eds., 2006); H. PATRICK GLENN, LEGAL TRADITIONS OF THE WORLD 56-83.

This Chapter focuses on the role of verbal insult in the customary law of Ghana. Ghana is the home of about twenty million people in six major ethnic groups and over 100 ethnolinguistic groups. Located in West Africa, on what is known as the Gold Coast, the people in this region experienced their first exposure to westerners in 1482, when the Portuguese built a permanent trading post. Later, the Portuguese relinquished the post to the Dutch. For the next 150 years, the British and Dutch competed for dominance in various trade ventures. Pursuant to a treaty in 1844 by which the coast Fanti people agreed to protect the British from the Ashanti people and to submit themselves to British jurisdiction for serious crimes, the British began to exert a legal presence. A question then arose as to whether English law would replace the customary laws that the various groups in Ghana had lived by for centuries.

The following excerpt by a Justice of the Supreme Court of Ghana frames the issues.

A. THE ROLE OF CUSTOMARY LAW IN GHANA

Justice Modibo Ocran

The Clash of Legal Cultures: The Treatment of Indigenous Law in Colonial and Post-Colonial Africa

39 Akron L. Rev. 465, 465-468 (2006)

. . . The story of the legal relationship between European and African legal systems that intrigues comparative lawyers starts in the 19th Century. As part of the Colonial Administration, the British naturally wanted to enforce law and order and to generally regulate the lives and habits of the people they conquered. This was not always easy for the British, both as a practical matter and as a matter of legal doctrine and ideology. They encountered a legal system quite different from their own legal traditions. They had to deal with a religion-based legal system simultaneously meant for secular application that was unlike other forms of religious law, such as Canon Law, which largely applied to the spiritual realm of life. They also faced hostile reaction from strong indigenous cultures that were not necessarily prepared to accept the assumptions of the Western cultural mind. Ultimately, the culture accepted the creation of legal pluralistic systems in which the English dominated, but indigenous law was maintained up to a certain point. In other parts of Africa, it was not simply the clash between European and indigenous cultural norms, but between European and Muslim or Islamic Law as well. . . .

At the start of the legal history that we are concerned with, the characteristics of African society were either pre-industrial or traditional. . . . Societies tended to be organized in small groupings, and "[t]he most important basis for [a] relationship was kinship.". . . The people were soaked in traditionalism and custom. Their mindset was: "[P]erform the ritual customs because your ancestors did so," and "stick with something that seems to work."

The starting point of custom is of course practice or long usage. In traditional African societies, custom became the principal, if not the only, source of law. Kings or chiefs occasionally issued edicts, but custom was decidedly the main source of law. The chief himself was bound by custom and indeed was the repository of custom. . . . Usage led to custom, and part of custom eventually became customary law. Customary law comes partially from the customs of the people, that is, that portion of customs that the people have accepted as community-governing principles, the violation of which would result in punishment. The rest of custom, that is non-legal custom, would not normally lead to punishment when violated, but could still effectively regulate norms of conduct. Custom itself emerged not simply from what was practiced, but also from the highly influential morals and religious beliefs of the people. . . . The core tenets of African customary law are its emphasis on collective responsibility, respect for the elderly, collective rights, and respect for long-established institutions.

. . . [T]his indigenous body of law began to face an assault from external influences in the form of Christian colonial power and Islamic religion. Would the new colonial powers reject African Law outright as somehow inconsistent with the primary imperative of colonialism to dominate the colonized people? If customary law was not to be accepted, could European law rule both European and non-European peoples in the enlarged colonial community? In any case, what should be the actual content of customary law in the new, multi-ethnic, African colonial states, where there are vastly different cultures and languages within one community? This was a problem, because if custom partially defines customary law, and if custom itself is something that emanates from the people, there would be as many customary laws as there were different communities.

Note

The English addressed the problem Justice Ocran describes by passing a statute in 1876 which provided that the common law, doctrines of equity and the statutes in force in England as of July,

1874, would apply in the colony of the Gold Coast. However, the statute also provided for the continued existence of customary law, so long as it was not "repugnant to natural justice, equity and good conscience . . . or incompatible . . . with any enactment of the Colonial legislature." Justice Ocran gives many examples of Ghanaian customary law that the British found repugnant and thus, inapplicable. Some examples stem from customary criminal laws such as those against witchcraft while others arise from animism (the attribution of a living soul to plants, inanimate objects, and natural phenomena.) An example of the latter includes the condemnation of "sexual intercourse in the leaves" among the Ashanti, who viewed this as a defilement of the Goddess Earth. They imposed both criminal and civil penalties for it, depending on the circumstances of the violation.

When Ghana gained independence in 1960 and as work began on a new Constitution for the young country, the same question about the respective roles of common law and customary laws persisted. By that time, Ghana had absorbed much of the common law tradition. On the other hand, the English "repugnancy" clauses were an affront to Ghanaian pride and culture, and the drafters of the Constitution saw no need to perpetuate them. The Constitution of Ghana reached a position of compromise, as is evident from the following excerpt.

CONSTITUTION OF THE REPUBLIC OF GHANA

Chapter Four (1992)

(1) The laws of Ghana shall comprise

a. this Constitution;

b. enactments made by or under the authority of the Parliament established by this Constitution; . . .

e. the common law

(2) The common law of Ghana shall comprise the rules of law generally known as the common law, the rules generally known as the doctrines of equity and the rules of customary law including those determined by the Superior Court of Judicature.

(3) For purposes of this article, "customary law" means the rules of law, which by custom are applicable to particular communities in Ghana.

Note

Other articles of the Constitution recognize the institution of chieftancy and its traditional councils under customary law, and charge the National House of Chiefs to undertake a study of customary laws with the goal of establishing unified rules and eliminating customs and usages that are "outmoded and socially harmful." Arts. 271 & 272. The Constitution also permits customary law to differ from, but not to conflict with, the national code. Some courts in Ghana resemble English common law courts while others are traditional tribal courts; the farther a village is from a city, the more likely customary law will predominate. In rural areas, each village has its own justice system. Serious criminal offenses are usually tried in the English-style courts.

B. ACTIONABILITY OF VERBAL INSULT UNDER CUSTOMARY LAW

With this background on the role of customary law in Ghana, we examine how the Ghanaian courts have approached the issue of verbal insults. The insults at issue often consist of statements that would not seem actionable under U.S. law, as described above, or under the traditional common law of defamation, which in Ghana bears a close resemblance to English law. Several cases illustrate the reach of customary law in this area. In one, the plaintiff was told during an angry exchange that "her vagina stinks." Judge Apaloo agreed with the district court that the words were "plain vituperation only," and stated, "The fact that the law of England provides no remedy is quite beside the point. The society of England is different from the society of Ghana. In this country, where words of abuse are taken seriously, it would in my opinion, be socially intolerable if customary law provided no sanctions against a man who finds pleasure in injuring the feelings of his neighbor by vituperation." *Wankiyiwaa v. Wereduwaa and Another* [1963] 1 GLR 332, High Court, Kumasi, 5 April 1963. This theme is further explored in the next opinion.

NKRUMAH AND ANOTHER v. MANU

[1971] 1 GLR 176-190
High Court, Kumasi
7 December 1970

TAYLOR, J.

[The parties were all Ghanaians and they agreed that the defendant had called the plaintiff a slave during a heated argument. A statute provided that legal issues should be determined according to common law unless the plaintiff was subject to a system of customary law and sought to have the dispute resolved under customary law. The legal issue was whether the applicable law was customary or common.]

. . . I must now move on to decide two things: first, whether the words uttered are defamatory under customary law and secondly, the applicable law, common or customary. It is now generally accepted that defamation under customary law is wider than under common law. Sarbah, in his Fanti Customary Laws (3d ed.) . . . generally indicated how extensive [customary defamation] is. . . . Dr. Danquah in the introduction to his cases in Akan Law was more specific:

> "Thus, although under the Common Law it is only in very exceptional cases that a plaintiff can succeed in an action for slander, the Customary Law gives full recognition to all claims for damages for insulting words or language used verbally against any person. A suit of this nature...covers serious assertions as that a person is an Odonkoba, 'son of a slave,' an 'obayifo,' a witch, and odutufo, 'one who has killed another by sympathetic magic, a poisoner,' down to such common place assertions as that another is a fool, or a beast such as an ass, or a silly idiot."

If I decide therefore that the applicable law is customary law I will be obliged to reduce the damages considerably because in this case the defamation clearly took place in the course of a heated quarrel. I must say though that it is about time the customary law of slander took on a more enlightened garb and moved so to speak with the demands of modern times. When village communities were small and the written word was unknown to customary law the only means of social and commercial intercourse was the spoken word. It was therefore essential for the preservation of the peace of those small communities that idle insults which ridicule and may therefore ruin a person be discouraged by the body politic. With the very drastic changes which modern civilization has imposed on community and rural life throughout the country it seems to me that the law has more serious problems to tackle than silly vituperations.

I would have thought that the conditions which engendered the customary remedy have disappeared and the customary view on the matter ought to be declared obsolete. Unfortunately this view is not borne out by the authorities ancient and modern. . . . In the introduction to his Cases in Akan Law, Dr. J.B. Danquah attempted this explanation of the psychological and sociological basis of the law of slander in its customary setting.

> "No one in Akan land would suffer an insult to his person which he would not suffer with impunity when offered to his body. The statement contains an element of truth, and the social psychologist who finds in this fact a proof of the African's greater and keener sensitiveness to insulting or abusive language would be doing useful service in broadening the amicable basis of inter-racial relations and co-operation. This difference of social outlook between the European and African codes of conduct and elegant address lies at the basis of many regrettable incidents which could not have happened had both sides known what was expected of them.
>
> "The delicate feelings of the average African are not half as blunted and atrophied as those of the average European, and where, for instance, an Englishman would not consider himself insulted, and would even if he did, receive no substantial help from the courts for being called a 'disgruntled Jacobite', an Akan man would receive full redress at law if anyone dared to cast a slur on his ancestry or said of him that he was not a true member of the Akan clans."

In a footnote to this observation, Dr. Danquah explained further that an assertion that an Akan man is not a member of the ancient Akan clans "is tantamount to saying the person referred to has no connexion with any royal house or that he is the descendant of a slave or a slave tribe." One can only hope that with the inevitable future break-up of our heterogeneous tribal groups implicit in the present efforts at a unitary state, and with the gradual process of inter-tribal marriage that these pompous tribal sentiments will eventually disappear. Until that event I must take the law as I find it.

[The court held that there was nothing on the record to show that the respondent had asked to have the issue determined according to customary law, nor that she had showed she was subject to customary law, and therefore, that the issue must be resolved on the basis of common law rules. On that basis, the court ruled that vulgar abuse uttered in the heat of passion was not actionable.]

Notes

1. Does customary law continue to be relevant in Ghana in the 21st century? According to Justice Ocran's article, excerpted in Section A above, it is. He states that the problems faced by the British in trying to synthesize common law and customary law in colonial Africa have not vanished. Even though the judiciary is almost entirely African, and therefore, experiences less of a cultural gap with the public, there are enormous class-based differences between the judiciary and the people they serve. Many judges are Western-educated. In addition, judges often do not come from the particular locality that they are serving and thus, have little knowledge of the customary law in the region. 39 AKRON L. REV. at 479.

2. The harmonization of customary law with the law of another culture or legal system is a challenge many other countries have faced. New Zealand has placed Maori custom in a position of honor and respect as a national tradition. The Spaniards confronted Aztec and Inca customary laws when they colonized Latin America. Like the English in Ghana, they considered such laws to be valid and enforceable so long as they did not conflict with Spanish laws or the Catholic Church. Indigenous law was found compatible in many instances and applied by the royal courts. Most often, though, lawmakers do not think highly of customary law because they constantly compare it to Western legal thinking and find it deficient in comparison. *See* Jan Kleinheisterkamp, *Development of Law in Latin America in* OXFORD HANDBOOK OF COMPARATIVE LAW 261 (Mathias Reimann & Reinhard Zimmerman eds., 2006) and T.W. Bennet, *Comparative Law and African Customary Law, in* OXFORD HANDBOOK OF COMPARATIVE LAW 658 (Mathias Reimann & Reinhard Zimmerman eds., 2006).

3. It may be difficult for a Western-educated lawyer to understand why calling someone an "ass" or a "hopeless lawyer" would be viewed as breaches of customary law. U.S. or English law treats these insults as trivial and not worthy of a court's expenditure of time. However, work in anthropology yields an explanation both about what is actionable and about the value of having courts give attention to the problem. T.W. Bennet, describing a study of Barotse people,[1] states:

> what might seem a petty quarrel about the infringement of a mere courtesy could well be the surface manifestation of a simmering conflict, fuelled by years of grievance. Moreover, because relationships were so intimate, disputes between kin generated intense emotion, and were quite likely to erupt into public displays of anger. In these circumstances, Barotse courts were expected to untangle all the complaints with a view to convincing the disputants that they ought to sink their differences so that the social harmony could be restored. . . . In fact, the very measure of an effective court in Africa is its willingness to engage in a thorough inquiry. The latitude allowed, however, is qualified by the court's overall purpose. The more distant the parties' relationship, the more likely that the court's purpose will be straightforward adjudication. . . . Conversely, where a court seeks to reconcile the parties, the immediate "legal" issues that might have precipitated litigation have little significance for the eventual outcome. The court must consider the parties' full relationship over a long period of time.

Bennet, *supra*, at 658-659.

4. The insult in issue in *Nkrumah v. Manu* is of particular interest. When the case was decided, slavery had long been abolished in Ghana, and Judge Taylor indicated that under the common law, the words were best characterized as vulgar abuse in the heat of passion which would not be actionable. Yet under customary law, calling someone a slave was a serious offense. Why is this so? The people of Ghana were heavily affected by slavery. Ghana was a major point of departure for slave ships and

---

[1] MAX GLUCKMAN, THE JUDICIAL PROCESS AMONG THE BAROTSE OF NORTHERN RHODESIA (1967).

the society was traumatized by the slave trade. It was not only foreign slave traders who participated in the slave trade. The Ashanti, for example, participated in the export of slaves as well as importing slaves from farther East to help build the Ashanti Empire. Being a slave or descending from one meant a disruption of the social order and a carried a distinct stigma that would lower the perception of one's family and clan. In a society that values the community and the elders of a group, the implication that one is not a member of a clan would be particularly offensive and disruptive of social cohesion. Kwame Anthony Appiah, who grew up in Kumasi, recalls his father's admonitions never to inquire about people's origins, and states that even today, "there are still slave descendants who work in the household of prosperous Ashanti without remuneration." Kwame Anthony Appiah, *A Slow Emancipation,* N.Y. TIMES, March 18, 2007 (magazine).

5. Although U.S. tort law is generally unreceptive to recognition of claims based on racial epithets that evoke longstanding images of subordination and inferiority, it does recognize that the context in which words are uttered can make a difference in how they are perceived. The Restatement (Second) of Torts, § 46, comments *e* and *f*, recognizes that conduct arising from an abuse of position of authority, such as that of a police officer, or targeting a plaintiff's particular susceptibility-(such as physical or mental infirmity) is more likely to be found extreme and outrageous. Ghanian customary law seems to reflect a much broader consciousness of context.

6. What harm do insults inflict, and what is the remedy available to a prevailing plaintiff? Here again, U.S. law and traditional customary law seem to differ. In American courts, we require either severe emotional distress, or actionable harm to reputation, or other pecuniary harm (depending on the cause of action); the usual remedy is compensatory damages. Under African customary law, the remedial focus is different. Indigenous African systems seek to balance opposing interests and to achieve compromise through mediation, with the goal of restoring balance and harmony through an outcome that will be acceptable to both parties to the dispute. CHARLES MWALIMU, THE NIGERIAN LEGAL SYSTEM, VOL. 1, PUBLIC LAW 95-96 (2005). The traditional remedies for insult could include public ridicule, pacification of the plaintiff and the community through an apology, and perhaps a small fine. The plaintiffs in some Ghanaian insult cases have sought higher compensatory damages on the theory that times have changed.

Chapter 3

THE ALIEN TORT STATUTE AND THE TORTURE VICTIM PROTECTION ACT

The Alien Tort Statute (also called the Alien Tort Act or the Alien Tort Claims Act) is a domestic law dating back to 1789 that makes certain intentionally tortious violations of customary international law – "the law of nations" – actionable in U.S. courts, no matter where the tort was committed. 28 U.S.C. § 1350. "To obtain relief under the [ATS], plaintiffs must be (1) an alien (2) suing for a tort (3) which was committed in violation of international law." *Aldana v. Del Monte Fresh Produce, N.A., Inc.*, 416 F.3d 1242 (11th Cir. 2005). In the first part of this Chapter, we look at Filartiga, the case that began the modern reemergence of the ATS, followed by an excerpt from Sosa, the 2004 Supreme Court case that circumscribes the statute's application while still "leaving the door ajar" for possible expansions.

The Torture Victim Protection Act of 1991 is broader than the ATS in one respect, in that it allows both aliens and U.S. citizens to sue in federal court. But it is narrower and more specific in another respect, creating a federal cause of action only against any individual, acting under the authority of any foreign nation, who intentionally subjects a person to "torture" or "extrajudicial killing." 28 U.S.C.A. §1350, note. The ATS and the TVPA thus overlap, but do not cover precisely the same ground, and a plaintiff may be able to plead both claims in a single action. In the second part of this Chapter, we set out the text of the TVPA and provide a brief analysis of that statute as applied to alien plaintiffs.

A. THE ALIEN TORT STATUTE

FILARTIGA v. PENA-IRALA

630 F.2d 876 (2d Cir. 1980).

IRVING R. KAUFMAN, Circuit Judge:

Upon ratification of the Constitution, the thirteen former colonies were fused into a single nation, one which, in its relations with foreign states, is bound both to observe and construe the accepted norms of international law, formerly known as the law of nations. Under the Articles of Confederation, the several states had interpreted and applied this body of doctrine as a part of their common law, but with the founding of the "more perfect Union" of 1789, the law of nations became preeminently a federal concern.

Implementing the constitutional mandate for national control over foreign relations, the First Congress established original district court jurisdiction over "all causes where an alien sues for a tort only (committed) in violation of the law of nations." Judiciary Act of 1789, ch. 20, § 9(b), 1 Stat. 73, 77 (1789), codified at 28 U.S.C. § 1350. Construing this rarely-invoked provision, we hold that deliberate torture perpetrated under color of official authority violates universally accepted norms of the international law of human rights, regardless of the nationality of the parties. Thus, whenever an alleged torturer is found and served with process by an alien within our borders, § 1350 provides federal jurisdiction. Accordingly, we reverse the judgment of the district court dismissing the complaint for want of federal jurisdiction.

I

The appellants, plaintiffs below, are citizens of the Republic of Paraguay. Dr. Joel Filartiga, a physician, describes himself as a longstanding opponent of the government of President Alfredo Stroessner, which has held power in Paraguay since 1954. His daughter, Dolly Filartiga, arrived in the United States in 1978 under a visitor's visa, and has since applied for permanent political asylum. The Filartigas brought this action in the Eastern District of New York against Americo Norberto Pena-Irala (Pena), also a citizen of Paraguay, for wrongfully causing the death of Dr.

Filartiga's seventeen-year old son, Joelito. Because the district court dismissed the action for want of subject matter jurisdiction, we must accept as true the allegations contained in the Filartigas' complaint and affidavits for purposes of this appeal.

The appellants contend that on March 29, 1976, Joelito Filartiga was kidnapped and tortured to death by Pena, who was then Inspector General of Police in Asuncion, Paraguay. Later that day, the police brought Dolly Filartiga to Pena's home where she was confronted with the body of her brother, which evidenced marks of severe torture. As she fled, horrified, from the house, Pena followed after her shouting, "Here you have what you have been looking for for so long and what you deserve. Now shut up." The Filartigas claim that Joelito was tortured and killed in retaliation for his father's political activities and beliefs.

Shortly thereafter, Dr. Filartiga commenced a criminal action in the Paraguayan courts against Pena and the police for the murder of his son. As a result, Dr. Filartiga's attorney was arrested and brought to police headquarters where, shackled to a wall, Pena threatened him with death. This attorney, it is alleged, has since been disbarred without just cause. . . .

[Pena entered the United States in 1978 on a visitor's visa, but remained after its expiration. Dolly Filartiga learned of Pena's presence and notified federal immigration authorities, who arrested Pena. Dolly caused Pena to be served with a summons and civil complaint, alleging that he had wrongfully caused Joelito's death by torture. In their suit the Filartigas sought compensatory and punitive damages of $10 million.] The cause of action is stated as arising under "wrongful death statutes; the U. N. Charter; the Universal Declaration on Human Rights; the U. N. Declaration Against Torture; the American Declaration of the Rights and Duties of Man; and other pertinent declarations, documents and practices constituting the customary international law of human rights and the law of nations," as well as 28 U.S.C. s 1350, Article II, sec. 2 and the Supremacy Clause of the U. S. Constitution. Jurisdiction is claimed under the general federal question provision, 18 U.S.C. § 1331 and, principally on this appeal, under the Alien Tort Statute, 28 U.S.C. § 1350. . . .

The Filartigas submitted the affidavits of a number of distinguished international legal scholars, who stated unanimously that the law of nations prohibits absolutely the use of torture as alleged in the complaint. Pena, in support of his motion to dismiss on the ground of forum non conveniens, submitted the affidavit of his Paraguayan counsel, Jose Emilio Gorostiaga, who averred that Paraguayan law provides a full and adequate civil remedy for the wrong alleged. Dr. Filartiga has not commenced such an action, however, believing that further resort to the courts of his own country would be futile. [The trial judge granted the motion to dismiss, after which Pena was ordered deported and returned to Paraguay.]

II

Appellants rest their principal argument in support of federal jurisdiction upon the Alien Tort Statute, 28 U.S.C. § 1350, which provides: "The district courts shall have original jurisdiction of any civil action by an alien for a tort only, committed in violation of the law of nations or a treaty of the United States." Since appellants do not contend that their action arises directly under a treaty of the United States, a threshold question on the jurisdictional issue is whether the conduct alleged violates the law of nations. In light of the universal condemnation of torture in numerous international agreements, and the renunciation of torture as an instrument of official policy by virtually all of the nations of the world (in principle if not in practice), we find that an act of torture committed by a state official against one held in detention violates established norms of the international law of human rights, and hence the law of nations.

The Supreme Court has enumerated the appropriate sources of international law. The law of nations "may be ascertained by consulting the works of jurists, writing professedly on public law; or by the general usage and practice of nations; or by judicial decisions recognizing and enforcing that law." United States v. Smith, 18 U.S. (5 Wheat.) 153, 160-61, 5 L.Ed. 57 (1820); Lopes v. Reederei Richard Schroder, 225 F.Supp. 292, 295 (E.D.Pa.1963). In Smith, a statute proscribing "the crime of piracy (on the high seas) as defined by the law of nations," 3 Stat. 510(a) (1819), was held sufficiently determinate in meaning to afford the basis for a death sentence. The Smith Court discovered among the works of Lord Bacon, Grotius, Bochard and other commentators a genuine consensus that rendered the crime "sufficiently and constitutionally defined." The Paquete Habana, 175 U.S. 677, 20

S.Ct. 290, 44 L.Ed. 320 (1900), reaffirmed that where there is no treaty, and no controlling executive or legislative act or judicial decision, resort must be had to the customs and usages of civilized nations; and, as evidence of these, to the works of jurists and commentators, who by years of labor, research and experience, have made themselves peculiarly well acquainted with the subjects of which they treat. Such works are resorted to by judicial tribunals, not for the speculations of their authors concerning what the law ought to be, but for trustworthy evidence of what the law really is. Modern international sources confirm the propriety of this approach.

Habana is particularly instructive for present purposes, for it held that the traditional prohibition against seizure of an enemy's coastal fishing vessels during wartime, a standard that began as one of comity only, had ripened over the preceding century into "a settled rule of international law" by "the general assent of civilized nations." Thus it is clear that courts must interpret international law not as it was in 1789, but as it has evolved and exists among the nations of the world today.

The requirement that a rule command the "general assent of civilized nations" to become binding upon them all is a stringent one. Were this not so, the courts of one nation might feel free to impose idiosyncratic legal rules upon others, in the name of applying international law. Thus, in Banco Nacional de Cuba v. Sabbatino, 376 U.S. 398, 84 S.Ct. 923, 11 L.Ed.2d 804 (1964), the Court declined to pass on the validity of the Cuban government's expropriation of a foreign-owned corporation's assets, noting the sharply conflicting views on the issue propounded by the capital-exporting, capital-importing, socialist and capitalist nations.

The case at bar presents us with a situation diametrically opposed to the conflicted state of law that confronted the Sabbatino Court. Indeed, to paraphrase that Court's statement, there are few, if any, issues in international law today on which opinion seems to be so united as the limitations on a state's power to torture persons held in its custody.

The United Nations Charter (a treaty of the United States, see 59 Stat. 1033 (1945)) makes it clear that in this modern age a state's treatment of its own citizens is a matter of international concern. It provides:

> With a view to the creation of conditions of stability and well-being which are necessary for peaceful and friendly relations among nations . . . the United Nations shall promote . . . universal respect for, and observance of, human rights and fundamental freedoms for all without distinctions as to race, sex, language or religion.

Id. Art. 55. And further: All members pledge themselves to take joint and separate action in cooperation with the Organization for the achievement of the purposes set forth in Article 55. Id. Art. 56.

While this broad mandate has been held not to be wholly self-executing, this observation alone does not end our inquiry. For although there is no universal agreement as to the precise extent of the "human rights and fundamental freedoms" guaranteed to all by the Charter, there is at present no dissent from the view that the guaranties include, at a bare minimum, the right to be free from torture. This prohibition has become part of customary international law, as evidenced and defined by the Universal Declaration of Human Rights, General Assembly Resolution 217 (III)(A) (Dec. 10, 1948) which states, in the plainest of terms, "no one shall be subjected to torture."[10] The General Assembly has declared that the Charter precepts embodied in this Universal Declaration "constitute basic principles of international law." G.A.Res. 2625 (XXV) (Oct. 24, 1970).

Particularly relevant is the Declaration on the Protection of All Persons from Being Subjected to Torture, General Assembly Resolution 3452, 30 U.N. GAOR Supp. (No. 34) 91, U.N.Doc. A/1034 (1975). . . . The Declaration expressly prohibits any state from permitting the dastardly and totally inhuman act of torture. Torture, in turn, is defined as "any act by which severe pain and suffering, whether physical or mental, is intentionally inflicted by or at the instigation of a public official on a person for such purposes as . . . intimidating him or other persons." The Declaration goes on to provide that "(w)here it is proved that an act of torture or other cruel, inhuman or degrading treatment or punishment has been committed by or at the instigation of a public official, the victim shall be afforded redress and

---

[10] Eighteen nations have incorporated the Universal Declaration into their own constitutions. 48 Revue Internationale de Droit Penal Nos. 3 & 4, at 211 (1977).

compensation, in accordance with national law." This Declaration, like the Declaration of Human Rights before it, was adopted without dissent by the General Assembly.

These U.N. declarations are significant because they specify with great precision the obligations of member nations under the Charter. Since their adoption, "(m)embers can no longer contend that they do not know what human rights they promised in the Charter to promote." Sohn, "A Short History of United Nations Documents on Human Rights," in The United Nations and Human Rights, 18th Report of the Commission (Commission to Study the Organization of Peace ed. 1968). Moreover, a U.N. Declaration is, according to one authoritative definition, "a formal and solemn instrument, suitable for rare occasions when principles of great and lasting importance are being enunciated." 34 U.N. ESCOR, Supp. (No. 8) 15, U.N. Doc. E/cn.4/1/610 (1962) (memorandum of Office of Legal Affairs, U.N. Secretariat). Accordingly, it has been observed that the Universal Declaration of Human Rights "no longer fits into the dichotomy of 'binding treaty' against 'non-binding pronouncement,' but is rather an authoritative statement of the international community." E. Schwelb, Human Rights and the International Community 70 (1964). Thus, a Declaration creates an expectation of adherence, and "insofar as the expectation is gradually justified by State practice, a declaration may by custom become recognized as laying down rules binding upon the States." 34 U.N. ESCOR, supra. Indeed, several commentators have concluded that the Universal Declaration has become, in toto, a part of binding, customary international law.

Turning to the act of torture, we have little difficulty discerning its universal renunciation in the modern usage and practice of nations. The international consensus surrounding torture has found expression in numerous international treaties and accords. E.g., American Convention on Human Rights, Art. 5, OAS Treaty Series No. 36 at 1, OAS Off. Rec. OEA/Ser 4 v/II 23, doc. 21, rev. 2 (English ed., 1975) ("No one shall be subjected to torture or to cruel, inhuman or degrading punishment or treatment"); International Covenant on Civil and Political Rights, U.N. General Assembly Res. 2200 (XXI)A, U.N. Doc. A/6316 (Dec. 16, 1966) (identical language); European Convention for the Protection of Human Rights and Fundamental Freedoms, Art. 3, Council of Europe, European Treaty Series No. 5 (1968), 213

U.N.T.S. 211 (semble). The substance of these international agreements is reflected in modern municipal i.e. national law as well. Although torture was once a routine concomitant of criminal interrogations in many nations, during the modern and hopefully more enlightened era it has been universally renounced. According to one survey, torture is prohibited, expressly or implicitly, by the constitutions of over fifty-five nations, including both the United States and Paraguay. Our State Department reports a general recognition of this principle: "There now exists an international consensus that recognizes basic human rights and obligations owed by all governments to their citizens . . . . There is no doubt that these rights are often violated; but virtually all governments acknowledge their validity." . . .

Having examined the sources from which customary international law is derived the usage of nations, judicial opinions and the works of jurists we conclude that official torture is now prohibited by the law of nations. The prohibition is clear and unambiguous, and admits of no distinction between treatment of aliens and citizens. . . . The treaties and accords cited above, as well as the express foreign policy of our own government, all make it clear that international law confers fundamental rights upon all people vis-a-vis their own governments. While the ultimate scope of those rights will be a subject for continuing refinement and elaboration, we hold that the right to be free from torture is now among them. We therefore turn to the question whether the other requirements for jurisdiction are met.

III

Appellee submits that even if the tort alleged is a violation of modern international law, federal jurisdiction may not be exercised consistent with the dictates of Article III of the Constitution. The claim is without merit. Common law courts of general jurisdiction regularly adjudicate transitory tort claims between individuals over whom they exercise personal jurisdiction, wherever the tort occurred. Moreover, as part of an articulated scheme of federal control over external affairs, Congress provided, in the first Judiciary Act, s 9(b), 1 Stat. 73, 77 (1789), for federal jurisdiction over suits by aliens where principles of international law are in issue. The constitutional basis for the Alien Tort Statute is the law of nations, which has always been part of the federal common law.

It is not extraordinary for a court to adjudicate a tort claim arising outside of its territorial jurisdiction. A state or nation has a legitimate interest in the orderly resolution of disputes among those within its borders, and where the lex loci delicti commissi is applied, it is an expression of comity to give effect to the laws of the state where the wrong occurred. Thus, Lord Mansfield in Mostyn v. Fabrigas, 1 Cowp. 161 (1774), quoted in McKenna v. Fisk, 42 U.S. (1 How.) 241, 248, 11 L.Ed. 117 (1843) said:

> [I]f A becomes indebted to B, or commits a tort upon his person or upon his personal property in Paris, an action in either case may be maintained against A in England, if he is there found . . . . (A)s to transitory actions, there is not a colour of doubt but that any action which is transitory may be laid in any county in England, though the matter arises beyond the seas.

Mostyn came into our law as the original basis for state court jurisdiction over out-of-state torts, and it has not lost its force in suits to recover for a wrongful death occurring upon foreign soil, as long as the conduct complained of was unlawful where performed. Here, where in personam jurisdiction has been obtained over the defendant, the parties agree that the acts alleged would violate Paraguayan law, and the policies of the forum are consistent with the foreign law, state court jurisdiction would be proper. Indeed, appellees conceded as much at oral argument.

Recalling that Mostyn was freshly decided at the time the Constitution was ratified, we proceed to consider whether the First Congress acted constitutionally in vesting jurisdiction over "foreign suits," alleging torts committed in violation of the law of nations. A case properly "aris(es) under the . . . laws of the United States" for Article III purposes if grounded upon statutes enacted by Congress or upon the common law of the United States. The law of nations forms an integral part of the common law, and a review of the history surrounding the adoption of the Constitution demonstrates that it became a part of the common law of the United States upon the adoption of the Constitution. Therefore, the enactment of the Alien Tort Statute was authorized by Article III.

During the eighteenth century, it was taken for granted on both sides of the Atlantic that the law of nations forms a part of the common law. 1 Blackstone, Commentaries 263-64 (1st Ed. 1765-69); 4 id. at 67.[19] Under the Articles of Confederation, the Pennsylvania Court of Oyer and Terminer at Philadelphia, per McKean, Chief Justice, applied the law of nations to the criminal prosecution of the Chevalier de Longchamps for his assault upon the person of the French Consul-General to the United States, noting that "(t)his law, in its full extent, is a part of the law of this state . . . ." Respublica v. DeLongchamps, 1 U.S. (1 Dall.) 113, 119, 1 L.Ed. 59 (1784). Thus, a leading commentator has written:

> It is an ancient and a salutary feature of the Anglo-American legal tradition that the Law of Nations is a part of the law of the land to be ascertained and administered, like any other, in the appropriate case. This doctrine was originally conceived and formulated in England in response to the demands of an expanding commerce and under the influence of theories widely accepted in the late sixteenth, the seventeenth and the eighteenth centuries. It was brought to America in the colonial years as part of the legal heritage from England. It was well understood by men of legal learning in America in the eighteenth century when the United Colonies broke away from England to unite effectively, a little later, in the United States of America.

Dickenson, "The Law of Nations as Part of the National Law of the United States," 101 U.Pa.L.Rev. 26, 27 (1952). . . .

[I]t was hardly a radical initiative for Chief Justice Marshall to state in The Nereide, 13 U.S. (9 Cranch) 388, 422, 3 L.Ed. 769 (1815), that in the absence of a congressional enactment, United States courts are "bound by the law of nations, which is a part of

---

[19] As Lord Stowell said in The Maria, 165 Eng.Rep. 955, 958 (Adm.1807): "In the first place it is to be recollected, that this is a Court of the Law of Nations, though sitting here under the authority of the King of Great Britain. It belongs to other nations as well as to our own; and what foreigners have a right to demand from it, is the administration of the law of nations, simply, and exclusively of the introduction of principles borrowed from our own municipal jurisprudence, to which it is well known, they have at all times expressed no inconsiderable repugnance."

the law of the land." These words were echoed in The Paquete Habana, supra, 175 U.S. at 700, 20 S.Ct. at 299: "[i]nternational law is part of our law, and must be ascertained and administered by the courts of justice of appropriate jurisdiction, as often as questions of right depending upon it are duly presented for their determination."

The Filartigas urge that 28 U.S.C. § 1350 be treated as an exercise of Congress's power to define offenses against the law of nations. While such a reading is possible, we believe it is sufficient here to construe the Alien Tort Statute, not as granting new rights to aliens, but simply as opening the federal courts for adjudication of the rights already recognized by international law. The statute nonetheless does inform our analysis of Article III, for we recognize that questions of jurisdiction "must be considered part of an organic growth part of an evolutionary process," and that the history of the judiciary article gives meaning to its pithy phrases. The Framers' overarching concern that control over international affairs be vested in the new national government to safeguard the standing of the United States among the nations of the world therefore reinforces the result we reach today.

Although the Alien Tort Statute has rarely been the basis for jurisdiction during its long history, in light of the foregoing discussion, there can be little doubt that this action is properly brought in federal court. This is undeniably an action by an alien, for a tort only, committed in violation of the law of nations. The paucity of suits successfully maintained under the section is readily attributable to the statute's requirement of alleging a "violation of the law of nations" (emphasis supplied) at the jurisdictional threshold. Courts have, accordingly, engaged in a more searching preliminary review of the merits than is required, for example, under the more flexible "arising under" formulation. Thus, the narrowing construction that the Alien Tort Statute has previously received reflects the fact that earlier cases did not involve such well-established, universally recognized norms of international law that are here at issue. . . .

Since federal jurisdiction may properly be exercised over the Filartigas' claim, the action must be remanded for further proceedings. Appellee Pena, however, advances several additional points that lie beyond the scope of our holding on jurisdiction. Both to emphasize the boundaries of our holding, and to clarify some of the issues reserved for the district court on remand, we will address these contentions briefly.

IV

. . . In the twentieth century the international community has come to recognize the common danger posed by the flagrant disregard of basic human rights and particularly the right to be free of torture. Spurred first by the Great War, and then the Second, civilized nations have banded together to prescribe acceptable norms of international behavior. From the ashes of the Second World War arose the United Nations Organization, amid hopes that an era of peace and cooperation had at last begun. Though many of these aspirations have remained elusive goals, that circumstance cannot diminish the true progress that has been made. In the modern age, humanitarian and practical considerations have combined to lead the nations of the world to recognize that respect for fundamental human rights is in their individual and collective interest. Among the rights universally proclaimed by all nations, as we have noted, is the right to be free of physical torture. Indeed, for purposes of civil liability, the torturer has become like the pirate and slave trader before him hostis humani generis, an enemy of all mankind. Our holding today, giving effect to a jurisdictional provision enacted by our First Congress, is a small but important step in the fulfillment of the ageless dream to free all people from brutal violence.

Notes

1. Were you at all surprised by the court's discussion of the relationship between customary international law and domestic common law? Can you articulate that relationship in a nutshell?

2. *Filartiga* says that adjudicating a claim under the Alien Tort Statute requires the court to explore whether the tort committed by the defendant violates a clear, unambiguous, well-established and basic principle of "the law of nations" (that is, customary international law). What sources does an American court consider in answering this question? Do these sources differ from sources courts examine in purely domestic torts cases? Is adjudication (and argumentation) of ATS claims more difficult than in cases involving purely domestic-law issues?

3. Why do you think the Founders gave aliens the right to sue in U.S. courts for these violations of customary international law? What does this say about the place of the new nation in the world? Does this still matter today?

4. *Kadic v. Karadzic*, 70 F.3d 232 (2d Cir. 1995), built on *Filartiga* and expanded the reach of the Alien Tort Statute to cover violations of the law of nations by private individuals. Radovan Karadzic, who self-identified as either "President of the self-proclaimed Republic of Srpska" or "not an official of any government," was found subject to liability under the ATS for genocide, war crimes, and crimes against humanity. "We do not agree that the law of nations, as understood in the modern era, confines its reach to state action," the court wrote. "Instead, we hold that certain forms of conduct violate the law of nations whether undertaken by those acting under the auspices of a state or only as private individuals." The court noted that piracy, one of the tortious acts clearly covered by the ATS at its inception, was most often a private act, rather than one committed by state actors.

5. *"Act of state," "political question" and "international comity" doctrines.* Plaintiffs in ATS cases may face a number of hurdles beyond proving the elements of the claim itself. One such barrier is the act of state doctrine, which prevents U.S. courts from inquiring into the validity of the public acts of a recognized foreign sovereign within its own territory. See *Banco Nacional de Cuba v. Sabbatino*, 376 U.S. 398, 84 S.Ct. 923, 11 L.Ed.2d 804 (1964). This doctrine reflects the concern that the judicial branch, by undertaking such an inquiry, will interfere with the executive branch's conduct of foreign policy. See *W.S. Kirkpatrick & Co. v. Environmental Tectonics Corp.*, 493 U.S. 400, 110 S.Ct. 701, 107 L.Ed.2d 816 (1990). A related doctrine is the political question doctrine, which requires a court to dismiss any case that would force the court to address "questions, in their nature political, or which are, by the constitution and laws, submitted to the executive." *Alperin v. Vatican Bank*, 410 F.3d 532 (9th Cir. 2005) (quoting *Marbury v. Madison*, 5 U.S. (1 Cranch.) 137, 2 L.Ed. 60 (1803). This doctrine, too, is a function of the separation of powers. See *Baker v. Carr*, 369 U.S. 186, 82 S.Ct. 691, 7 L.Ed.2d 663 (1962) (setting forth six factors, the presence of any one of which

forces dismissal on political question grounds,[*] and noting that issues relating to foreign relations "frequently turn on standards that defy judicial application, or involve the exercise of discretion demonstrably committed to the executive or legislature"). Finally, the international comity doctrine allows courts to decline to exercise jurisdiction that is otherwise properly asserted by deferring to the laws or interests of a foreign country. As the Supreme Court has explained, international comity "refers to the spirit of cooperation in which a domestic tribunal approaches the resolution of cases touching the laws and interests of other sovereign states." *Societe Nationale Industrielle Aerospatiale v. United States Dist. Court*, 482 U.S. 522, 107 S.Ct. 2542, 96 L.Ed.2d 461 (1987). None of these doctrines is an absolute bar to all ATS cases, but courts must be mindful of all three when adjudicating such claims. See *Sosa*, 542 U.S. at 761 (Breyer, J., concurring) (stressing the importance of a court's considering international comity when deciding to exercise jurisdiction in an ATS case).

6. *Suing U.S. government employees and officials.* An ATS or Torture Victim Protection Act claim brought by an alien against the an employee or official of the United States government runs squarely into the Westfall Act, 28 U.S.C. § 2679(b)(1), a federal statute that "affords federal employees absolute immunity from tort liability for negligent or wrongful acts or omissions they commit while acting within the scope of their employment." *In re: Iraq and Afghanistan Detainees Litigation*, 479 F.Supp.2d 85 (D.D.C. 2007). When the Attorney General certifies that a particular employee was acting within the scope of employment when the tort occurred, the action is converted into one against the United States itself. "The litigation is thereafter governed by the Federal Tort Claims Act." *Osborn v. Haley*, 127 S.Ct. 881, 166 L.Ed. 2d 819 (2007). The FTCA, 28 U.S.C.§ 2671 et seq., however, contains express limitations on governmental liability – such as a retention of immunity for assault and battery and false

---

[*]The six factors are: (1) a textually demonstrable constitutional commitment of the issue to a coordinate political department; or (2) a lack of judicially discoverable and manageable standards for resolving it; or (3) the impossibility of deciding without an initial policy determination of a kind clearly for nonjudicial discretion; or (4) the impossibility of a court's undertaking independent resolution without expressing lack of the respect due coordinate branches of government; or (5) an unusual need for unquestioning adherence to a political decision already made; or (6) the potentiality of embarrassment from multifarious pronouncements by various departments on one question. *Baker v. Carr*, 369 U.S. at 217.

imprisonment, and for acts occurring in a foreign country – that essentially renders governmental liability an impossibility in ATS and TVPA cases. Plaintiffs may also run headlong into the political question doctrine, described in Note 5 above, See, e.g., *Gonzales-Vera v. Kissinger*, 449 F.3d 1260 (D.C. Cir. 2006) (holding ATS case against former Secretary of State and National Security Advisor nonjusticiable under the political question doctrine), and the state secrets doctrine, which provides that the U.S. government may "prevent the disclosure of information in a judicial proceeding if 'there is a reasonable danger' that such disclosure 'will expose military matters which, in the interests of national security, should not be divulged.'" *El-Masri v. United States*, 479 F.3d 296 (4th Cir. 2007) (dismissing ATS suit alleging CIA's "extraordinary rendition" of plaintiff, a German citizen) (quoting *United States v. Reynolds*, 345 U.S. 1, 73 S.Ct. 528, 97 L.Ed. 727 (1953)).

SOSA v. ALVAREZ-MACHAIN

542 U.S. 692, 124 S.Ct. 2739, 159 L.Ed.2d 718 (2004).

Justice SOUTER delivered the opinion of the Court.

. . . In 1985, an agent of the Drug Enforcement Administration (DEA), Enrique Camarena-Salazar, was captured on assignment in Mexico and taken to a house in Guadalajara, where he was tortured over the course of a 2-day interrogation, then murdered. Based in part on eyewitness testimony, DEA officials in the United States came to believe that respondent Humberto Alvarez-Machain (Alvarez), a Mexican physician, was present at the house and acted to prolong the agent's life in order to extend the interrogation and torture. [In 1990 a federal grand jury indicted Alvarez for murder, and a warrant was issued for his arrest. After the Mexican government failed to assist in bringing him to the U.S., the DEA approved a plan to hire Mexican nationals to seize him in Mexico and bring him to the U.S. A group of Mexicans, including Jose Francisco Sosa, abducted Alvarez at his home, held him overnight in a motel, and brought him to Texas, where Alvarez was arrested. Alvarez's 1992 criminal trial ended with a judgment of acquittal.]

In 1993, after returning to Mexico, Alvarez began the civil action before us here. He sued Sosa, Mexican citizen and DEA operative Antonio Garate-Bustamante, five unnamed Mexican civilians, the United States, and four DEA agents. So far as it matters here, Alvarez sought damages from the United States under the FTCA [the Federal Tort Claims Act], alleging false arrest, and from Sosa under the ATS [Alien Tort Statute], for a violation of the law of nations. . . . The District Court granted the Government's motion to dismiss the FTCA claim, but awarded summary judgment and $25,000 in damages to Alvarez on the ATS claim. A three-judge panel of the Ninth Circuit then affirmed the ATS judgment, but reversed the dismissal of the FTCA claim. A divided en banc court came to the same conclusion. . . .

II

[The petitioner's FTCA claim fails because the liability asserted here falls within the FTCA exception to waiver of sovereign immunity for claims "arising in a foreign country," 28 U.S.C. § 2680(k).] The FTCA "was designed primarily to remove the sovereign immunity of the United States from suits in tort and, with certain specific exceptions, to render the Government liable in tort as a private individual would be under like circumstances." *Richards v. United States*, 369 U.S. 1, 6, 82 S.Ct. 585, 7 L.Ed.2d 492 (1962); *see also* 28 U.S.C. § 2674. . . . But the Act also limits its waiver of sovereign immunity in a number of ways. . . .

Here the significant limitation on the waiver of immunity is the Act's exception for "[a]ny claim arising in a foreign country," § 2680(k), a provision that on its face seems plainly applicable to the facts of this action. . . . For a plaintiff injured in a foreign country . . . the presumptive choice in American courts under the traditional rule would have been to apply foreign law to determine the tortfeasor's liability. *See, e.g., Day & Zimmermann, Inc. v. Challoner*, 423 U.S. 3, 96 S.Ct. 167, 46 L.Ed.2d 3 (1975) (per curiam) (noting that Texas would apply Cambodian law to wrongful-death action involving explosion in Cambodia of an artillery round manufactured in United States); *Thomas v. FMC Corp.*, 610 F.Supp. 912 (M.D.Ala.1985) (applying German law to determine American manufacturer's liability for negligently designing and manufacturing a Howitzer that killed decedent in Germany); *Quandt v. Beech Aircraft Corp.*, 317 F.Supp. 1009

(D.Del.1970) (noting that Italian law applies to allegations of negligent manufacture in Kansas that resulted in an airplane crash in Italy); *Manos v. Trans World Airlines*, 295 F.Supp. 1170 (N.D.Ill.1969) (applying Italian law to determine American corporation's liability for negligent manufacture of a plane that crashed in Italy).

. . . The application of foreign substantive law exemplified in these cases was, however, what Congress intended to avoid by the foreign country exception. . . . The object being to avoid application of substantive foreign law, Congress evidently used the modifier "arising in a foreign country" to refer to claims based on foreign harm or injury, the fact that would trigger application of foreign law to determine liability. . . .

III

Alvarez has also brought an action under the ATS against petitioner Sosa, who argues (as does the United States supporting him) that there is no relief under the ATS because the statute does no more than vest federal courts with jurisdiction, neither creating nor authorizing the courts to recognize any particular right of action without further congressional action. Although we agree the statute is in terms only jurisdictional, we think that at the time of enactment the jurisdiction enabled federal courts to hear claims in a very limited category defined by the law of nations and recognized at common law. We do not believe, however, that the limited, implicit sanction to entertain the handful of international law cum common law claims understood in 1789 should be taken as authority to recognize the right of action asserted by Alvarez here.

. . . [The parties here make extensive arguments about the history of the ATS; each contends that history supports its position. Scholars are not in complete agreement about the scope of the ATS.] Still, the history does tend to support two propositions. First, there is every reason to suppose that the First Congress did not pass the ATS as a jurisdictional convenience to be placed on the shelf for use by a future Congress or state legislature that might, someday, authorize the creation of causes of action or itself decide to make some element of the law of nations actionable for the benefit of foreigners. . . . There is too much in the historical record to believe that Congress would have enacted the ATS only to leave it lying fallow indefinitely.

The second inference to be drawn from the history is that Congress intended the ATS to furnish jurisdiction for a relatively modest set of actions alleging violations of the law of nations. Uppermost in the legislative mind appears to have been offenses against ambassadors; violations of safe conduct were probably understood to be actionable, and individual actions arising out of prize captures and piracy may well have also been contemplated. But the common law appears to have understood only those three of the hybrid variety as definite and actionable, or at any rate, to have assumed only a very limited set of claims. [Citing Blackstone's Commentaries.] . . .

IV

We think it is correct, then, to assume that the First Congress understood that the district courts would recognize private causes of action for certain torts in violation of the law of nations, though we have found no basis to suspect Congress had any examples in mind beyond those torts corresponding to Blackstone's three primary offenses: violation of safe conducts, infringement of the rights of ambassadors, and piracy. We assume, too, that no development in the two centuries from the enactment of § 1350 to the birth of the modern line of cases beginning with *Filartiga v. Pena-Irala*, 630 F.2d 876 (C.A.2 1980), has categorically precluded federal courts from recognizing a claim under the law of nations as an element of common law; Congress has not in any relevant way amended § 1350 or limited civil common law power by another statute. Still, there are good reasons for a restrained conception of the discretion a federal court should exercise in considering a new cause of action of this kind. Accordingly, we think courts should require any claim based on the present-day law of nations to rest on a norm of international character accepted by the civilized world and defined with a specificity comparable to the features of the 18th-century paradigms we have recognized. This requirement is fatal to Alvarez's claim. . . .

B

[We should exercise] great caution in adapting the law of nations to private rights. . . . [Jurisdiction under the ATS] was originally understood to be available to enforce a small number of international norms that a federal court could properly recognize as within the common law enforceable without further statutory authority. . . . [Yet we are persuaded] that the judicial power should be exercised on the understanding that the door is still ajar subject to vigilant doorkeeping, and thus open to a narrow class of international norms today. . . . For two centuries we have affirmed that the domestic law of the United States recognizes the law of nations. *See, e.g., Sabbatino*, 376 U.S., at 423, 84 S.Ct. 923 ("[I]t is, of course, true that United States courts apply international law as a part of our own in appropriate circumstances"); *The Paquete Habana*, 175 U.S., at 700, 20 S.Ct. 290 ("International law is part of our law, and must be ascertained and administered by the courts of justice of appropriate jurisdiction, as often as questions of right depending upon it are duly presented for their determination"); *The Nereide*, 9 Cranch 388, 423, 3 L.Ed. 769 (1815) (Marshall, C.J.) ("[T]he Court is bound by the law of nations which is a part of the law of the land"). It would take some explaining to say now that federal courts must avert their gaze entirely from any international norm intended to protect individuals.

We think an attempt to justify such a position would be particularly unconvincing in light of what we know about congressional understanding bearing on this issue lying at the intersection of the judicial and legislative powers. The First Congress, which reflected the understanding of the framing generation and included some of the Framers, assumed that federal courts could properly identify some international norms as enforceable in the exercise of § 1350 jurisdiction. We think it would be unreasonable to assume that the First Congress would have expected federal courts to lose all capacity to recognize enforceable international norms simply because the common law might lose some metaphysical cachet on the road to modern realism. Later Congresses seem to have shared our view. The position we take today has been assumed by some federal courts for 24 years, ever since the Second Circuit decided *Filartiga v. Pena-Irala*, 630 F.2d 876 (C.A.2 1980) . . . .

. . . [N]othing Congress has done is a reason for us to shut the door to the law of nations entirely. It is enough to say that Congress may do that at any time (explicitly, or implicitly by treaties or statutes that occupy the field), just as it may modify or cancel any judicial decision so far as it rests on recognizing an international norm as such.

C

We must still, however, derive a standard or set of standards for assessing the particular claim Alvarez raises, and for this action it suffices to look to the historical antecedents. Whatever the ultimate criteria for accepting a cause of action subject to jurisdiction under § 1350, we are persuaded that federal courts should not recognize private claims under federal common law for violations of any international law norm with less definite content and acceptance among civilized nations than the historical paradigms familiar when § 1350 was enacted. *See, e.g., United States v. Smith*, 5 Wheat. 153, 163-180, n. a, 5 L.Ed. 57 (1820) (illustrating the specificity with which the law of nations defined piracy). This limit upon judicial recognition is generally consistent with the reasoning of many of the courts and judges who faced the issue before it reached this Court. *See Filartiga, supra*, at 890 ("[F]or purposes of civil liability, the torturer has become – like the pirate and slave trader before him – hostis humani generis, an enemy of all mankind"); *Tel-Oren*, 726 F.2d 774, 781 (C.A.D.C. 1984) (Edwards, J., concurring) (suggesting that the "limits of section 1350's reach" be defined by "a handful of heinous actions-each of which violates definable, universal and obligatory norms"); *see also In re Estate of Marcos Human Rights Litigation*, 25 F.3d 1467, 1475 (C.A.9 1994) ("Actionable violations of international law must be of a norm that is specific, universal, and obligatory"). And the determination whether a norm is sufficiently definite to support a cause of action should (and, indeed, inevitably must) involve an element of judgment about the practical consequences of making that cause available to litigants in the federal courts.

Thus, Alvarez's detention claim must be gauged against the current state of international law, looking to those sources we have long, albeit cautiously, recognized. . . . To begin with, Alvarez cites two well-known international agreements that, despite their moral authority, have little utility under the standard set out in this opinion. He says that his abduction by Sosa was an "arbitrary arrest" within the meaning of the Universal Declaration of Human Rights (Declaration), G.A. Res. 217A (III), U.N. Doc. A/810 (1948). And he traces the rule against arbitrary arrest not only to the Declaration, but also to article nine of the International Covenant on Civil and Political Rights (Covenant), Dec. 16, 1966, 999 U.N.T.S. 171, to which the United States is a party, and to various other conventions to which it is not. [Article nine provides that "[n]o one shall be subjected to arbitrary arrest or detention," that "[n]o one shall be deprived of his liberty except on such grounds and in accordance with such procedure as are established by law," and that "[a]nyone who has been the victim of unlawful arrest or detention shall have an enforceable right to compensation."] But the Declaration does not of its own force impose obligations as a matter of international law. *See* Humphrey, *The UN Charter and the Universal Declaration of Human Rights,* in The International Protection of Human Rights 39, 50 (E. Luard ed. 1967) (quoting Eleanor Roosevelt calling the Declaration "a statement of principles . . . setting up a common standard of achievement for all peoples and all nations" and "not a treaty or international agreement . . . impos[ing] legal obligations"). And, although the Covenant does bind the United States as a matter of international law, the United States ratified the Covenant on the express understanding that it was not self-executing and so did not itself create obligations enforceable in the federal courts. Accordingly, Alvarez cannot say that the Declaration and Covenant themselves establish the relevant and applicable rule of international law. He instead attempts to show that prohibition of arbitrary arrest has attained the status of binding customary international law.

Here, it is useful to examine Alvarez's complaint in greater detail. As he presently argues it, the claim does not rest on the cross-border feature of his abduction. Although the District Court granted relief in part on finding a violation of international law in taking Alvarez across the border from Mexico to the United States, the Court of Appeals rejected that ground of liability for failure to identify a norm of requisite force prohibiting a forcible abduction across a border. Instead, it relied on the conclusion that the law of the United States did not authorize Alvarez's arrest. . . It is this position that Alvarez takes now: that his arrest was arbitrary and as such forbidden by international law not because it infringed the prerogatives of Mexico, but because no applicable law authorized it.

Alvarez thus invokes a general prohibition of "arbitrary" detention defined as officially sanctioned action exceeding positive authorization to detain under the domestic law of some government, regardless of the circumstances. Whether or not this is an accurate reading of the Covenant, Alvarez cites little authority that a rule so broad has the status of a binding customary norm today. He certainly cites nothing to justify the federal courts in taking his broad rule as the predicate for a federal lawsuit, for its implications would be breathtaking. His rule would support a cause of action in federal court for any arrest, anywhere in the world, unauthorized by the law of the jurisdiction in which it took place, and would create a cause of action for any seizure of an alien in violation of the Fourth Amendment, supplanting the actions under Rev. Stat. § 1979, 42 U.S.C. § 1983, and *Bivens v. Six Unknown Fed. Narcotics Agents*, 403 U.S. 388, 91 S.Ct. 1999, 29 L.Ed.2d 619 (1971), that now provide damages remedies for such violations. It would create an action in federal court for arrests by state officers who simply exceed their authority; and for the violation of any limit that the law of any country might place on the authority of its own officers to arrest. And all of this assumes that Alvarez could establish that Sosa was acting on behalf of a government when he made the arrest, for otherwise he would need a rule broader still.

Alvarez's failure to marshal support for his proposed rule is underscored by the Restatement (Third) of Foreign Relations Law of the United States (1986), which says in its discussion of customary international human rights law that a "state violates international law if, as a matter of state policy, it practices, encourages, or condones ... prolonged arbitrary detention." Although the Restatement does not explain its requirements of a "state policy" and of "prolonged" detention, the implication is clear. Any credible invocation of a principle against arbitrary detention that the civilized world accepts as binding customary international law requires a factual basis beyond relatively brief detention in excess of positive authority. Even the Restatement's limits are only the beginning of the enquiry, because although it is easy to say that some policies of prolonged arbitrary detentions are so bad that those who enforce them become enemies of the human race, it may be harder to say which policies cross that line with the certainty afforded by Blackstone's three common law offenses. In any event, the label would never fit the reckless policeman who botches his warrant, even though that same officer might pay damages under municipal law.

Whatever may be said for the broad principle Alvarez advances, in the present, imperfect world, it expresses an aspiration that exceeds any binding customary rule having the specificity we require. Creating a private cause of action to further that aspiration would go beyond any residual common law discretion we think it appropriate to exercise. It is enough to hold that a single illegal detention of less than a day, followed by the transfer of custody to lawful authorities and a prompt arraignment, violates no norm of customary international law so well defined as to support the creation of a federal remedy.

The judgment of the Court of Appeals is *Reversed.*

[Concurring opinions omitted.]

Notes

1. The *Sosa* Court says that the ATS is jurisdictional only, and does not create a cause of action. But what does this mean? The ATS itself gives the federal courts jurisdiction over aliens' claims that a defendant committed a tort that violates "the law of nations." To determine jurisdiction, then, the courts must conclude that the tort at issue is in fact actionable as a violation of customary international law. Is this any different from saying that the ATS creates a cause of action for violations of customary international law committed against aliens? See *Aldana v. Del Monte Fresh Produce, N.A., Inc.*, 416 F.3d 1242 (11th Cir. 2005) (stating that Sosa stands for the proposition that the ATS "is jurisdictional in nature but that it also provides a cause of action 'for the modest number of international law violations with a potential for personal liability at the time [of its] enactment.'"

2. *Sosa* reaffirms the basic approach taken in *Filartiga,* but holds that "courts should require any claim based on the present-day law of nations to rest on a norm of international character accepted by the civilized world and defined with a specificity comparable to the features of the 18th-century paradigms we have recognized." These 18th century paradigms – the torts the drafters of the ATS would have had in mind in 1789 – are "violation of safe conducts, infringement of the rights of ambassadors, and piracy." What do you think of this formulation? Should the court have read "the law of nations" more flexibly? Why was the Court this cautious?

3. At the same time, the Court said that "the judicial power should be exercised on the understanding that the door is still ajar subject to vigilant doorkeeping, and thus open to a narrow class of international norms today." Does this provide sufficient flexibility for lower courts to further expand the ATS? Does the Court give sufficient guidance on how large this "class of international norms today" might be?

4. The key question in cases after *Sosa* is perhaps not all that different from that which had to be addressed before *Sosa* was decided: has the alien plaintiff alleged a tort that violates a norm of customary international law sufficiently definite to support a cause of action?" *Filartiga* had held that the defendant's conduct had to violate well-established and universally-recognized rules of customary international law, and other courts had applied that test before the Supreme Court's decision in *Sosa*. In *Flores v. Southern Peru Copper Corp.*, 414 F.3d 233 (2d Cir. 2003), the court added that the current law of nations "is composed only of those rules that States universally abide by, or accede to, out of a sense of legal obligation and mutual concern. The *Flores* court went on to hold that the plaintiffs' assertion that the defendant infringed upon their customary international law "right to life," "right to health," and right to "sustainable development" were either "insufficiently definite" or, in the case of the last purported right, not a recognized international norm. Applying its own version of the test, the *Sosa* Court held that a one-day detention did not violate such a norm. What if Sosa had been held for months? What if he had been tortured during his detention? Does the Court's many favorable references to *Filartiga* answer that last question?

5. Those who predicted that *Sosa* would sound the death knell for ATS cases have been proven wrong, at least for now. Numerous cases continue to wind their way though the federal courts, and some have succeeded. Litigation typically centers on the particular norm of international law allegedly violated, and whether it is sufficiently definite. The assassination of El Salvadoran Archbishop Romero was held actionable under the ATS in *Doe v. Rafael Saravia*, 348 F.Supp.2d 1112 (E.D. Cal. 2004). Acts of genocide and crimes against humanity have been held to violate the law of nations. See *Almog v. Arab Bank, PLC*, 471 F.Supp.2d 257 (E.D.N.Y. 2007). Claims of torture have succeeded. See, e.g., *Aldana v. Del Monte Fresh Produce, N.A.*, Inc., 416 F.3d 1242 (11th Cir. 2005) (but holding that "non-torture claims" were not actionable); *Chavez v. Carranza*, 413 F.Supp.2d 891 (W.D. Tenn. 2005)(defendants' beating of plaintiff until he

agreed to confess to a killing was "torture" and thus actionable). But such conduct as statutory rape of a 16-year old has been held not actionable. *Cisneros v. Aragon*, 485 F.3d 1226 (10th Cir. 2007) (noting that "the law of nations, particularly that subset of that law enforceable under the ATS, does not include a norm simply because the norm is enshrined in the domestic law of all civilized societies"). And in *Taveras v. Taveraz*, 477 F.3d 767 (6th Cir. 2007), the court held that a cross-border parental child abduction by a defendant who had custody did not violate the "law of nations."

6. *Aiding and abetting liability.* ATS suits against corporations or financial institutions are usually founded on a theory of aiding and abetting. Two lawyer-analysts conclude that "the Sosa Court's underlying analysis tends to case serious doubt on the viability of aiding and abetting and other forms of secondary liability." Kristin Linsley Myles & Daniel P. Collins, *The Future of International Human Rights Litigation*, 32:3 Litigation 40, 45 (Spring 2006). But some post-Sosa lower courts have imposed such liability. See *Almog v. Arab Bank, PLC*, 471 F.Supp.2d 257 (E.D.N.Y. 2007) (collecting cases, and noting that "[g]oing back over 200 years, contemporaneous with the enactment of the ATS, aider and abetter liability was contemplated under the ATS); see also *Kiobel v. Royal Dutch Petroleum Co.*, 456 F.Supp.2d 457 (S.D.N.Y. 2005) ("Where a cause of action for violation of an international norm is viable under the ATS, claims for aiding and abetting that violation are viable as well."); *Mujica v. Occidental Petroleum Corp.*, 381 F.Supp.2d 1164 (C.D. Cal. 2005) (in dictum, noting that ATS allows for aiding and abetting liability in claim of torture).

B. THE TORTURE VICTIM PROTECTION ACT

THE TORTURE VICTIM PROTECTION ACT

PUB. L. NO. 102-256, 106 STAT. 73,
codified at 28 U.S.C. § 1350 note

§ SECTION 1. SHORT TITLE.

This Act may be cited as the "Torture Victim Protection Act of 1991."

§ SEC. 2. ESTABLISHMENT OF CIVIL ACTION.

(a) LIABILITY.—An individual who, under actual or apparent authority, or color of law, of any foreign nation—

(1) subjects an individual to torture shall, in a civil action, be liable for damages to that individual; or
(2) subjects an individual to extrajudicial killing shall, in a civil action, be liable for damages to the individual's legal representative, or to any person who may be a claimant in an action for wrongful death.

(b) EXHAUSTION OF REMEDIES.—A court shall decline to hear a claim under this section if the claimant has not exhausted adequate and available remedies in the place in which the conduct giving rise to the claim occurred.

(c) STATUTE OF LIMITATIONS.—No action shall be maintained under this section unless it is commenced within 10 years after the cause of action arose.

§ SEC. 3. DEFINITIONS.

(a) EXTRAJUDICIAL KILLING.—For the purposes of this Act, the term "extrajudicial killing" means a deliberated killing not authorized by a previous judgment pronounced by a regularly constituted court affording all the judicial guarantees which are recognized as indispensable by civilized peoples. Such term, however, does not include any such killing that, under international law, is lawfully carried out under the authority of a foreign nation.

(b) TORTURE.—For the purposes of this Act—

(1) the term "torture" means any act, directed against an individual in the offender's custody or physical control, by which severe pain or suffering (other than pain or suffering arising only from or inherent in, or incidental to, lawful sanctions), whether physical or mental, is intentionally inflicted on that individual for such purposes as obtaining from that individual or a third person information or a confession, punishing that individual for an act that individual or a third person has committed or is suspected of having committed, intimidating or coercing that individual or a third person, or for any reason based on discrimination of any kind; and

(2) mental pain or suffering refers to prolonged mental harm caused by or resulting from—

(A) the intentional infliction or threatened infliction of severe physical pain or suffering;
(B) the administration or application, or threatened administration or application, of mind altering substances or other procedures calculated to disrupt profoundly the senses or the personality;
(C) the threat of imminent death; or
(D) the threat that another individual will imminently be subjected to death, severe physical pain or suffering, or the administration or application of mind altering substances or other procedures calculated to disrupt profoundly the senses or personality.

Notes

1. With the Torture Victim Protection Act, Congress codified the core holding of *Filartiga*, expressly authorizing a cause of action for official torture and extrajudicial killing, and extended the right to sue to non-aliens (that is, to U.S. citizens and U.S. nationals). Federal jurisdiction over Torture Victim Act cases rests on general federal-question grounds, rather than on the Alien Tort Statute.

2. The TVPA and the ATS overlap to a degree, as you can see: an alien who was tortured, or the heirs of an alien who was subjected to extrajudicial killing, by an individual acting under authority (apparent or actual) of any foreign nation, could sue on

both theories. But the TVPA was not intended to limit or supplant the ATS, and they do not cover precisely the same ground, even with respect to alien plaintiffs. More specifically, first, "the law of nations" referenced in the ATS covers a broader set of wrongs than just "torture" or "extrajudicial killing." Second, the ATS covers a broader set of defendants than individuals acting under color of foreign law.

3. Since the passage of the TVPA in 1991, and especially since the *Sosa* decision was handed down in 2004, federal courts have addressed many aspects of the precise relationship between the TVPA and the ATS. Some of these issues remain unresolved. For example, where an alien is suing only for torture and killing by a former foreign official, must that plaintiff bring the claim only under the TVPA, and not under the ATS – thus becoming subject to the TVPA's exhaustion-of-local-remedies requirement? (The *Sosa* Court expressly left open the exhaustion of remedies question, commenting, "We would certainly consider this requirement in an appropriate case." *Sosa*, 542 U.S. at 733 n.21.) The court in *Enahoro v. Abubakar*, 408 F.3d 877 (7th Cir. 2005), so held. But other courts have disagreed, saying that state-sponsored torture is actionable under both the ATS and the TVPA, see *Aldana v. Del Monte Fresh Produce, N.A., Inc.*, 416 F.3d 1242 (11th Cir. 2005); *Kadic v. Karadzic*, 70 F.3d 232 (2d Cir. 1995), and that the exhaustion requirement in the TVPA does not apply to ATS cases in any event, see *Jean v. Dorelien*, 431 F.3d 776 (11th Cir. 2005). The *Aldana* court rested its conclusion in part on the idea that the TVPA's statutory definition of "torture" does not apply to the ATS at all. The ATS, remember, allows an alien to sue for a tort "committed in violation of the law of nations." Whether a tort violates "the law of nations" is determined by looking to international law, not domestic law. Thus, the *Aldana* court concluded, "a plaintiff may bring distinct claims for torture under each statute. . . . These two definitions suggest each statute provides a means to recover for torture as that term separately draws its meaning from each statute."

4. Other issues with respect to the relationship between the TVPA and the ATS appear to have been largely resolved. For example, the ten-year statute of limitations in the TVPA has been generally held to apply to the ATS, even though the ATS itself contains no express limitation. See, e.g., *Cabello v. Fernandez-Larios*, 402 F.3d 1148 (11th Cir. 2005); *Papa v. United States*, 281 F.3d 1004 (9th Cir. 2002).

5. *Suing a foreign government.* Notice that none of the cases in this Chapter are suits against foreign governments. The reason for that is that U.S. courts have jurisdiction over such suits only where the foreign government's immunity is removed by some particular provision of the Foreign Sovereign Immunities Act. The FSIA, its germane exceptions, and its relationship to the ATS, are addressed in Chapter 10. Suffice it to say for now that if an alien's tort suit is against a foreign government, he or she will face significant and perhaps insurmountable jurisdictional barriers.

Chapter 4

THE ANTI-TERRORISM ACT

GILMORE v. PALESTINIAN INTERIM SELF-GOVERNMENT AUTHORITY

422 F.Supp.2d 96 (D.D.C. 2006)

KESSLER, District Judge.

Plaintiffs are various family members of Esh Kodesh Gilmore, who Plaintiffs allege was killed in a terrorist shooting on October 30, 2000 in Jerusalem, Israel. Defendants are the Palestinian Interim Self-Government Authority ("PA"), the Palestine Liberation Organization ("PLO"), Yasser Arafat, and several other individual Defendants Plaintiffs allege were responsible for planning and carrying out the shooting. Plaintiffs bring suit under the Anti-Terrorism Act of 1991 ("ATA"), 18 U.S.C. § 2331, et seq., for international terrorism, and related torts. This matter is before the Court on Defendants' Revised Motion to Dismiss. Upon consideration of the Motion, Opposition, Reply, Surreply, and the entire record herein, Defendants' Motion is granted in part and denied in part.

I. Background

Plaintiffs base their lawsuit on the Antiterrorism Act of 1991, which provides a cause of action for United States nationals injured by an act of international terrorism. 18 U.S.C. § 2333(a). Plaintiffs also allege wrongful death, negligence, and intentional and negligent infliction of emotional distress.

For purposes of this Motion, the facts can be briefly stated. Plaintiffs allege that Defendants are responsible for "the planning and execution of terrorist bombings and shootings against civilians worldwide." They further allege that on October 30, 2000, several of the individual Defendants, who were associated with the PLO and the PA, "arrived at the offices of the National Insurance Institute on Asfani Street in Jerusalem, entered the building and without warning or provocation murdered," their family member, Esh Kodesh Gilmore, a United States citizen, by gunfire. At the time of his death, Gilmore was 25 years old, married, and father of a one-year old girl.

Defendants have moved to dismiss, claiming Plaintiffs' Complaint presents a non-justiciable political question, lack of subject matter jurisdiction based on Defendants' sovereign status, failure to state a claim upon which relief can be granted, and lack of personal jurisdiction over the individually named Defendants.

II. Standard of Review

. . . A motion to dismiss tests not whether the plaintiff will prevail on the merits, but instead whether the plaintiff has properly stated a claim in the Complaint. See Fed.R.Civ.P. 12(b)(6). Accordingly, the factual allegations of the complaint must be presumed true and liberally construed in favor of the plaintiff. . . .

III. Analysis

A. Plaintiffs' Complaint Presents Justiciable Issues Rather than Political Questions

Defendants first argue that Plaintiffs' Complaint should be dismissed because their allegations "have nothing to do with the death of the decedent," but rather, "amount to an all-out political attack upon the PA, the PLO, President Arafat, and senior Palestinian officials over decades and of such wide scope as to be nonjusticiable, raising issues that are not appropriate for or capable of judicial resolution." Defendants assert that "the judicial process is not equipped to assess the actions of a distant and foreign functioning government and its officials in this way over a period of decades. . . ."

Defendants fail to address the fact that this lawsuit was brought under a statute specifically designed to provide a civil cause of action in federal court for terrorist acts taken against American nationals abroad. The ATA provides:

> Action and jurisdiction. -- Any national of the United States injured in his or her person, property, or business by reason of an act of international terrorism, or his or her estate, survivors, or heirs, may sue therefor in any appropriate district court of the United States and shall recover threefold the damages he or she sustains and the cost of the suit, including attorney's fees.

18 U.S.C. § 2333(a). Enactment of the ATA makes it clear that both Congress and the Executive have "expressly endorsed the concept of suing terrorist organizations in federal court," and therefore this Court need not delve into an in-depth political question analysis here. Klinghoffer v. S.N.C. Achille Lauro, 937 F.2d 44, 49 (2d Cir.1991). Moreover, through the express language of the ATA and the application of common law tort principles, the Court has clear and manageable standards by which to properly adjudicate Plaintiffs' claims. See Ungar v. The Palestinian Authority, 402 F.3d 274, 281 (1st Cir. 2005).

The courts which have addressed this precise issue have squarely held that ATA claims brought against the PLO and the PA do not constitute non-justiciable political questions. See, e.g., Biton v. Palestinian Interim Self-Government Authority, 310 F.Supp.2d 172, 184-85 (D.D.C.2004); Ungar, 402 F.3d at 282; Klinghoffer, 937 F.2d at 49-50; Knox v. Palestine Liberation Organization, 306 F.Supp.2d 424, 448-49 (S.D.N.Y.2004). Defendants fail to discuss, no less distinguish, any of these cases. . . .

Whatever the merits of Defendants' contentions about the political situation between the Israelis and the Palestinians, it does not necessarily follow that Plaintiffs' claims constitute a non-justiciable political question. As the Second Circuit noted in Klinghoffer, in which the PLO made nearly the exact same non-justiciability argument, the doctrine "is one of 'political questions,' not one of 'political cases.' The fact that the issues before us arise in a politically charged context does not convert what is essentially an ordinary tort suit into a non-justiciable political question." 937 F.2d at 49 (citing Baker v. Carr, 369 U.S. 186, 217, 82 S.Ct. 691, 7 L.Ed.2d 663 (1962)). As in Klinghoffer, this case "is essentially an ordinary tort suit," despite its tragic facts. Consequently, Defendants' Motion with respect to non-justiciability must be denied.

B. Palestine Is Not a State and Therefore Is Not Entitled to Sovereign Immunity

Defendants next argue that "Palestine is an entity that meets the definition of a state under U.S. and international law," and therefore is immune from suit under 18 U.S.C. Section 2337(2). That section of the ATA provides that "[n]o action shall be maintained," against "a foreign state, an agency of a foreign state, or an officer or employee of a foreign state or an agency thereof acting within his or her official capacity or under color of legal authority." To determine whether a defendant is immune from suit because it is a "state," within the meaning of United States and international law, courts have looked to Section 201 of the Restatement (3d) of Foreign Relations Law of the United States, which provides: "Under international law, a state is an entity that has a defined territory and a permanent population, under the control of its own government, and that engages in, or has the capacity to engage in, formal relations with other such entities."

Defendants have the burden of establishing a prima facie case of sovereign immunity. With respect to the required elements under the Restatement, Defendants make a blanket assertion that "[t]he State of Palestine has a defined territory in the West Bank, Gaza Strip and East Jerusalem, a permanent population numbering in the millions under the control of its own government and engages in and has the capacity to engage in foreign relations with other states." At the very least, Defendants fail to establish that Palestine has the capacity to engage in formal relations with other sovereign states. . . . Several courts have considered this precise issue in depth, and have concluded that Defendants lack the capacity to engage in foreign relations. . . . In light of Defendants' failure to satisfy one of the criteria for statehood, it is not necessary for the Court to examine Plaintiffs' remaining arguments for why Palestine does not possess the attributes of statehood as outlined in the Restatement. . . . Thus, Defendants fail to meet their evidentiary burden to establish sovereign immunity.

C. Plaintiff's Complaint Sufficiently States a Claim for International Terrorism under the ATA

Defendants next assert that Plaintiffs fail to state a claim under the ATA. They argue that "Palestinian resistance and self defense in the occupied territories against Israeli occupation and oppression are neither coercion nor intimidation [and] ... do not constitute terrorism."

The plain words of Plaintiffs' Complaint make it clear that Defendants' argument has no merit. Plaintiffs allege that the murder of Esh Kodesh Gilmore was "planned and carried out" by several of the individual Defendants, "pursuant to prior authorization, instructions and directives of Defendants PA, PLO and ARAFAT." Plaintiffs also allege that Defendants' actions were "intended to intimidate or coerce a civilian population, and to influence the policy of a government by intimidation or coercion, within the meaning of 18 U.S.C. § 2331." These allegations, which must be taken as true at this early stage of the litigation, are more than sufficient to state a claim for international terrorism under the ATA.

Defendants' argument that Plaintiffs have failed to show that Defendants' motivation was intentional, in accordance with the definition of international terrorism in Section 2331 of the ATA, also must fail. "International terrorism" is defined in the ATA as:

> activities that –
>
> (A) involve violent acts or acts dangerous to human life that are a violation of the criminal laws of the United States or of any State, or that would be a criminal violation if committed within the jurisdiction of the United States or of any State;
>
> (B) appear to be intended –
> (i) to intimidate or coerce a civilian population;
> (ii) to influence the policy of a government by intimidation or coercion; or
> (iii) to affect the conduct of a government by mass destruction, assassination, or kidnapping; and
>
> (C) occur primarily outside the territorial jurisdiction of the United States, or transcend national boundaries in terms of the means by which they are accomplished, the persons they appear intended to intimidate or coerce, or the locale in which their perpetrators operate or seek asylum.

18 U.S.C. § 2331(A)-(C).

It is well-settled that the issue of intent is one for the jury to decide, and not an appropriate basis for ruling on a motion to dismiss. Accordingly, Defendants' Motion to Dismiss based on failure to state a claim must be denied.

D. The Court Lacks Personal Jurisdiction over the Individual Defendants

Finally, Defendants claim that none of the named individual Defendants have any connection to the United States, and therefore the Court may not exercise personal jurisdiction over them. . . .

Plaintiffs contend that, "the exercise of jurisdiction is consistent with the Constitution and laws of the United States," under a specific personal jurisdiction analysis outlined in a line of cases arising under the Antiterrorism and Effective Death Penalty Act of 1996 ("AEDPA"), an amendment to the Foreign Sovereign Immunities Act, which provides an exception to a foreign state's sovereign immunity in certain limited circumstances.

In [the AEDPA cases], the courts held that the act of committing a terrorist act against a United States national abroad, even if the defendant did not have actual contacts with the United States, constituted sufficient minimum contacts to satisfy due process for personal jurisdiction purposes. In Eisenfeld, for example, the court held that "a foreign state that causes the death of a United States national through an act of state-sponsored terrorism has the requisite 'minimum contacts' with the United States so as not to offend 'traditional notions of fair play and substantial justice.' "

Plaintiffs' argument that the personal jurisdiction analysis used in the AEDPA cases should be applied to the facts of this case must be rejected. The ATA and the AEDPA differ in significant respects.

First, in rejecting the same arguments that Plaintiffs make here, Judge Collyer noted in Biton:

> [t]here is one very simple reason why a district court may exercise personal jurisdiction over a foreign state defendant under the FSIA but not a similarly-situated individual defendant under the ATA. Section 1330(b) of the FSIA provides that 'personal jurisdiction over a foreign state shall exist as to every claim for relief over which the district courts have jurisdiction ... where service has been made

under section 1608 of this title' ... The ATA, in contrast, does not contain such an explicit grant of personal jurisdiction.

Second, unlike the present case, the AEDPA cases Plaintiffs cite were brought against states and state officials. . . . Therefore, the courts addressing the AEDPA claims did not have to consider the individual interests and freedoms protected by the due process analysis for personal jurisdiction which are presented in this case. . . .

Therefore, Plaintiffs must satisfy the Court that it has personal jurisdiction under Federal Rule of Civil Procedure 4(k)(2). [Plaintiffs must prove that] the federal courts' exercise of personal jurisdiction over the defendant must not offend the Constitution or other federal law. [Plaintiffs here] do not provide any evidence whatsoever to show that haling the individually named Defendants into this Court would "not offend the Constitution." Plaintiffs do not even allege that the individual Defendants had any contact with the United States. Without such a proffer, the Court is not satisfied that the individually named Defendants' "conduct and connection with the forum State are such that [they] should reasonably anticipate being haled into court there." Therefore, Defendants' Motion to Dismiss the individual Defendants for lack of personal jurisdiction must be granted.

IV. Conclusion

Accordingly, for the foregoing reasons, Defendants' Motion to Dismiss is granted in part and denied in part. Plaintiffs' claims against the individually named Defendants are dismissed. Defendants' Motion is denied with respect to subject matter jurisdiction, failure to state a claim, and justiciability.

Notes

1. *Elements of a claim under the Anti-Terrorism Act (ATA).* A claim under the ATA requires proof that (1) the injured person is a U.S. national (2) injured in his or her person, property or business (3) by reason of (4) an act of international terrorism. How does this differ from the elements of claims under the Alien Tort Claims Act and the Torture Victim Protection Act (both considered in Chapter 3)?

2. Is the ATA essentially an intentional tort claim, or will negligence suffice for liability? Does the text of the statute itself provide an answer?

3. *The "act of war" exception.* Section 2336(a) of the ATA states that "No action shall be maintained under section 2333 of this title for injury or loss by reason of an act of war." An "act of war" is defined in section 2331(4) as "any act occurring in the course of – (A) declared war; (B) armed conflict, whether or not war has been declared, between two or more nations; or (C) armed conflict between military forces of any origin." The statute itself, in other words, distinguishes between "international terrorism" and "war," making injuries caused by the former actionable and those caused by the latter non-actionable. One court has said that they key in ATA cases is often whether the tortfeasors are members of a "military force," which denotes the force "of a nation." Thus al Qaeda is not a "military force" and acts of violence by al Qaeda are acts of terrorism rather than acts of war. *Morris v. Khadr*, 415 F.Supp.2d 1323 (D. Utah 2006). See also *Estate of Klieman v. Palestine Authority*, 424 F.Supp.2d 153 (D.D.C. 2006) (holding that "as a matter of law, an act that violates established norms of warfare and armed conflict under international law is not an act occurring in the course of armed conflict. An armed attack on a civilian bus, such as the one plaintiffs have alleged in the complaint, violates these established norms."); *Biton v. Palestinian Interim Self-Government Authority*, 412 F.Supp.2d 1 (D.D.C. 2005) (bombing of a bus containing "only children and teachers" is not an "act of war" as a matter of law).

4. *Emotional distress recoveries.* Can a plaintiff sue for the emotional distress of losing a loved one to a terrorist act? Courts have said yes, as long as the emotional injury was "by reason of" the international terrorist act. See, e.g., *Biton v. Palestinian Interim Self-Government Authority*, 310 F.Supp.2d 172 (D.D.C. 2004) (holding that purely emotional harm is an "injur[y] in . . . her person" under the ATA, noting "[i]t seems unlikely that Congress would have considered damage to a car to constitute an 'injury' for purposes of the ATA but not emotional trauma and a loss of companionship from the death of a spouse occurring in the same attack. Which would you rather lose, a car or a spouse?").

5. What if the person physically killed or injured was not a U.S. national, but the plaintiff – perhaps that person's spouse – is suing for her own emotional distress caused by the attack? Does that fit the elements of the ATA? See *Biton*, 310 F.Supp. 2d at 181 ("If Mrs. Biton sues as the principal victim herself . . . she may be

able to state a claim if she can allege a cognizable injury that arose by reason of an act of international terrorism.")

6. *Damages.* The ATA itself provides that a prevailing plaintiff "shall recover threefold the damages he or she sustains and the cost of suit, including attorney's fees." Damages in ATA cases may run into the millions. See, e.g., *Ungar v. Palestine Liberation Organization,* 402 F.3d 274 (1st Cir. 2005) (upholding $116 million damages award); *Knox v. Palestine Liberation Organization,* 442 F.Supp.2d 62 (S.D.N.Y. 2006) (awarding damages of over $192 million); *Morris v. Khadr,* 415 F.Supp.2d 1323 (D. Utah 2006)(awarding damages of over $102 million).

7. Many damages awards in ATA cases will be uncollectible, either because the defendant has no money or because the plaintiff cannot reach the funds to satisfy the judgment. What, then, is the point of bringing a claim like this?

BOIM v. QURANIC LITERACY INSTITUTE AND HOLY LAND FOUNDATION FOR RELIEF AND DEVELOPMENT

291 F.3d 1000 (7th Cir. 2002).

ROVNER, Circuit Judge.

[The parents of a U.S. citizen murdered in Israel by Hamas terrorists sued several individuals and organizations for the loss of their son. Two of the organizational defendants moved to dismiss the complaint. The district court denied the motion, and the two defendants filed this interlocutory appeal.]

I.

We derive the facts from the allegations of the complaint. . . . We may affirm the dismissal of that complaint only if it appears beyond doubt that the plaintiffs can prove no set of facts in support of their claim that would entitle them to relief. [David Boim held dual citizenship in the U.S. and Israel. His parents, Joyce and Stanley Boim, are U.S. citizens.] In 1996, the Boims were living in Israel, where seventeen-year-old David was studying at a yeshiva. On May 13, 1996, David was murdered as he waited with other students at a bus stop near Beit El in the West Bank. He was struck by bullets fired from a passing car, and was pronounced dead within an hour of the shooting. . . . [Both killers were known member of the military wing of Hamas.] Hamas was designated a terrorist organization by President William Jefferson Clinton in 1995 by Executive Order. In 1997, Hamas was designated a foreign terrorist organization pursuant to 8 U.S.C. § 1189.

The Boims allege that Hamas' military wing depends on foreign contributions, with approximately one-third of its multi-million dollar annual budget coming from fund-raising in North America and Western Europe. The Boims believe that the Quranic Literacy Institute ("QLI") and the Holy Land Foundation for Relief and Development (AHLF"), along with other defendants not involved in this appeal, are the main fronts for Hamas in the United States. They allege that these organizations' allegedly humanitarian functions mask their core mission of raising and funneling money and other resources to Hamas operatives in support of terrorist activities. . . .

According to the Boims, money flows from American contributors to Hamas in a three-step process: first, the front organizations solicit contributions; second, the leaders arrange for the money to be laundered and wired overseas; and third, Hamas operatives in Gaza and the West Bank use the money to finance terrorist activities. Because it is illegal to provide financial support to recognized terrorist groups, the money flows through a series of complicated transactions, changing hands a number of times, and being commingled with funds from the front organizations' legitimate charitable and business dealings. The funds are laundered in a variety of ways, including through real estate deals and through Swiss bank accounts. The Boims allege that money raised by HLF and QLI was transferred to Hamas terrorists using these various methods in order to finance terrorist activities. Hamas used the money raised in this way to purchase weapons to carry out terrorist attacks, including the attack on David Boim. . . .

[The Boims bring their suit under the Anti-Terrorism Act, 18 U.S.C. § 2331 et seq. They charge that all of the defendants are civilly liable for David's murder. They allege that HLF and QLI aided, abetted and financed the two men who actually murdered their son.] They assert that the organizational defendants provided material support or resources to Hamas as those terms are defined in 18 U.S.C. §§ 2339A and 2339B. The Boims seek compensation for the extreme physical pain David suffered before his death, and for the cost of his funeral and the loss of accretion to his estate due to his death at age seventeen. They also seek damages for their own extreme mental anguish and loss of the society of their son. They ask for $100,000,000 compensatory damages, $100,000,000 punitive damages, plus costs and attorney's fees, and request the trebling of damages pursuant to the statute. . . .

II.

[T]he district court correctly certified three issues for [interlocutory] appeal:

(1) Does funding, *simpliciter*, of an international terrorist organization constitute an act of terrorism under 18 U.S.C. § 2331?

(2) Does 18 U.S.C. § 2333 incorporate the definitions of international terrorism found in 18 U.S.C. §§ 2339A and 2339B?

(3) Does a civil cause of action lie under 18 U.S.C. §§ 2331 and 2333 for aiding and abetting international terrorism? . . .

A.

The plaintiffs' first theory is that the simple provision of funds to Hamas by QLI and HLF constitutes an act of international terrorism because it "involve[s] violent acts or acts dangerous to human life." The Boims liken payments to Hamas to murder for hire: the person who pays for the murder does not himself commit a violent act, but the payment Ainvolves" violent acts in the sense that it brings about the violent act and provides an incentive for someone else to commit it. The Boims urge us to adopt a very broad definition of "involves" that would include any activity that touches on and supports a violent act. They argue that David's murder was indisputably a violent act, and we have no quarrel with that premise. But they further argue that the provision of money or in-kind services to persons outside the country who set up the infrastructure used to recruit and train David's murderers, buy their weapons, and compensate their families also "involves" violent acts. The defendants, in turn, urge us to read the statute to hold liable only those who actually commit a violent act.

. . . The controversy here centers on the definition of international terrorism, and in particular on the definition of the word "involve," which is susceptible to many meanings. The statutory definition of international terrorism in section 2331(1) is drawn verbatim from the Foreign Intelligence Surveillance Act,

50 U.S.C. § 1801(c) ("FISA"). No court has yet expounded on the meaning or scope of "international terrorism" as it is used in FISA either, so we are not aided by that origin. . . . [W]e agree with the district court that we must look to the structure, context and legislative history of the statute to determine what Congress intended.

The government, in its very helpful amicus curiae brief, delineates some of the legislative history of sections 2331 and 2333. That history, in combination with the language of the statute itself, evidences an intent by Congress to codify general common law tort principles and to extend civil liability for acts of international terrorism to the full reaches of traditional tort law. In particular, the statute itself contains all of the elements of a traditional tort: breach of a duty (i.e., committing an act of international terrorism); injury to the person, property or business of another; and causation (injured "by reason of"). Although the statute defines the class of plaintiffs who may sue, it does not limit the class of defendants, and we must therefore look to tort law and the legislative history to determine who may be held liable for injuries covered by the statute.

The legislative record is replete with references to the then-recent decision in Klinghoffer v. Palestine Liberation Organization, 739 F.Supp. 854 (S.D.N.Y.1990), vacated, 937 F.2d 44 (2d Cir.1991). Leon Klinghoffer was a U.S. citizen who was murdered in a terrorist attack on a cruise ship in the Mediterranean Sea. The district court found that his survivors' claims were cognizable in federal court under federal admiralty jurisdiction and the Death on the High Seas Act because the tort occurred in navigable waters. The repeated favorable references to Klinghoffer indicate a desire on the part of Congress to extend this liability to land-based terrorism that occurred in a foreign country.

The statute clearly is meant to reach beyond those persons who themselves commit the violent act that directly causes the injury. The Senate report on the bill notes that "[t]he substance of [an action under section 2333] is not defined by the statute, because the fact patterns giving rise to such suits will be as varied and numerous as those found in the law of torts." . . . [T]his history indicates an intent by Congress to allow a plaintiff to recover from anyone along the causal chain of terrorism.

But to the extent that the Boims urge a reading of the statute that would lead to liability for merely giving money to Hamas, a group which then sponsored a terrorist act in the manner the Boims have alleged, we agree with the district court, the defendants and the government that those allegations would be inadequate. To say that funding simpliciter constitutes an act of terrorism is to give the statute an almost unlimited reach. Any act which turns out to facilitate terrorism, however remote that act may be from actual violence and regardless of the actor's intent, could be construed to "involve" terrorism. Without also requiring the plaintiffs to show knowledge of and intent to further the payee's violent criminal acts, such a broad definition might also lead to constitutional infirmities by punishing mere association with groups that engage in terrorism. . . .

Additionally, the statute itself requires that in order to recover, a plaintiff must be injured "by reason of" an act of international terrorism. The Supreme Court has interpreted identical language to require a showing of proximate cause. See Holmes v. Securities Investor Protection Corp., 503 U.S. 258, 265-68, 112 S.Ct. 1311, 117 L.Ed.2d 532 (1992) (interpreting "by reason of" language in civil RICO provision to require a showing that the defendant's conduct proximately caused the plaintiff's injury). Foreseeability is the cornerstone of proximate cause, and in tort law, a defendant will be held liable only for those injuries that might have reasonably been anticipated as a natural consequence of the defendant's actions. In the circumstances of this case, the Boims cannot show that David Boim was injured "by reason of" the defendants' payments to Hamas in the traditional tort sense of causation unless they can also show that murder was the reasonably foreseeable result of making the donation. To hold the defendants liable for donating money without knowledge of the donee's intended criminal use of the funds would impose strict liability. Nothing in the language of the statute or its structure or history supports that formulation. The government, in its amicus brief, maintains that funding may be enough to establish liability if the plaintiff can show that the provider of funds was generally aware of the donee's terrorist activity, and if the provision of funds substantially assisted the terrorist act in question. We will consider the government's proposed standard separately in our discussion of aiding and abetting liability. For now we note only that the complaint cannot be sustained on the theory that the defendants themselves committed an act of international terrorism when they donated unspecified amounts of money to Hamas, neither knowing nor suspecting that Hamas would in turn financially support the persons who murdered David Boim. In the very least, the plaintiffs must be able to show that murder was a reasonably foreseeable result of making a donation. Thus, the Boims' first theory of liability under section 2333, funding simpliciter of a terrorist organization, is insufficient because it sets too vague a standard, and because it does not require a showing of proximate cause.

B.

The Boims' second theory of liability is that the defendants' violation of sections 2339A and 2339B, the criminal counterparts to section 2333, gives rise to civil liability under section 2333. . . .

In 1994, Congress passed 18 U.S.C. § 2339A, which criminalizes the provision of material support to terrorists. . . . "Material support or resources" is a defined term:

> In this section, the term "material support or resources" means currency or other financial securities, financial services, lodging, training, safehouses, false documentation or identification, communications equipment, facilities, weapons, lethal substances, explosives, personnel, transportation, and other physical assets, except medicine or religious materials.

18 U.S.C. § 2339A(b). Two years later, Congress extended criminal liability to those providing material support to foreign terrorist organizations:

> Whoever, within the United States or subject to the jurisdiction of the United States, knowingly provides material support or resources to a foreign terrorist organization, or attempts or conspires to do so, shall be fined under this title or imprisoned not more than 10 years, or both.

18 U.S.C. § 2339B(a)(1). Section 2339B adopts the definition of "material support or resources" provided in section 2339A, and looks to 8 U.S.C. § 1189 for the definition of "terrorist organization."

. . .When it passed sections 2339A and 2339B, Congress undoubtedly intended that the persons providing financial support to terrorists should also be held criminally liable for those violent acts. Indeed, as we have already noted, the Congressional record for section 2333 indicates an intention to cut off the flow of money in support of terrorism generally. Sections 2339A and 2339B further this goal by imposing criminal liability for financial support of terrorist activities and organizations. The fact that Congress imposed lesser criminal penalties for the financial supporters indicates perhaps that they found the financiers less dangerous or less culpable than the terrorists they finance, but it does not in any way indicate that Congress meant to limit civil liability to those who personally committed acts of terrorism. On the contrary, it would be counterintuitive to conclude that Congress imposed criminal liability in sections 2339A and 2339B on those who financed terrorism, but did not intend to impose civil liability on those same persons through section 2333.

Section 2339A prohibits the provision of material support for an extensive list of violent crimes associated with terrorism-assassination, kidnapping, arson, destruction of aircraft -- that make clear what types of conduct Congress had in mind when it defined "international terrorism" in section 2331(1) as not just the violent acts themselves, but also "activities that involve violent acts or acts dangerous to human life." There is no textual, structural or logical justification for construing the civil liability imposed by section 2333 more narrowly than the corresponding criminal provisions. . . .

We hasten to add that, although proof of a criminal violation under sections 2339A or 2339B might satisfy the definition of international terrorism under section 2333, such proof is not necessary to sustain a section 2333 claim. As we discuss in the context of aiding and abetting, we believe Congress intended for civil liability for financing terrorism to sweep more broadly than the conduct described in sections 2339A and 2339B. . . . For civil liability, section 2333 requires that the plaintiff be injured "by reason of" the act of international terrorism. Because we believe Congress intended to import standard tort law into section 2333, causation may be demonstrated as it would be in traditional tort law. Congress has made clear, though, through the criminal liability imposed in sections 2339A and 2339B, that even small donations made knowingly and intentionally in support of terrorism may meet the standard for civil liability in section 2333. Congress' goal of cutting off funding for terrorism would be seriously compromised if terrorist organizations could avoid liability by simply pooling together small donations to fund a terrorist act. . . .

C.

We turn next to the Boims' theory that HLF and QLI may be held civilly liable under section 2333 for aiding and abetting an act of international terrorism. Under this theory, the Boims urge us to find that aiding and abetting a violent act is conduct that "involves" a violent act as that word is used in section 2331(1). . . . The Boims also contend that section 2333 explicitly extends liability to aiders and abettors because it extends civil liability to "activities that involve violent acts ... that are a violation of the criminal laws of the United States." Because 18 U.S.C. § 2 criminalizes aiding and abetting the commission of a felony, the Boims maintain there is no doubt Congress intended to include liability for aiding and abetting in section 2333. The government, in its amicus brief, adds that the language and legislative history of section 2333 indicate an intent by Congress to import into section 2333 civil tort law principles as expressed in the Restatement Second of Torts, and as applied in the cases. . . .

As we will discuss below, although the words "aid and abet" do not appear in the statute, Congress purposely drafted the statute to extend liability to all points along the causal chain of terrorism. It is not much of a leap to conclude that Congress intended to extend section 2333 liability beyond those persons directly perpetrating acts of violence. Indeed, the statute itself defines international terrorism so broadly – to include activities that "involve" violent acts – that we must construe it carefully to meet the constitutional standards regarding vagueness and First Amendment rights of association.

[T]he language and legislative history of section 2333 evidence an intent to import general tort law principles into the statute. . . [T]he language of section 2333 tracks the traditional elements of tort law as expressed in the Restatement, and the legislative history expressly references tort principles in setting out the perimeters of Congress' intent. . . .

Congress also expressed an intent in section 2333 to make civil liability at least as extensive as criminal liability. The statute defining "international terrorism" includes activities that "involve violent acts or acts dangerous to human life that are a violation of the criminal laws of the United States or of any State, or that would be a criminal violation if committed within the jurisdiction of the United States or of any State." This language, embracing activities that "involve" violent acts, taken at face value would certainly cover aiding and abetting violent acts. Remember, too, the criminal laws include 18 U.S.C. § 2, which creates liability for aiding and abetting violations of any other criminal provisions. By incorporating violations of any criminal laws that involve violent acts or acts dangerous to human life, Congress was expressly including aiding and abetting to the extent that aiding and abetting "involves" violence. . . . Aiding and abetting, which is surely subsumed in the definition of acts that "involve" certain criminal violations, is a well known and well defined doctrine. That Congress did not use the words "aid and abet" in the statute is not determinative when it did use words broad enough to include all kinds of secondary liability. . . .

Finally, if we failed to impose liability on aiders and abettors who knowingly and intentionally funded acts of terrorism, we would be thwarting Congress' clearly expressed intent to cut off the flow of money to terrorists at every point along the causal chain of violence. . . . Congress' purpose here could not be met unless liability attached beyond the persons directly involved in acts of violence. The statute would have little effect if liability were limited to the persons who pull the trigger or plant the bomb because such persons are unlikely to have assets, much less assets in the United States, and would not be deterred by the statute. Also, and perhaps more importantly, there would not be a trigger to pull or a bomb to blow up without the resources to acquire such tools of terrorism and to bankroll the persons who actually commit the violence. Moreover, the organizations, businesses and nations that support and encourage terrorist acts are likely to have reachable assets that they wish to protect. The only way to imperil the flow of money and discourage the financing of terrorist acts is to impose liability on those who knowingly and intentionally supply the funds to the persons who commit the violent acts. . . .

III.

In short, we answer the three questions certified by the district court as follows: funding, *simpliciter*, of a foreign terrorist organization is not sufficient to constitute an act of terrorism under 18 U.S.C. § 2331. However, funding that meets the definition of aiding and abetting an act of terrorism does create liability under sections 2331 and 2333. Conduct that would give rise to criminal liability under section 2339B is conduct that "involves" violent acts or acts dangerous to human life, and therefore may meet the definition of international terrorism as that term is used in section 2333.

. . . The plaintiffs have not yet had an opportunity to develop the facts of their case. Today we hold that dismissal would be premature at this stage of the litigation because we can envision a set of facts in support of the claim they have alleged that would entitle them to relief.

Affirmed.

Notes

1. After the Seventh Circuit's opinion in *Boim* was rendered, the case was back in the trial court. In 2004 the trial court granted summary judgment for the plaintiffs against all but one of the organizational defendants, finding the evidence sufficient to prove that most of the organizational defendants had provided material support to a terrorist group in violation of the ATA. *Boim v. Quranic Literacy Institute*, 340 F.Supp.2d 885 (N.D. Ill. 2004). Later that year, the case went to trial before a jury against the one remaining organizational defendant, QLI. The jury returned a verdict against QLI for $52 million; the trial court then trebled the award, pursuant to the statute, to $156 million. QLI's motion for a new trial was denied shortly thereafter. *Boim v. Quranic Literacy Institute*, 2005 WL 433463 (N.D. Ill.).

2. *"Material support" and aiding and abetting liability.* Notice that providing "material support" to a terrorist group is a primary violation of the ATA, under sections 2339B and 2333(a). Aiding and abetting a violation of the ATA is secondary liability, but liability nonetheless. Courts have thus far agreed with the Seventh Circuit's *Boim* opinion that Congress intended to allow for aiding and abetting liability in the ATA. Courts have used the definition of aiding and abetting in the Restatement (Second) of Torts § 876(b), which requires that the plaintiff prove that the defendant "knows the other's conduct constitutes a breach of duty and gives substantial assistance or encouragement to the other so to conduct himself." Thus an act such as "the mere maintenance of a bank account and the receipt or transfer of funds" does not fit this definition. See *Weiss v. National Westminster Bank, PLC*, 453 F.Supp.2d 609 (E.D.N.Y. 2006); *In re: Terrorist Attacks on September 11, 2001*, 349 F.Supp.2d 765 (S.D.N.Y. 2005) ("there can be no bank liability for injuries caused by money routinely passing through the bank"). On the other hand, where a defendant served in a leadership role in al Qaeda and "encouraged his son to perpetrate terror," that defendant can be liable under the ATA for aiding and abetting. *Morris v. Khadr*, 415 F.Supp.2d 1323 (D. Utah 2006).

3. If Congress has criminalized giving material support to terrorists, and aiding and abetting terrorist violence, why do the plaintiffs here care whether the Anti-Terrorism Act creates a private cause of action for the same tortious activities?

Chapter 5

LIABILITY OF PARENTS AND CHILDREN

A. PARENTAL LIABILITY FOR TORTS OF CHILDREN: *GARDIEN* LIABILITY

Students of American tort law learn early on that as a general rule, parents are not vicariously liable for the torts of their children. This rule stands in marked contrast to well-established rules imposing vicarious (or strict) liability on employers for the torts of their employees. To be sure, many states have statutes that modify the common law to impose vicarious liability on parents, but the reach of the statutes is very limited. Frequently the damages permitted by a statute are capped at a low amount, or liability is imposed only for certain types of activities (such as driving) or only when the court concludes the child acted with a high level of culpability, such as wanton or willful conduct. See DAN B. DOBBS & PAUL T. HAYDEN, TORTS AND COMPENSATION 53-54 (5th Ed. 2005).

One possible explanation for the common law rule is that it, like other areas of U.S. tort law, reflects the value placed on individualism. Despite the fact that a child is brought into the world by his or her parents and is under their control and supervision for at least eighteen years, U.S. courts would find it unfair to consider parent and child as a unit for liability purposes. They are keenly aware that children have their own will and that they act independently of their parents.

In France, parents may be held strictly liable for the torts of children under a principle known as *gardien* liability. *Gardien* liability originates in Article 1384 of the French Civil Code, and it applies to a wide variety of circumstances. The basic idea is that the guardian of a thing (be it a piece of equipment or a child) is responsible for the harm it causes. This subsection will introduce you to the French Civil Code and give you some insights about this important part of tort law.

FRENCH CIVIL CODE, ARTICLE 1384*

A person is liable not only for the damages he causes by his own act, but also for that which is caused by the acts of persons for whom he is responsible, or by things which are in his custody. . . .

(4) The father and mother, in so far as they exercise "parental authority," are jointly and severally liable for the damage caused by their minor children who live with them.

Martin Shapiro

COURTS: A COMPARATIVE AND POLITICAL ANALYSIS

137-40 (1981)

[What Anglo-American legal systems call tort is referred to in civil law systems as noncontractual obligation, because when one person injures another, there is an obligation to compensate the injured party. The obligation is created by the act of injury, which is called a *delict*.]

ARTICLES 1382 AND 1383: LIABILITY FOR FAULT

The Civil Code has five brief articles on delict. They illustrate the point that. . . the French code often announces general legal principles rather than stating specific legal rules. Articles 1382 and 1383 say that a person is responsible for the damage done by his acts when he was at fault, negligent, or imprudent. Together they total forty-five words and constitute the entire basic code law on delict.

---

* Translated in Legifrance (trans. Georges Rouhette & Anne Barton).

ARTICLE 1384 AND LIABILITY WITHOUT FAULT

. . . Articles 1384, 1385 and 1386 create exceptions to the basic principle [of liability for wrongful or negligent acts]. It is in the tension between 1382-83, on the one hand, and 1384, on the other, that French courts have made their most innovative bodies of case law.

While there is much flag waving about the revolutionary break of the Code Napoleon from the law of pre-revolutionary France, in fact the code relied heavily on French legal traditions. Thus, 1382 and 1383 are revolutionary, at least in the sense of introducing a single, simple, sweeping rule. But 1384-86 introduce a series of exceptions to the principle which are in reality a compendium of minor pre-Revolutionary legal rules that followed no particular principle. Thus, 1386 provides that the owner of a building is responsible for injuries caused by its collapse, and 1385 provides for the liability of the owners of animals for the damage they do. Both of these articles obviously derive from older rules of special liability for the owners of buildings and animals. Both deviate from 1382-83 because owners of these particular things are liable even if they have not acted wrongfully or negligently.

The crucial deviation, however, is 1384. It sets up a number of categories of persons who are liable, not only for their own wrongful or negligent acts, but for the acts of others. Parents are declared responsible for the acts of their children, employers for those of their employees, and teachers and artisans for their students and apprentices. Article 1384 also declares that persons are responsible not only for the acts of persons for whom they are responsible but for damages caused by things "under their guard."

The phrase "things under guard" is hardly self-explanatory. One traditional theory was that it referred only to the animals and buildings that are the subject of 1385 and 1386. . . . The phrase obviously has enormous potential for judicial choice, for it would allow the judges to throw nearly any accident caused by both a person and a thing under either 1382 or 1384.

FACT-FINDING FRENCH STYLE

What difference does it make, however, whether a tort case comes under 1382 or 1384? In fact, it makes an enormous difference, but to understand why, we must look briefly at the way French courts handle questions of fact. . . . French fact-finding traditions arose in the context of professional judges and religious courts. There was great emphasis on the moral obligation of the judge to be absolutely certain he had discovered the true facts. For instance, medieval English criminal courts did not hesitate to convict a person who continued to profess his innocence if the jury believed him to be guilty. At the same period in France, criminal courts required a confession before they would convict and in theory at least required that even a confession be corroborated by other evidence. Modern French courts will very, very frequently simply conclude that there is not enough evidence to reach a factual conclusion. Often they refuse to make an authoritative finding of facts in situations in which an English or American court would hold that, for purposes of deciding the case, whatever version of the facts is most probably true will be taken as true. . . .

Faced with the proclivity of French courts to avoid conclusive findings of fact, plaintiffs who bring suit under 1382 are at a serious disadvantage. Unless they can get the court to make a finding of willful fault or negligence, they cannot win, and the court will frequently say simply that it cannot tell whether there was or was not fault or negligence. Even apart from these proclivities of French courts, the requirement that a plaintiff prove not only that the defendant's act caused the injury but also that he acted willfully or negligently is an onerous one that even Anglo-American plaintiffs often fail to meet.

ARTICLE 1384 AND THE PRESUMPTION OF RESPONSIBILITY

Unlike 1382, article 1384 does not require that the plaintiff prove that the defendant was at fault, because it imposes liability without fault. French courts very early established the rule that 1384 entailed a presumption of responsibility, a presumption that could not be overcome even if the defendant could prove that he had not been at fault. Thus, if a plaintiff could manage to bring the defendant under 1384 rather than 1382, he could win even if the court found itself unable to establish the facts conclusively. Indeed, the plaintiff could win under 1384 even if the defendant could prove he had done nothing wrong. In a legal tradition that makes it very hard for the plaintiff to establish the facts necessary to win, a legal presumption of those facts is of incredible value.

[French courts included industrial accidents under 1384 until passage of the Workers' Compensation Law. Section 1384 also includes automobile accidents, as the car is "under the guard" of the driver.]

Notes

1. Does the author's explanation surprise you? It highlights the importance of understanding the context of legal principles in a system of foreign law. Without context, it is hard to correctly discern what policy justifications are embodied in a code or in the judicial decisions of a country. Even then, it is a difficult task unless one can read the commentaries of legal scholars, for the French courts and legislature do not provide the extensive analysis one finds in U.S. opinions.

2. It is a common misconception that courts in civil law countries merely apply the code and do no original thinking about what it means. The courts' interpretation of the French Civil Code dispels that stereotype. Professor Shapiro explains in his book that the forty-five words of the French Civil Code on delict are far too broad and general to cover the issues, and that French judges, like common law judges, have had to propose and elaborate rules. Given the fact that in civil law systems, cases lack the precedential value they carry in the common law systems, do you think French judges have even greater freedom to create and explore the law of delict than their common law counterparts?

3. Even if it is difficult to prove fault under French law, the French courts could have insisted upon it in cases involving parental liability for torts of children if they were convinced this was the only fair basis for permitting compensation. So how did the French happen to come to the opposite conclusion? When the Civil Code was adopted in 1804, Article 1384(4) was understood to apply to instances where there *was* fault on the part of parents, such as inadequate supervision of their children. Parents could be relieved of liability if they proved they had not committed any wrongful acts. The imposition of strict liability is actually of recent origin, beginning with the *Bertrand* case, reproduced below. The justifications for the change, as provided by French scholars, include an interest in compensating the victim of damage and recognition that underage children pose risks to the community by reason of their youth and lack of experience.

4. Though expansive, liability is not completely unlimited. The Code conditions liability on co-habitation of parent and child, and this requirement has forced judges to decide what to do when, for example, parents are divorced or the child lives at boarding school or with grandparents or friends. In the instance of divorce, the parent with legal custody is the one who will be held strictly liable, and in the instance where children are living away from

home, the parents are held strictly liable regardless, so long as the child's legal residence is with the parents. The only way parents can now escape liability under Article 1384(4) is to show that a *force majeure* [Act of God, or natural disaster] prevented them from taking action to avoid an act of their child that caused damage. Laurence Francoz-Terminal, Fabien Lafay, Olivier Moréteau & Caroline Pellerin-Rugliano, *Children as Tortfeasors Under French Law, in* CHILDREN IN TORT LAW, PART I: CHILDREN AS TORTFEASORS, 193 (Miquel Martín-Casals ed., 2006).

BERTRAND v. DOMINGUES

Cour de cassation [cass. ass. plén]
[highest court of original jurisdiction]
Bordeaux, 19 fevrier 1997, D. 1997, 265†

Whereas according to the judgment under attack (Court of Appeal, Bordeaux, October 4, 1994) there was a collision on May 24, 1989 between a bicycle ridden by Sebastien X . . ., aged twelve, and the motorcycle of Mr. Domingues, who was injured and claimed compensation from Mr. Jean-Claude X . . ., father of the child, as being civilly responsible for him, and his insurer . . . intervened. . . .

On the legal second ground put forward:

Whereas the judgment is criticized for holding Mr. X . . . liable whereas, according to the ground of his [the father's] appeal, the presumption of liability of the parents of a child under the article 1384, paragraph 4 of the Civil Code, can be rebutted not only by proof of *force majeure* or fault of the victim, but also when the parents prove that they were not at fault in the supervision or education of the child; by refusing to inquire whether Mr. X . . . had proved the absence of any fault of supervision on the ground that only the *force majeure* or the fault of the victim could exonerate him from the strict liability imposed by the article 1384, paragraph 4 of the Civil Code, the Court of Appeal had violated article 1384, paragraph 4 of the Civil Code;

Whereas the decision was right to state that only the *force majeure* or the fault of the victim could exonerate Mr. X . . . from the strict liability for the damage caused by his resident minor

† Translation by Clemence George

son, the Court of Appeal had no need to inquire into any possible fault in the father's supervision;

Therefore the legal ground put forward is declared unfounded;

. . .

Therefore: Dismiss the appeal.

Note

The French courts have continued to affirm this unique strict liability doctrine in subsequent cases, as indicated in the following excerpt.

Miguel Martín-Casals

Cass. Ass. Pleniere, 13 deciembre 2002, Bull.civ.AP, No. 3, J.C.P. G2003 II, 10010: Parental Liability for the Acts of Their Children

12 Eur. Rev. of Private L. 691, 692-693 (2004)

French case law has thus established a strict liability regime for parents, and not only because fault of the parents is not a condition for their liability. If this were the case, we could be saying that it has established a vicarious liability regime. The first step, i.e., doing away with the condition of fault or negligence of the parents and establishing *de facto* a regime of vicarious liability for the acts of their children, has almost been taken up by case law in Italy, where parents can hardly ever reverse the burden of proof, and even more clearly in Spain, where courts have rendered it impossible for parents to escape liability by proving their diligence. Moreover, in Spain specific legal provisions have introduced a system of vicarious liability of parents for the acts of their children when these acts also qualify as a crime or a misdemeanor.

French law has gone a step further and has established a strict liability regime considering that for the parents to be liable it is irrelevant whether the child has been at fault—in the case that he has tortious capacity—and also whether he would have been at fault if he had been an adult—when he does not have such a capacity.

Notes

1. The strictness of the French approach is evidenced in cases subsequent to *Bertrand.* One involved a boy who lost his balance during a sports training class and fell on one of his classmates, kicking him in the head. Another involved a rugby player who was tackled by one player and fell on a third player, injuring him. Do you concur with parental liability in these instances?

2. In another part of the article excerpted above, Martín-Casals criticizes the fairness of the French approach. He questions whether it is wise to treat *gardien* liability of parents the same way one would treat liability for animals or dangerous things. He points out the societal interest in raising children and contrasts animals or dangerous activities, which are kept for the benefit of keeper. Martín-Casals also suggests that this rule may run counter to society's interest in holding children other than the very young responsible for their own acts. He suggests it is appropriate to recognize that after a certain age parents can no longer reasonably be expected to control children. Do you agree? Might imposing strict liability on parents produce a safer society?

3. The PRINCIPLES OF EUROPEAN TORT LAW Art. 6:101 (2005), proposes that a person in charge of a minor should be held liable for damage caused unless the person in charge shows conformity to the required standard of conduct in supervision. This position represents the prevailing view of representatives of many European countries who met over a period of years to compare their countries' approaches to this and other questions.

B. LIABILITY OF CHILDREN FOR THEIR OWN TORTS

Students of U.S. law are often surprised to read cases in which small children are held liable for such things as moving a chair an adult was planning to sit in, or for tossing keys in a game of Monkey-in-the-Middle. Despite the general willingness to impose liability on children, there are, as a practical matter, a few limits. Some states, by statute, do not permit very young children to be held liable in tort at all. See 1 DAN B. DOBBS, THE LAW OF TORTS § 124, at 293 (2000). Further, with intentional torts, courts may find that very young children do not have the capacity to formulate the required intent – although if they are capable, they are usually not immune from suit due to age alone. With regard to negligence liability, babies and toddlers are generally considered incapable of negligence; however, in most states, children of kindergarten age or older may be sued. The child standard of care, which requires a child to act as a reasonable child of like age, experience, intelligence and maturity would act, protects children from liability for lapses in skill or judgment that would certainly lead to liability for an adult.

When one studies the law in other countries, it quickly becomes apparent that they approach this question differently from the U.S., and from one another. An interesting starting point is the law of France. One might think that because parents are held liable for the torts of minors under Article 1384, children themselves would not be held accountable. However, this is entirely wrong, as children may be held strictly liable as *gardiens* under Article 1384, as well as under the fault-based liability of Articles 1382 and 1383.

This is a relatively recent development in French law. Prior to 1984, French law required that a person must be capable of understanding a wrongful act. Children were presumed incapable of doing so and were not held responsible under either the fault-based or *gardien* articles. In 1968, the French legislature had stated that mentally ill persons would become fully liable, but it was not until 1984 that the same rule was applied to children. The following case, *Sabatier*, is one of the most important on this point.

ARRÊT SABATIER

Cass. Civ., 12 Decembre 1984 *

[Seven-year-old Jean-Claude Sabatier, was playing in the school yard with Nicolas Desprats, who also seven years of age. Jean-Claude pushed Nicolas. He fell, hit a bench and was injured.]

. . .Whereas the judgment is criticized for holding Jean-Claude Sabatier solely responsible for Nicolas Desprats' physical injuries without discussion of the ability of a seven-year-old to discern the consequences of his acts;. . .

But whereas the decision established that the minor Jean-Claude Sabatier pushed Nicolas Desprats on a school bench with such violence that it led his spleen to burst with resulting internal hemorrhage;

. . . [T]he Court of Appeal did not have to verify if the minor Jean-Claude Sabatier was capable of discerning the consequences of his acts to conclude that he was at fault.

Therefore the legal ground put forward is declared unfounded;

---

* Translation by Clemence George.

Therefore: Dismiss the appeal.

Note

Even if French law makes children fully capable of fault, it would be possible to mitigate this harshness through the standard of care. This is the way U.S. courts handle the issue, taking into account a child's age, intelligence, maturity and experience. French law, however, does not modify the standard of care, as the following excerpt explains.

Christian Von Bar

THE COMMON EUROPEAN LAW OF TORTS*

Volume I, pp. 93-95 (1998)

The most important aspect of these rulings seems to be the following. In negligence, the simple fact that the ability to reason has ceased to be a precondition for liability does not answer an equally important question: what standard of care should be required of a child or juvenile? Should he be judged by reference to the diligence to be expected of a person of the same age in similar circumstances, or that of the *bon père de famille?* [good father of the family]. Nearly all scholars who have analyzed the more recent French rulings agree that the question was, or at least should have been, answered by applying the stringent standard of care demanded of the *bon père de famille.* The current position of French judge-made law is therefore that a civil *faute* is determined solely by the act committed: the age of the tortfeasor, his character, intelligence and ethical capacity are of no relevance. . . . In other words, liability is based on objective misconduct, and is independent of fault. Although, unlike in cases of true strict liability, the question of whether even the *bon père de famille* could reasonably have been expected to act lawfully, or whether the act of the child could be considered reasonable from the point of view of an adult, is still an issue, nobody seems to remember that fathers too were once children.

The frequently used argument that adults are treated no differently from children, i.e., they too are subject to a strict duty of care, cannot justify the course embarked upon by the *Cour de Cassation.* For to deprive children of the protection of the requirement of *discernement* is to place a heavy responsibility on them before their lives have begun. As for the standard of care, one should always bear in mind that a child cannot act other than as a child. . . .

Note

In contrast to French law, most other European countries are highly protective of children, though their approaches differ quite markedly from one another. Dutch law exemplifies a particularly protective approach, as the following description reveals.

Willem H. van Boom

Children as Tortfeasors under Dutch Law, *in* CHILDREN IN TORT LAW PART 1: CHILDREN AS TORTFEASORS

Miguel Martín-Casals, ed. (2006) pp. 296-297

The 1992 Dutch Civil Code introduced a groundbreaking new principle on the liability of children. Under art 6:162 BW (*Burgerlijk Wetboek*), a wrongful act can only induce liability if the act is *imputable.** Under art. 6:164 BW, however, imputability of the acts of children younger than fourteen years is fully excluded. As a result children younger than fourteen are completely exempt from any tortious liability. Therefore, the fixed minimum age is fourteen years.

However, the injured party is not left without compensation. In most cases of wrongful infliction of damage by children, the parents are strictly liable. Art. 6:169 BW states that parents can be held liable if the wrongful act – omissions not included – would have been imputable to the child if, at the time of the act, it had already reached the age of fourteen. . . .

When answering this question, one must ask himself whether a prudent person of average age could and should have acted otherwise. . . . It must be noted, however, that any physical or mental disabilities of tortfeasors of fourteen years and older do not stand in the way of liability. . . .

Notes

1. Some European countries, notably Austria, Belgium and the Czech Republic, utilize a subjective standard of care for children. In Austria, for example, a plaintiff must prove that the

*Editors' note: The concept of imputability is a difficult one. The term is codified at 6:162 BW, paragraph 3, which, as translated by Van Boom and others, provides: "[a] wrongful act can be imputed to its author if it results from his fault or from a cause for which he is answerable according to law or common opinion." Van Boom explains that word "law" refers to a statutory basis and "common opinion" refers to an unwritten source of legal and moral authority as expressed in case law. *Id.* at 293-94. Wrongfulness and imputability are thus separate required elements.

minor was able to realize the wrongfulness of his behavior, and a judge would consider the minor's age, stage of development and surrounding circumstances. The Czech Republic recognizes that proving subjective fault of a child may be difficult for victims, and places the burden of proof on the defendant to demonstrate absence of fault. *See* Miguel Maríin-Casals, *Comparative Overview*, in CHILDREN AS TORTFEASORS, *supra*, at 427-28.

2. Mexico's approach to the question of liability of children and parents represents an intermediate view. The Código Civil Federal, Art. 1911, provides that a person who lacks capacity but causes injury must be answerable for it, unless the responsibility falls on those who are responsible for that person. Article 1922 of the Code states that neither the parents nor the tutors have an obligation to respond to harm and prejudice caused by those with incapacity who are under their care and vigilance if they prove that it would have been impossible for them to avoid the harm. Another variation, the Civil Code of Argentina, Art. 1114, imposes joint and several liability for damage caused by minor children that live with parents, without prejudice to liability of the children if they are over ten years old. As is true in Mexico, parents are not liable for the damage caused by the acts of children if it would be impossible for them to prevent such acts. Art. 1116. Both Argentina and Mexico make clear that the occurrence of acts outside the presence of the parents will not exempt them if it appears they were negligent in failing to supervise.

3. Do you think French law, through its rather stringent rules for placing responsibility on children and its strict *gardien* liability, motivates greater parental supervision of children? Or would this incentive only play a role in a society with far more litigation than is present in France?

4. Does the Dutch system of shielding children younger than fourteen from liability and imposing strict liability on their parents treat parents unfairly? Do Argentina and Mexico have it right when they allow the parents to exculpate themselves by proving they were not negligent in their supervision?

5. How do you think that the U.S. combination of extensive potential liability of children and very limited parental responsibility compares in terms of fairness and its practical impact to the approaches other countries take?

Chapter 6

THE WARSAW CONVENTION

The international treaty commonly known as the Warsaw Convention[1] governs the rights of passengers, shippers and carriers in most aspects of international air transportation, including the conditions under which most international air passengers may sue for personal injuries and property damage. It was promulgated in 1929, after the completion of negotiations in Warsaw, Poland (hence the common name). The United States Senate ratified the Convention in 1934. Since that time four agreements have modified various aspects of the original Convention, most notably damages caps and defenses: the Hague Protocol of 1955; the Montreal Agreement of 1966; the Guatemala City Protocol of 1971; and the Montreal Protocol No. 4 of 1998. Not all of the countries that are signatory to the original Convention have ratified all of the subsequent modifications, creating some sticky interpretive issues that must remain beyond the scope of our inquiry here. About 135 countries have either signed or abide by the Convention (or one or more of the subsequent agreements, or both), making it one of the most widely-adopted international treaties in world history.

Pursuant to Article VI of the U.S. Constitution, "all treaties made . . . under the authority of the United States, shall be the supreme law of the land," along with the Constitution itself and federal law, "and the judges in every state shall be bound

[1] Its formal name is the Multilateral Convention for the Unification of Certain Rules Relating to International Transportation by Air, codified in 49 Stat. 3000, T.S. No. 876 (1934), note following 49 U.S.C.App. § 1502.

thereby." Thus the Warsaw Convention is the law of this land, on an equal footing with our purely domestic law.

Requirements for carrier liability. Where the Convention applies (that is, where the flight is "international," and where a ticket has been delivered, stating that the Convention applies), a carrier is liable to a passenger where there is an "accident" on board the aircraft, or in the course of embarking or disembarking, that causes "damage." Fault of the airline is not required.[2]

Limitations on liability. Why, if the Convention sets up a strict liability scheme, is there so much litigation by plaintiffs trying to argue that the Convention does *not* apply? The answer is that the Convention limits airlines' monetary liability rather dramatically, at least compared to domestic American tort law. The current cap, set by the 1966 Montreal Agreement, is $75,000 per passenger. Punitive damages are not allowed, either. The damages cap is lifted if the carrier commits "willful misconduct."

Venue and Jurisdiction. Where the Convention applies, a plaintiff is not free to choose the most favorable forum in which to bring a damages suit. Instead, the Convention itself provides that a plaintiff must bring suit within the territory of one of the High Contracting Parties,[3] before the court located in either (1) the domicile of the carrier; or (2) the carrier's principal place of business; or (3) the place where the carrier has a place of business through which the contract has been made; or (4) the place of destination. Art. 28(1). Notice that neither the domicile of the plaintiff nor the place of the flight's origin is an authorized venue. Article 28 sets the outer limits of a court's jurisdiction over a Warsaw Convention case. See, e.g., *Petrie v. Spantax, S.A.*, 756 F.2d 263 (2d Cir. 1985) (affirming dismissal of suit by heirs of a Spanish national killed on a round-trip flight from Spain to New York and back on a Spanish airline; Spain is the only proper venue and U.S. courts have no jurisdiction).

---

[2] Art. 20 of the Convention states that "the carrier shall not be liable if he proves that he and his agents have taken all necessary measures to avoid the damage or that it was impossible for him to take such measures," thus giving carriers an affirmative defense of due care. But later amendments and carrier agreements have removed this defense for damage to passengers and baggage, leaving it in place only where damage is caused by "delay." Liability for harms to passengers and baggage, then, is effectively strict liability.

[3] A High Contracting Party is a country that has either ratified or which adheres to the Convention.

Scope. The Warsaw Convention applies only to "international transportation," a term defined by Article 1(2) as any trip in which, "according to the contract made by the parties, the place of departure and the place of destination" are either within the territories of two "High Contracting Parties or within the territory of a single High Contracting Party, if there is an agreed stopping place within a territory . . . of another power, even though that power is not a party to this convention." This means that not all international flights are subject to the Convention; if a flight either originates or terminates in a non-Convention country, the Convention cannot apply. Thus, for example, since Taiwan does not adhere to the Convention, one-way flights to and from that country are not covered – leaving the parties to argue about which country's substantive law should apply when an injury or loss occurs. See, e.g., *Mingtai Fire & Marine Ins. Co. v. United Parcel Service*, 177 F.3d 1142 (9th Cir. 1999). But this same provision also means that a round-trip flight to and from a Convention country – say, a flight from Los Angeles to Taiwan and back, or from Mexico (a Convention country) to Thailand (a non-Convention country) to Japan and back to Mexico – is subject to the Convention, even where the injury occurs in the non-Convention country. See, e.g, *Chagnon v. Japan Air Lines*, 661 F.Supp. 224 (C.D. Cal 1987) (flight between Thailand and Japan was subject to Warsaw Convention because that leg was part of a round-trip flight to and from Mexico).

Even a flight between two points within one country might be subject to the Warsaw Convention, if a leg of this flight has included a stop in another country and the domestic portion was purchased in a single transaction with the international portion. See, e.g. *Duff v. Trans World Airlines, Inc.*, 527 N.E.2d 498 (Ill. App. 1988) (flight from New York to Chicago covered by the Warsaw Convention where that flight was merely the last leg in an international flight between Spain and Chicago). If passengers are on a truly separate "side trip" within one country while on a broader international trip, however, the Warsaw Convention will not apply. See, e.g., *Coyle v. P.T. Garuda Indonesia*, 363 F.3d 979 (9th Cir. 2004) (crash on trip between two Indonesian cities was not part of victims' overall international travel itinerary; thus Warsaw Convention was inapplicable).

As you can probably tell just from this introduction, the Warsaw Convention, in all its complexity, occupies an extremely important part of the field of global tort law. Case law under the Convention is voluminous, both inside the United States and in the courts of other nations that have ratified or observe it.

Litigation often centers on the interpretation and application of various operative terms in the Convention and its later modifications, but several cases have addressed more basic questions about the scope of the Convention and its relation to domestic tort law. In the rest of this Chapter we highlight some of the key issues that have been brought before U.S. courts in recent years.

A. THE "ACCIDENT" REQUIREMENT

AIR FRANCE v. SAKS

470 U.S. 392, 105 S.Ct. 1338, 84 L.Ed.2d 289 (1985).

Justice O'CONNOR delivered the opinion of the Court.

Article 17 of the Warsaw Convention makes air carriers liable for injuries sustained by a passenger "if the accident which caused the damage so sustained took place on board the aircraft or in the course of any of the operations of embarking or disembarking." We granted certiorari to resolve a conflict among the Courts of Appeals as to the proper definition of the word "accident" as used in this international air carriage treaty.

I

On November 16, 1980, respondent Valerie Saks boarded an Air France jetliner in Paris for a 12-hour flight to Los Angeles. The flight went smoothly in all respects until, as the aircraft descended to Los Angeles, Saks felt severe pressure and pain in her left ear. The pain continued after the plane landed, but Saks disembarked without informing any Air France crew member or employee of her ailment. Five days later, Saks consulted a doctor who concluded that she had become permanently deaf in her left ear.

Saks filed suit against Air France in California state court, alleging that her hearing loss was caused by negligent maintenance and operation of the jetliner's pressurization system. The case was removed to the United States District Court for the Central District of California. After extensive discovery, Air France moved for summary judgment on the ground that respondent could not prove that her injury was caused by an "accident" within the meaning of the Warsaw Convention. The term "accident," according to Air France, means an "abnormal, unusual or unexpected occurrence aboard the aircraft." All the available evidence, including the postflight reports, pilot's affidavit, and passenger testimony, indicated that the aircraft's pressurization system had operated in the usual manner. Accordingly, the airline contended that the suit should be dismissed because the only alleged cause of respondent's injury-normal operation of a pressurization system-could not qualify as an "accident." In her opposition to the summary judgment motion, Saks acknowledged that "[t]he sole question of law presented ... by the parties is whether a loss of hearing proximately caused by normal operation of the aircraft's pressurization system is an 'accident' within the meaning of Article 17 of the Warsaw Convention. . . . " She argued that "accident" should be defined as a "hazard of air travel," and that her injury had indeed been caused by such a hazard.

[The district court granted summary judgment for Air France, and a divided Ninth Circuit panel reversed. The Ninth Circuit panel concluded that the Warsaw convention imposes absolute liability on airlines for injuries proximately caused by the risks inherent in air travel, and defined "accident" as "an occurrence associated with the operation of an aircraft which takes place between the time any person boards the aircraft with the intention of flight and all such persons have disembarked. . . ." 724 F.2d at 1385.] We disagree with the definition of "accident" adopted by the Court of Appeals, and we reverse.

II

Air France is liable to a passenger under the terms of the Warsaw Convention only if the passenger proves that an "accident" was the cause of her injury. The narrow issue presented is whether respondent can meet this burden by showing that her injury was caused by the normal operation of the aircraft's pressurization system. The proper answer turns on interpretation of a clause in an international treaty to which the United States is a party. "[T]reaties are construed more liberally than private agreements, and to ascertain their meaning we may look beyond the written words to the history of the treaty, the negotiations, and the practical construction adopted by the parties." *Choctaw Nation of Indians v. United States,* 318 U.S. 423, 431-432, 63 S.Ct. 672, 677-678, 87 L.Ed. 877 (1943). The analysis must begin, however, with the text of the treaty and the context in which the written words are used.

A

Article 17 of the Warsaw Convention establishes the liability of international air carriers for harm to passengers. Article 18 contains parallel provisions regarding liability for damage to baggage. The governing text of the Convention is in the French language. . . . The official American translation of this portion of the text, which was before the Senate when it ratified the Convention in 1934, reads as follows:

Article 17

> The carrier shall be liable for damage sustained in the event of the death or wounding of a passenger or any other bodily injury suffered by a passenger, *if the accident which caused the damage* so sustained took place on board the aircraft or in the course of any of the operations of embarking or disembarking.

Article 18

> (1) The carrier shall be liable for damage sustained in the event of the destruction or loss of, or of damage to, any checked baggage or any goods, *if the occurrence which caused the damage* so sustained took place during the transportation by air.

Two significant features of these provisions stand out in both the French and the English texts. First, Article 17 imposes liability for injuries to passengers caused by an "accident," whereas Article 18 imposes liability for destruction or loss of baggage caused by an "occurrence." This difference in the parallel language of Articles 17 and 18 implies that the drafters of the Convention understood the word "accident" to mean something different than the word "occurrence," for they otherwise logically would have used the same word in each article. The language of the Convention accordingly renders suspect the opinion of the Court of Appeals that "accident" means "occurrence."

Second, the text of Article 17 refers to an accident *which caused* the passenger's injury, and not to an accident which *is* the passenger's injury. In light of the many senses in which the word "accident" can be used, this distinction is significant. As Lord Lindley observed in 1903:

> "The word 'accident' is not a technical legal term with a clearly defined meaning. Speaking generally, but with reference to legal liabilities, an accident means any unintended and unexpected occurrence which produces hurt or loss. But it is often used to denote any unintended and unexpected loss or hurt apart from its cause; and if the cause is not known the loss or hurt itself would certainly be called an accident. The word 'accident' is also often used to denote both the cause and the effect, no attempt being made to discriminate between them." *Fenton v. J. Thorley & Co.,* [1903] A.C. 443, 453.

In Article 17, the drafters of the Warsaw Convention apparently did make an attempt to discriminate between "the cause and the effect"; they specified that air carriers would be liable if an accident *caused* the passenger's injury. The text of the Convention thus implies that, however we define "accident," it is the *cause* of the injury that must satisfy the definition rather than the occurrence of the injury alone. American jurisprudence has long recognized this distinction between an accident that is the *cause* of an injury and an injury that is itself an accident. See *Landress v. Phoenix Mutual Life Ins. Co.,* 291 U.S. 491, 54 S.Ct. 461, 78 L.Ed. 934 (1934).

While the text of the Convention gives these two clues to the meaning of "accident," it does not define the term. Nor is the context in which the term is used illuminating. To determine the meaning of the term "accident" in Article 17 we must consider its French legal meaning. This is true not because "we are forever chained to French law" by the Convention, see *Rosman v. Trans World Airlines, Inc.,* 34 N.Y.2d 385, 394, 358 N.Y.S.2d 97, 102, 314 N.E.2d 848, 853 (1974), but because it is our responsibility to give the specific words of the treaty a meaning consistent with the shared expectations of the contracting parties. We look to the French legal meaning for guidance as to these expectations because the Warsaw Convention was drafted in French by continental jurists. See Lowenfeld & Mendelsohn, The United States and the Warsaw Convention, 80 Harv.L.Rev. 497, 498-500 (1967).

A survey of French cases and dictionaries indicates that the French legal meaning of the term "accident" differs little from the meaning of the term in Great Britain, Germany, or the United States. Thus, while the word "accident" is often used to refer to the *event* of a person's injury, it is also sometimes used to describe a *cause* of injury, and when the word is used in this latter sense, it is usually defined as a fortuitous, unexpected, unusual, or unintended event. See 1 Grand Larousse de La Langue Francaise 29 (1971) (defining "accident" as "Evénement fortuit et fâcheux, causant des dommages corporels ou matériels"); *Air France v. Haddad, Judgment of June 19, 1979,* Cour d'appel de Paris, Première Chambre Civile, 1979 Revue Francaise de Droit Aérien 327, 328, appeal rejected, *Judgment of February 16, 1982,* Cour de Cassation, 1982 Bull.Civ. I 63. This parallels British and American jurisprudence. See *Fenton v. J. Thorley & Co., supra; Landress v. Phoenix Mutual Life Ins. Co., supra; Koehring Co. v. American Automobile Ins. Co.,* 353 F.2d 993 (CA7 1965). The text of the Convention consequently suggests that the passenger's injury must be caused by an unexpected or unusual event.

B

This interpretation of Article 17 is consistent with the negotiating history of the Convention, the conduct of the parties to the Convention, and the weight of precedent in foreign and American courts. . . .

In determining precisely what causes can be considered accidents, we "find the opinions of our sister signatories to be entitled to considerable weight." *Benjamins v. British European Airways,* 572 F.2d 913, 919 (CA2 1978), cert. denied, 439 U.S. 1114, 99 S.Ct. 1016, 59 L.Ed.2d 79 (1979). While few decisions are precisely on point, we note that, in *Air France v. Haddad, Judgment of June 19, 1979,* Cour d'appel de Paris, Première Chambre Civile, 1979 Revue Francaise de Droit Aérien, at 328, a French court observed that the term "accident" in Article 17 of the Warsaw Convention embraces causes of injuries that are fortuitous or unpredictable. European legal scholars have generally construed the word "accident" in Article 17 to require that the passenger's injury be caused by a sudden or unexpected event other than the normal operation of the plane. See, *e.g.,* O. Riese & J. Lacour, Précis de Droit Aérien 264 (1951) (noting that Swiss and German law require that the damage be caused by an accident, and arguing that an accident should be construed as an event which is sudden and independent of the will of the carrier); 1 C. Shawcross & K. Beaumont, Air Law ¶ VII(148) (4th ed. 1984) (noting that the Court of Appeals for the Third Circuit's definition of accident accords with some English definitions and "might well commend itself to an English court"). These observations are in accord with American decisions which, while interpreting the term "accident" broadly, *Maugnie v. Compagnie Nationale Air France,* 549 F.2d, at 1259, nevertheless refuse to extend the term to cover routine travel procedures that produce an injury due to the peculiar internal condition of a passenger. See, *e.g. Abramson v. Japan Airlines Co.,* 739 F.2d 130 (CA3 1984) (sitting in airline seat during normal flight which aggravated hernia not an "accident"), cert. pending, No. 84-939; *MacDonald v. Air Canada,* 439 F.2d 1402 (CA5 1971) (fainting while waiting in the terminal for one's baggage not shown to be caused by an "accident"); *Scherer v. Pan American World Airways, Inc.,* 54 App.Div.2d 636, 387 N.Y.S.2d 580 (1976) (sitting in airline seat during normal flight which aggravated thrombophlebitis not an "accident").

III

We conclude that liability under Article 17 of the Warsaw Convention arises only if a passenger's injury is caused by an unexpected or unusual event or happening that is external to the passenger. This definition should be flexibly applied after assessment of all the circumstances surrounding a passenger's injuries. For example, lower courts in this country have interpreted Article 17 broadly enough to encompass torts committed by terrorists or fellow passengers. See *Evangelinos v. Trans World Airlines, Inc.,* 550 F.2d 152 (CA3 1977) (en banc) (terrorist attack); *Day v. Trans World Airlines, Inc.,* 528 F.2d 31 (CA2 1975) (en banc) (same), cert. denied, 429 U.S. 890, 97 S.Ct. 246, 50 L.Ed.2d 172 (1976); *Krystal v. British Overseas Airways Corp.,* 403 F.Supp. 1322 (CD Cal.1975) (hijacking); *Oliver v. Scandinavian Airlines System,* 17 CCH Av.Cas. 18,283 (Md.1983) (drunken passenger falls and injures fellow passenger). In cases where there is contradictory evidence, it is for the trier of fact to decide whether an "accident" as here defined caused the passenger's injury. But when the injury indisputably results from the passenger's own internal reaction to the usual, normal, and expected operation of the aircraft, it has not been caused by an accident, and Article 17 of the Warsaw Convention cannot apply. The judgment of the Court of Appeals in this case must accordingly be reversed.

We recognize that any standard requiring courts to distinguish causes that are "accidents" from causes that are "occurrences" requires drawing a line, and we realize that "reasonable [people] may differ widely as to the place where the line should fall." *Schlesinger v. Wisconsin,* 270 U.S. 230, 241, 46 S.Ct. 260, 262, 70 L.Ed. 557 (1926) (Holmes, J., dissenting). We draw this line today only because the language of Articles 17 and 18 requires it, and not because of any desire to plunge into the "Serbonian bog" that accompanies attempts to distinguish between causes that are accidents and injuries that are accidents. See *Landress v. Phoenix Mutual Life Ins. Co.,* 291 U.S., at 499, 54 S.Ct., at 463 (Cardozo, J., dissenting). Any injury is the product of a chain of causes, and we require only that the passenger be able to prove that some link in the chain was an unusual or unexpected event external to the passenger. Until Article 17 of the Warsaw Convention is changed by the signatories, it cannot be stretched to impose carrier liability for injuries that are not caused by accidents. It remains "[o]ur duty ... to enforce the ... treaties of the United States, whatever they might be, and ... the Warsaw Convention remains the supreme law of the land." *Reed,* 555 F.2d, at 1093.

Our duty to enforce the "accident" requirement of Article 17 cannot be circumvented by reference to the Montreal Agreement of 1966. It is true that in most American cases the Montreal Agreement expands carrier liability by requiring airlines to waive their right under Article 20(1) of the Warsaw Convention to defend claims on the grounds that they took all necessary measures to avoid the passenger's injury or that it was impossible to take such measures. Because these "due care" defenses are waived by the Montreal Agreement, the Court of Appeals and some commentators have characterized the Agreement as imposing "absolute" liability on air carriers. See Lowenfeld & Mendelsohn, 80 Harv.L.Rev., at 599. As this case demonstrates, the characterization is not entirely accurate. It is true that one purpose of the Montreal Agreement was to speed settlement and facilitate passenger recovery, but the parties to the Montreal Agreement promoted that purpose by specific provision for waiver of the Article 20(1) defenses. They did not waive other provisions in the Convention that operate to qualify liability, such as the contributory negligence defense of Article 21 or the "accident" requirement of Article 17. See *Warshaw,* 442 F.Supp., at 408.

Under the Warsaw Convention as modified by the Montreal Agreement, liability can accordingly be viewed as "absolute" only in the sense that an airline cannot defend a claim on the ground that it took all necessary measures to avoid the injury. The "accident" requirement of Article 17 is distinct from the defenses in Article 20(1), both because it is located in a separate article and because it involves an inquiry into the nature of the event which *caused* the injury rather than the care taken by the airline to avert the injury. While these inquiries may on occasion be similar, we decline to employ that similarity to repeal a treaty provision that the Montreal Agreement on its face left unaltered. . . .

The judgment of the Court of Appeals is reversed, and the case is remanded for further proceedings consistent with this opinion.

It is so ordered.

Notes

1. How does the "accident" requirement differ from any elements of domestic torts you have studied? Is it fair to say that the Warsaw Convention has spawned interpretive case law that is different from anything you would find in the common law of torts?

2. Justice O'Connor's precise formulation of "accident" – "an unexpected or unusual event or happening that is external to the passenger" – has been utilized in a number of courts in foreign countries as well. As the Court of Appeal of the Supreme Court of Victoria, Australia, said, "[C]ounsel for the respondent were unable to take us to any decision in any jurisdiction, common law or civil, where the definition given in *Saks* had been disapproved." *Qantas Ltd v. Povey*, 2003 WL 23000692 (Vict., Austl., Ct. of App.), [2003] ALMD 6602, 11 VR 642, [2003] VSCA 227. Perhaps this is not surprising since the Court drew on foreign sources in formulating the definition of "accident" in the first place – and was attempting to follow "sister nations" in the interests of uniformity.

3. Whether a particular happening aboard an aircraft is "unexpected or unusual" is not always self-evident. Saks holds that normal changes in cabin pressure during flight are neither unexpected nor unusual. How about injuries caused by turbulence? Courts have drawn a distinction between light or moderate turbulence, which is not unusual, and severe turbulence, which might be. Compare *Koor v. Air Canada*, 2001 WL 452006 (Ont., Can., Super. Ct. of Justice) (passenger fell in lavatory during light or moderate turbulence; not an "accident") with *Magan v. Lufthansa German Airlines*, 339 F.3d 158 (2d Cir. 2003) (passenger fell during severe turbulence; issue of fact on whether this was an "accident"). How about faulty cleaning of the plane? See, e.g., *Waxman v. C.I.S. Mexicana de Aviacion S.A. de C.V.*, 13 F.Supp.2d 508 (S.D.N.Y. 1998) (cleaning crew's failure to remove a hypodermic needle protruding from the fabric in the seat in front of the plaintiff was an "accident"). For scores of examples,

see Kurtis A. Kemper, Annot., *What Constitutes Accident Under Warsaw Convention – Global Cases*, 4 A.L.R.FED.2d 1 (2005).

4. The requirement that the happening be "external to the passenger" has led most courts to conclude that a passenger's development of deep vein thrombosis (which is probably not "unexpected or unusual," either) is not an "accident" for which compensation is owed. See, e.g., *Rodriguez v. Ansett Austl. Ltd.*, 383 F.3d 914 (9th Cir. 2004); *Povey v. Qantas Airways Ltd.*, 2005 WL 1460709 (Austl.), 223 CLR 189, [2005] HCA 33; *In re Deep Vein Thrombosis and Air Travel Group Litigation*, [2006] 1 A.C. 495 (H.L.), [2006] 1 All. Eng. Rep. 786, 2005 WL 3299091. Courts have also held that an airline's failure to warn of the risks of developing deep vein thrombosis is not an "accident," either. See, e.g., *Caman v. Continental Airlines, Inc.*, 455 F.3d 1087 (9th Cir. 2006); *Blansett v. Continental Airlines, Inc.*, 379 F.3d 177 (5th Cir. 2004); *In re Deep Vein Thrombosis and Air Travel Group Litigation*, [2006] 1 A.C. 495 (H.L.), [2006] 1 All. Eng. Rep. 786, 2005 WL 3299091. But would it be an "accident" if a passenger suffered injury because of a misplaced built-in lumbar support in his seat? See *Malaysian Airline Systems Berhad v. Krum*, 2005 WL 2278945 (Vict., Austl., Ct. of App.), [2005] VSCA 232 (yes).

5. *Failure to assist.* In *Olympic Airways v. Husain*, 540 U.S. 644, 124 S.Ct. 1221, 157 L.Ed.2d 1146 (2004), an airline flight attendant refused to assist a passenger who was complaining about being seated near smokers despite his severe allergy to smoke. The passenger ultimately died. The Court held that the carrier's action (or inaction) was an "accident" because it was "unexpected and usual," given that it violated carrier policy, and (quoting the Ninth Circuit's opinion below) represented a "failure to act in the face of a known, serious risk" even where "reasonable alternatives exist that would substantially minimize the risk and implementing those alternatives would not unreasonably interfere with the normal, expected operation of the airplane."

6. Can an intentional tort be considered an "accident" under Article 17? Courts have said yes – some noting that to hold otherwise would immunize airlines from liability for intentional acts but not less culpable acts. See *Carey v. United Airlines*, 255 F.3d 1044 (9th Cir. 2001); *Bernardi v. Apple Vacations*, 236 F.Supp.2d 465 (E.D. Pa. 2002); *Naral-Torres v. Northwest Airlines Inc.*, 1998 WL 1717959 (Ont., Can., Gen. Div. 1998).

7. *Causation.* Carrier liability follows only where an "accident" causes a legally-cognizable harm. How strong must the causal

link be? Plaintiff need only prove that "some link in the chain of causation" was an "accident;" every injury has multiple causes and that fact cannot defeat liability. See *Air France v. Saks*, 470 U.S. 392, 105 S.Ct. 1338, 84 L.Ed.2d 289 (1985) ("Any injury is the product of a chain of causes."); *Olympic Airways v. Husain*, 540 U.S. 644, 124 S.Ct. 1221, 157 L.Ed.2d 1146 (2004) (recognizing that decedent's death was due to both "the exposure to the smoke and the refusal to assist the passenger").

B. REMEDIAL EXCLUSIVITY AND LEGALLY-COGNIZABLE HARM

EL AL ISRAEL AIRLINES, LTD. v. TSENG

525 U.S. 155, 119 S.Ct. 662, 142 L.Ed.2d 576 (1999).

Justice GINSBURG delivered the opinion of the Court.

Plaintiff-respondent Tsui Yuan Tseng was subjected to an intrusive security search at John F. Kennedy International Airport in New York before she boarded an El Al Israel Airlines May 22, 1993 flight to Tel Aviv. Tseng seeks tort damages from El Al for this occurrence. The episode-in-suit, both parties now submit, does not qualify as an "accident" within the meaning of the treaty popularly known as the Warsaw Convention, which governs air carrier liability for "all international transportation." Tseng alleges psychic or psychosomatic injuries, but no "bodily injury," as that term is used in the Convention. Her case presents a question of the Convention's exclusivity: When the Convention allows no recovery for the episode-in-suit, does it correspondingly preclude the passenger from maintaining an action for damages under another source of law, in this case, New York tort law?

The exclusivity question before us has been settled prospectively in a Warsaw Convention protocol (Montreal Protocol No. 4) recently ratified by the Senate.[2] In accord with the protocol, Tseng concedes, a passenger whose injury is not compensable under the Convention (because it entails no "bodily injury" or was

---

[2]Montreal Protocol No. 4 to Amend the Convention for the Unification of Certain Rules Relating to International Carriage By Air, signed at Warsaw on October 12, 1929, as amended by the Protocol Done at the Hague on September 8, 1955 (hereinafter Montreal Protocol No. 4), reprinted in S. Exec. Rep. No. 105-20, pp. 21-32 (1998).

not the result of an "accident") will have no recourse to an alternate remedy. We conclude that the protocol, to which the United States has now subscribed, clarifies, but does not change, the Convention's exclusivity domain. We therefore hold that recovery for a personal injury suffered "on board [an] aircraft or in the course of any of the operations of embarking or disembarking," Art. 17, 49 Stat. 3018, if not allowed under the Convention, is not available at all.

The Court of Appeals for the Second Circuit ruled otherwise. In that court's view, a plaintiff who did not qualify for relief under the Convention could seek relief under local law for an injury sustained in the course of international air travel. 122 F.3d 99 (1997). [The Federal Courts of Appeals have divided on the treaty interpretation question at issue.] We granted certiorari, and now reverse the Second Circuit's judgment. Recourse to local law, we are persuaded, would undermine the uniform regulation of international air carrier liability that the Warsaw Convention was designed to foster.

I

We have twice reserved decision on the Convention's exclusivity. In *Air France v. Saks,* 470 U.S. 392, 105 S.Ct. 1338, 84 L.Ed.2d 289 (1985), we concluded that a passenger's injury was not caused by an "accident" for which the airline could be held accountable under the Convention, but expressed no view whether that passenger could maintain "a state cause of action for negligence." *Id.,* at 408, 105 S.Ct. 1338. In *Eastern Airlines, Inc. v. Floyd,* 499 U.S. 530, 111 S.Ct. 1489, 113 L.Ed.2d 569 (1991), we held that mental or psychic injuries unaccompanied by physical injuries are not compensable under Article 17 of the Convention, but declined to reach the question whether the Convention "provides the exclusive cause of action for injuries sustained during international air transportation." We resolve in this case the question on which we earlier reserved judgment.

At the outset, we highlight key provisions of the treaty we are interpreting. Chapter I of the Warsaw Convention, entitled "Scope-Definitions," declares in Article 1(1) that the "[C]onvention shall apply to all international transportation of persons, baggage, or goods performed by aircraft for hire." 49 Stat. 3014. Chapter III, entitled "Liability of the Carrier," defines in Articles 17, 18, and 19 the three kinds of liability for which the Convention provides. Article 17 establishes the conditions of liability for personal injury to passengers:

> "The carrier shall be liable for damage sustained in the event of the death or wounding of a passenger or any other bodily injury suffered by a passenger, if the accident which caused the damage so sustained took place on board the aircraft or in the course of any of the operations of embarking or disembarking."

Article 18 establishes the conditions of liability for damage to baggage or goods. Article 19 establishes the conditions of liability for damage caused by delay. Article 24, referring back to Articles 17, 18, and 19, instructs:

> "(1) In the cases covered by articles 18 and 19 any action for damages, however founded, can only be brought subject to the conditions and limits set out in this convention.
>
> "(2) In the cases covered by article 17 the provisions of the preceding paragraph shall also apply, without prejudice to the questions as to who are the persons who have the right to bring suit and what are their respective rights."

II

With the key treaty provisions as the backdrop, we next describe the episode-in-suit. On May 22, 1993, Tsui Yuan Tseng arrived at John F. Kennedy International Airport (hereinafter JFK) to board an El Al Israel Airlines flight to Tel Aviv. In conformity with standard El Al preboarding procedures, a security guard questioned Tseng about her destination and travel plans. The guard considered Tseng's responses "illogical," and ranked her as a "high risk" passenger. Tseng was taken to a private security room where her baggage and person were searched for explosives and detonating devices. She was told to remove her shoes, jacket, and sweater, and to lower her blue jeans to midhip. A female security guard then searched Tseng's body outside her clothes by hand and with an electronic security wand.

After the search, which lasted 15 minutes, El Al personnel decided that Tseng did not pose a security threat and allowed her to board the flight. Tseng later testified that she "was really sick and very upset" during the flight, that she was "emotionally traumatized and disturbed" during her month-long trip in Israel, and that, upon her return, she underwent medical and psychiatric treatment for the lingering effects of the body search.

Tseng filed suit against El Al in 1994 in a New York state court of first instance. Her complaint alleged a state-law personal injury claim based on the May 22, 1993 episode at JFK. Tseng's pleading charged, *inter alia,* assault and false imprisonment, but alleged no bodily injury. El Al removed the case to federal court.

The District Court, after a bench trial, dismissed Tseng's personal injury claim. That claim, the court concluded, was governed by Article 17 of the Warsaw Convention, which creates a cause of action for personal injuries suffered as a result of an "accident ... in the course of any of the operations of embarking or disembarking," Tseng's claim was not compensable under Article 17, the District Court stated, because Tseng "sustained no bodily injury" as a result of the search, and the Convention does not permit "recovery for psychic or psychosomatic injury unaccompanied by bodily injury," citing Eastern Airlines, Inc. v. Floyd, 499 U.S. 530, 111 S.Ct. 1489, 113 L.Ed.2d 569 (1991). The District Court further concluded that Tseng could not pursue her claim, alternately, under New York tort law; as that court read the Convention, Article 24 shields the carrier from liability for personal injuries not compensable under Article 17.

The Court of Appeals reversed in relevant part. The Second Circuit concluded first that no "accident" within Article 17's compass had occurred; in the Court of Appeals' view, the Convention drafters did not "ai[m] to impose close to absolute liability" for an individual's "personal reaction" to "routine operating procedures," measures that, although "inconvenien[t] and embarass [ing]," are the "price passengers pay for ... airline safety." In some tension with that reasoning, the Second Circuit next concluded that the Convention does not shield the very same "routine operating procedures" from assessment under the diverse laws of signatory nations (and, in the case of the United States, States within one Nation) governing assault and false imprisonment.

Article 24 of the Convention, the Court of Appeals said, "clearly states that resort to local law is precluded only where the incident is 'covered' by Article 17, meaning where there has been an accident, either on the plane or in the course of embarking or disembarking, which led to death, wounding or other bodily injury." The court found support in the drafting history of the Convention, which it construed to "indicate that national law was intended to provide the passenger's remedy where the Convention did not expressly apply." The Second Circuit also rejected the argument that allowance of state-law claims when the Convention does not permit recovery would contravene the treaty's goal of uniformity. . . .

III

We accept it as given that El Al's search of Tseng was not an "accident" within the meaning of Article 17, for the parties do not place that Court of Appeals conclusion at issue. . . . The parties do not dispute that the episode-in-suit occurred in international transportation in the course of embarking.

Our inquiry begins with the text of Article 24, which prescribes the exclusivity of the Convention's provisions for air carrier liability. "[I]t is our responsibility to give the specific words of the treaty a meaning consistent with the shared expectations of the contracting parties." *Saks,* 470 U.S., at 399, 105 S.Ct. 1338. "Because a treaty ratified by the United States is not only the law of this land, see U.S. Const., Art. II, § 2, but also an agreement among sovereign powers, we have traditionally considered as aids to its interpretation the negotiating and drafting history (*travaux préparatoires*) and the postratification understanding of the contracting parties." *Zicherman,* 516 U.S., at 226, 116 S.Ct. 629.

Article 24 provides that "cases covered by article 17" – or in the governing French text, "les cas prévus à l'àrticle 17" – may "only be brought subject to the conditions and limits set out in th[e] [C]onvention." That prescription is not a model of the clear drafter's art. We recognize that the words lend themselves to divergent interpretation.

In Tseng's view, and in the view of the Court of Appeals, "les cas prévus à l'àrticle 17" means those cases in which a passenger could actually maintain a claim for relief under Article 17. So read, Article 24 would permit any passenger whose personal injury suit did not satisfy the liability conditions of Article 17 to pursue the claim under local law.

In El Al's view, on the other hand, and in the view of the United States as *amicus curiae,* "les cas prévus à l'àrticle 17" refers generically to all personal injury cases stemming from occurrences on board an aircraft or in embarking or disembarking, and simply distinguishes that class of cases (Article 17 cases) from cases involving damaged luggage or goods, or delay (which Articles 18 and 19 address). So read, Article 24 would preclude a passenger from asserting any air transit personal injury claims under local law, including claims that failed to satisfy Article 17's liability conditions, notably, because the injury did not result from an "accident," see *Saks,* 470 U.S., at 405, 105 S.Ct. 1338, or because the "accident" did not result in physical injury or physical manifestation of injury, see *Floyd,* 499 U.S., at 552, 111 S.Ct. 1489.

Respect is ordinarily due the reasonable views of the Executive Branch concerning the meaning of an international treaty. See *Sumitomo Shoji America, Inc. v. Avagliano,* 457 U.S. 176, 184-185, 102 S.Ct. 2374, 72 L.Ed.2d 765 (1982) ("Although not conclusive, the meaning attributed to treaty provisions by the Government agencies charged with their negotiation and enforcement is entitled to great weight."). We conclude that the Government's construction of Article 24 is most faithful to the Convention's text, purpose, and overall structure.

A

The cardinal purpose of the Warsaw Convention, we have observed, is to "achiev[e] uniformity of rules governing claims arising from international air transportation." *Floyd,* 499 U.S., at 552, 111 S.Ct. 1489; see *Zicherman,* 516 U.S., at 230, 116 S.Ct. 629. The Convention signatories, in the treaty's preamble, specifically "recognized the advantage of regulating in a uniform manner the conditions of ... the liability of the carrier." To provide the desired uniformity, Chapter III of the Convention sets out an array of liability rules which, the treaty declares, "apply to all international transportation of persons, baggage, or goods performed by aircraft." In that Chapter, the Convention describes and defines the three areas of air carrier liability (personal injuries in Article 17, baggage or goods loss, destruction, or damage in Article 18, and damage occasioned by delay in Article 19), the conditions exempting air carriers from liability (Article 20), the monetary limits of liability (Article 22), and the circumstances in which air carriers may not limit liability (Articles 23 and 25). Given the Convention's comprehensive scheme of liability rules and its textual emphasis on uniformity, we would be hard put to conclude that the delegates at Warsaw meant to subject air carriers to the distinct, nonuniform liability rules of the individual signatory nations. . . .

A complementary purpose of the Convention is to accommodate or balance the interests of passengers seeking recovery for personal injuries, and the interests of air carriers seeking to limit potential liability. Before the Warsaw accord, injured passengers could file suits for damages, subject only to the limitations of the forum's laws, including the forum's choice-of-law regime. This exposure inhibited the growth of the then-fledgling international airline industry. See *Floyd,* 499 U.S., at 546, 111 S.Ct. 1489; Lowenfeld & Mendelsohn, The United States and the Warsaw Convention, 80 Harv. L.Rev. 497, 499-500 (1967). Many international air carriers at that time endeavored to require passengers, as a condition of air travel, to relieve or reduce the carrier's liability in case of injury. See Second International Conference on Private Aeronautical Law, October 4-12, 1929, Warsaw, Minutes 47 (R. Horner & D. Legrez transls. 1975) (hereinafter Minutes). The Convention drafters designed Articles 17, 22, and 24 of the Convention as a compromise between the interests of air carriers and their customers worldwide. In Article 17 of the Convention, carriers are denied the contractual prerogative to exclude or limit their liability for personal injury. In Articles 22 and 24, passengers are limited in the amount of damages they may recover, and are restricted in the claims they may pursue by the conditions and limits set out in the Convention.

Construing the Convention, as did the Court of Appeals, to allow passengers to pursue claims under local law when the Convention does not permit recovery could produce several anomalies. Carriers might be exposed to unlimited liability under diverse legal regimes, but would be prevented, under the treaty, from contracting out of such liability. Passengers injured physically in an emergency landing might be subject to the liability caps of the Convention, while those merely traumatized in the same mishap would be free to sue outside of the Convention for potentially unlimited damages. The Court of Appeals' construction of the Convention would encourage artful pleading by plaintiffs seeking to opt out of the Convention's liability scheme when local law promised recovery in excess of that prescribed by the treaty. Such a reading would scarcely advance the predictability that adherence to the treaty has achieved worldwide.[12]

The Second Circuit feared that if Article 17 were read to exclude relief outside the Convention for Tseng, then a passenger

[12]The Court of Appeals recognized that the Convention aimed to "balance the interests of the passenger and the carrier," but concluded that, with the "increasing strength of the airline industry, the balance has properly shifted away from protecting the carrier and toward protecting the passenger." Postratification adjustments, however, are appropriately made by the treaty's signatories.

injured by a malfunctioning escalator in the airline's terminal would have no recourse against the airline, even if the airline recklessly disregarded its duty to keep the escalator in proper repair. As the United States pointed out in its *amicus curiae* submission, however, the Convention addresses and concerns, only and exclusively, the airline's liability for passenger injuries occurring "on board the aircraft or in the course of any of the operations of embarking or disembarking." "[T]he Convention's preemptive effect on local law extends no further than the Convention's own substantive scope." A carrier, therefore, "is indisputably subject to liability under local law for injuries arising outside of that scope: *e.g.*, for passenger injuries occurring before 'any of the operations of embarking' " or disembarking.

Tseng raises a different concern. She argues that air carriers will escape liability for their intentional torts if passengers are not permitted to pursue personal injury claims outside of the terms of the Convention. But we have already cautioned that the definition of "accident" under Article 17 is an "unusual event ... *external to the passenger*," and that "[t]his definition should be flexibly applied." *Saks,* 470 U.S., at 405, 105 S.Ct. 1338 (emphasis added). In *Saks,* the Court concluded that no "accident" occurred because the injury there – a hearing loss – "indisputably result[ed] from *the passenger's own internal reaction* to the usual, normal, and expected operation of the aircraft." As we earlier noted, see *supra,* at 670, n.9, Tseng and El Al chose not to pursue in this Court the question whether an "accident" occurred, for an affirmative answer would still leave Tseng unable to recover under the treaty; she sustained no "bodily injury" and could not gain compensation under Article 17 for her solely psychic or psychosomatic injuries.

B

The drafting history of Article 17 is consistent with our understanding of the preemptive effect of the Convention. The preliminary draft of the Convention submitted to the conference at Warsaw made air carriers liable "in the case of death, wounding, or any other bodily injury suffered by a traveler." In the later draft that prescribed what is now Article 17, airline liability was narrowed to encompass only bodily injury caused by an "accident." It is improbable that, at the same time the drafters narrowed the conditions of air carrier liability in Article 17, they intended, in Article 24, to permit passengers to skirt those conditions by pursuing claims under local law. . . .[13]

C

Montreal Protocol No. 4, ratified by the Senate on September 28, 1998,[14] amends Article 24 to read, in relevant part: "In the carriage of passengers and baggage, any action for damages, however founded, can only be brought subject to the conditions and limits set out in this Convention....."[15] Both parties agree that, under the amended Article 24, the Convention's preemptive effect is clear: The treaty precludes passengers from bringing actions under local law when they cannot establish air carrier liability under the treaty. Revised Article 24, El Al urges and we agree, merely clarifies, it does not alter, the Convention's rule of exclusivity.

Supporting the position that revised Article 24 provides for preemption not earlier established, Tseng urges that federal preemption of state law is disfavored generally, and particularly when matters of health and safety are at stake. Tseng overlooks in this regard that the nation-state, not subdivisions within one nation, is the focus of the Convention and the perspective of our treaty partners. Our home-centered preemption analysis, therefore, should not be applied, mechanically, in construing our international obligations.

---

[13] Sir Alfred Dennis of Great Britain stated at the Warsaw Conference that Article 24 is "a very important stipulation which touches the very substance of the Convention, because [it] excludes recourse to common law." Minutes 213.

[14] See 144 Cong. Rec. S11059 (Sept. 28, 1998). The President signed the instrument of ratification for Montreal Protocol No. 4 on November 5, 1998. The Protocol will enter into force in the United States on March 4, 1999.

[15] Article 24, as amended by Montreal Protocol No. 4, provides:

"1. In the carriage of passengers and baggage, any action for damages, however founded, can only be brought subject to the conditions and limits set out in this Convention, without prejudice to the question as to who are the persons who have the right to bring suit and what are their respective rights.

"2. In the carriage of cargo, any action for damages, however founded, whether under this Convention or in contract or in tort or otherwise, can only be brought subject to the conditions and limits of liability set out in this Convention without prejudice to the question as to who are the persons who have the right to bring suit and what are their respective rights. Such limits of liability constitute maximum limits and may not be exceeded whatever the circumstances which gave rise to the liability."

Decisions of the courts of other Convention signatories corroborate our understanding of the Convention's preemptive effect. In *Sidhu,* the British House of Lords considered and decided the very question we now face concerning the Convention's exclusivity when a passenger alleges psychological damages, but no physical injury, resulting from an occurrence that is not an "accident" under Article 17. See 1 All E. R., at 201, 207. Reviewing the text, structure, and drafting history of the Convention, the Lords concluded that the Convention was designed to "ensure that, in all questions relating to the carrier's liability, it is the provisions of the [C]onvention which apply and that the passenger does not have access to any other remedies, whether under the common law or otherwise, which may be available within the particular country where he chooses to raise his action." Courts of other nations bound by the Convention have also recognized the treaty's encompassing preemptive effect.[16] The "opinions of our sister signatories," we have observed, are "entitled to considerable weight." *Saks*, 470 U.S., at 404, 105 S.Ct. 1338 (internal quotation marks omitted). The text, drafting history, and underlying purpose of the Convention, in sum, counsel us to adhere to a view of the treaty's exclusivity shared by our treaty partners.

For the reasons stated, we hold that the Warsaw Convention precludes a passenger from maintaining an action for personal

---

[16] See, *e.g., Gal v. Northern Mountain Helicopters Inc.,* Dkt. No. 3491834918, 1998 B.C.T.C. Lexis 1351, *15-*16 (July 22, 1998) (Hunter, J., in chambers) (reviewing claim for personal injuries sustained during helicopter crash, a judge of the Supreme Court of British Columbia concluded: "The Warsaw Convention remedy pursuant to Article 17 is exclusive.... [T]he plaintiff has no claim except for that permitted under the Warsaw Convention."); *Naval-Torres v. Northwest Airlines Inc.,* 159 D.L.R. (4th) 67, 73, 77 (1998) (Sharpe, J.) (considering claim of bodily injury from exposure, in flight, to second-hand smoke, a judge of the Ontario Court (General Division) rejected passenger's contention that she "is entitled in law to pursue any common law or statutory claims which exist apart from any claims she may have under the *Convention,*" and concluded that "where a claim falls within the reach of the *Convention,* the *Convention* is exhaustive of the rights of the plaintiff"); *Emery Air Freight Corp. v. Nerine Nurseries Ltd.,* [1997] 3 N.Z.L.R. 723, 735-736, 737 (concluding that action for damage to goods "must comply with the conditions and limits set out in the [C]onventio[n]," New Zealand Court of Appeal recalled the "general purpose of the [C]onventio[n] ... to protect carriers operating across international boundaries from the vagaries of local laws and to impose a uniform regime upon them and upon those dealing with them"); *Seagate Technology Int'l v. Changi Int'l Airport Servs. Pte Ltd.,* [1997] 3 S.L.R. 1, 9 (considering claim of lost goods, Singapore Court of Appeal noted: Articles 17, 18, and 19 "form the sole foundation of the carrier's liability in respect of loss or damage falling within the scope of those articles. In such cases, the party seeking satisfaction from the carrier need not and, in fact, cannot plead his case in common law or otherwise.").

injury damages under local law when her claim does not satisfy the conditions for liability under the Convention. Accordingly, we reverse the judgment of the Second Circuit.

It is so ordered.

[Dissent of Justice Stevens omitted.]

Notes

1. The Warsaw Convention was designed to accomplish two major goals: creating a uniform legal regime applicable to damages claims on international air flights, and limiting carriers' liability "in order to foster the growth of the fledgling commercial airline industry. . . . The passengers themselves could be said to assume some of the risk that this nascent technology might engender their lives." Paul Stephen Dempsey, *International Air Cargo & Baggage Liability and the Tower of Babel*, 36 GEO. WASH. INT'L L. REV. 239, 247 (2004). Do these goals retain their vitality today?

2. Are you convinced that the Warsaw Convention should preempt state tort law? Would anything bad happen if it did not? Would resort to local tort law undermine the goal of uniformity? How?

3. The Warsaw Convention certainly achieves a measure of uniformity across national borders, but there is still a role for the local law of each nation. As the Supreme Court put it in *Zicherman v. Korean Air Lines Co.*, 516 U.S. 217, 116 S.Ct. 629, 133 L.Ed.2d 596 (1996), "Articles 17 and 24(2) of the Warsaw Convention permit compensation only for legally cognizable harm, but leave the specification of what harm is legally cognizable to the domestic law applicable under the forum's choice-of-law rules." Article 24(2), quoted in the *Tseng* case, provides that cases covered by article 17 shall be determined "without prejudice to the questions as to who are the persons who have the right to bring suit and what are their respective rights." Justice Scalia, writing for the Court in *Zicherman*, said, "The most natural reading of this Article is that, in an action brought under Article 17, the law of the Convention does not affect the substantive questions of who may bring suit and what they may be compensated for. Those questions are to be answered by the domestic law selected by the courts of the contracting states." That is to say that "the Convention left to domestic law the questions of who may recover

and what compensatory damages are available to them. . . ." Indeed, some countries outside the U.S. have adopted domestic legislation specifying the types of damages that can be recovered in a Warsaw Convention case.

4. In *Eastern Airlines, Inc. v. Floyd,* 499 U.S. 430, 111 S.Ct. 1489, 113 L.Ed.2d 569 (1991), cited in *Tseng,* the Court held that purely emotional distress, without accompanying physical injury, is not a recoverable type of damage in a Warsaw Convention case. The Court looked to the French text of Article 17, which uses the term *lesion corporelle,* and after exploring French legislation, caselaw and scholarly writings, concluded the term could mean only "bodily injury." The Court stressed also that most signatory nations would likely find strict liability for purely emotional harm controversial in light of their own domestic legal systems.

5. After *Floyd,* most lower courts in this country have concluded that emotional distress is recoverable in Warsaw Convention cases only where the mental suffering flows from physical injuries as opposed to, say, the fear of dying in the plane accident. This has proved to be a difficult burden for plaintiffs to meet. See, e.g., *Erlich v. American Airlines, Inc.*, 360 F.3d 366 (2d Cir. 2004) (holding that recoverable mental injuries must be caused by bodily injuries, not merely accompany them); *Bobian v. Czech Airlines,* 93 Fed. Appx. 406 (3d Cir. 2004) (rejecting claims of post-traumatic stress disorder where there were no physical injuries); *In re Air Crash at Little Rock, Arkansas, on June 1, 1999 (Lloyd v. American Airlines, Inc.*), 291 F.3d 503 (8th Cir. 2002) (plaintiff failed to prove that her PTSD and depression "flow[ed] from the injuries to her legs and the smoke inhalation," as opposed to her fear of imminent death); *Carey v. United Airlines,* 255 F.3d 1044 (9th Cir. 2001) (holding that plaintiff cannot recover for emotional distress simply by showing physical manifestations of that distress).

6. Note that when a plaintiff's "injury" is found to be purely emotional, and thus not compensable under the Convention, the preemptive effect of the Convention means that the plaintiff cannot recover at all, even under state tort law. See *Fishman by Fishman v. Delta Air Lines, Inc.*, 132 F.3d 183 (2d Cir. 1998) (commenting that "when Mrs. Fishman emphasizes that the only harm she suffered is emotional, she proves too much"). Of course, state law in the U.S. is hardly consistent when it comes to recovery of purely emotional distress – although it is hardly as restrictive as the Warsaw Convention. Thus in a domestic air flight not subject to the Warsaw Convention a plaintiff might

recover in one state but not another, largely because of differences in state law. Compare *Atlantic Coast Airlines v. Cook*, 857 N.E.2d 989 (Ind. 2006) (no recovery for mental distress suffered on board an air flight, absent a "physical impact" with the plaintiff), with *Quill v. Trans World Airlines*, 361 N.W.2d 438 (Minn.App.1985) (negligent infliction of emotional distress claim stated where plane dove 34,000 feet in an uncontrolled tailspin). Is "uniformity" more important in international treaty interpretation than in ordinary domestic state-law tort cases? Why or why not?

7. Under *Zicherman*, referenced in Note 3 above, why shouldn't U.S. courts feel free to allow purely emotional damages in Warsaw Convention cases? Isn't that the kind of decision left to each contracting state under Article 24?

C. "WILLFUL ACT" EXCLUSION

KOIRALA v. THAI AIRWAYS INTERNATIONAL, LTD.

126 F.3d 1205 (9th Cir. 1997).

THOMAS, Circuit Judge:

On July 31, 1992, Thai Airways International ("Thai Airways") Flight TG-311 crashed into a mountainside while attempting to land at Tribhuvan International Airport in Kathmandu, Nepal, killing all 113 people aboard. In this case, we examine whether the crash was the result of "wilful misconduct" on the part of the flight crew, lifting the Warsaw Convention's $75,000 cap on damages for personal injury. We agree with the district court that it was.

I

Flight TG-311 was a regularly scheduled flight from Bangkok, Thailand to Kathmandu, Nepal. Tribhuvan International Airport in Kathmandu has the reputation of being one of the most difficult airports in the world in which to land. It is situated in a valley surrounded by very high mountains, requiring a steep approach to land and the full extension of the wing flaps during the entire descent. Kathmandu air traffic control has no radar. Instead, air traffic controllers determine aircraft location and provide instructions to aircraft using air-to-ground and ground-to-air radio communications. Flight TG-311 Captain Preeda Suttimai and First Officer Phunthat Boonyayej (collectively "the flight crew" or "the crew") were properly licensed and certified, and both had substantial experience flying into Kathmandu.

On the night of the crash, the weather in Kathmandu was cloudy and rainy. The flight crew had little visibility and were entirely dependent upon navigational instruments to fly the aircraft. At 06:46:07 Coordinated Universal Time, Tribhuvan air traffic control authorized the captain to execute a landing approach. The aircraft was at this time flying at heading 022, twenty-two degrees east of due north. When the crew attempted to configure the airplane for landing, they discovered at 06:47:34 that the wing flaps failed to extend properly, rendering landing too dangerous to attempt. The crew requested permission to divert the aircraft to Calcutta, but before air traffic control responded, the wing flaps extended properly at 06:49:05. By this time, however, the aircraft had traveled too far north and was too high to begin a descent toward the runway.

From 06:49:08 until 06:50:21, the captain asked air traffic control four times for clearance to turn left and fly south to point "Romeo," a navigational position approximately forty-one miles south of Tribhuvan International Airport from which the aircraft had made its initial approach, to attempt another landing approach. Although a left turn under these circumstances was a reasonable and safe action for the airplane, air traffic control did not respond to the captain's repeated requests.

At approximately 06:50:50, without requesting or obtaining clearance from air traffic control, the flight crew began a climbing right turn. The first officer notified air traffic control at 06:51:55 of the right turn and the crew's intention to climb to 18,000 feet and return to point Romeo. Air traffic control ordered the aircraft to descend to 11,500 feet and maintain that altitude, and the flight crew complied with that instruction.

Six separate times from 06:52:06 to 06:59:39, air traffic control authorized the aircraft to head south and return to point Romeo. Instead of turning 180 degrees and heading south on heading 202, as was their stated intention, the flight crew mistakenly turned the aircraft full circle, 360 degrees, and unknowingly continued heading north toward the mountains surrounding Kathmandu on heading 022. From the time the aircraft completed the 360 degree turn, at approximately 06:54:41, the flight crew believed they had executed only a 180 degree turn and were heading south, despite the fact that all the navigational instruments on the instrument panel constantly indicated the northerly heading of the aircraft.

The crew had apparently become preoccupied from approximately 06:54:12 with their unsuccessful efforts to input and display the location of point Romeo on the computerized Flight Management System ("FMS"). They were unable to display point Romeo on the FMS because the system was incapable of displaying navigational points located behind the aircraft. As point Romeo was located to the south of the aircraft and the aircraft was heading north, the FMS was unable to display the location of the navigational point. However, the crew believed they were heading south and could not understand why they were unable to display the location of point Romeo on the FMS.

The crew continued to attempt to program the FMS and to operate under the misconception that they were heading south for approximately six minutes, until at least 06:59:56. At 06:59:58, the first officer realized the aircraft was heading north and attempted to communicate this fact to the captain, who did not understand the warning. Twenty-eight seconds later, at 07:00:26, the aircraft crashed into the side of a mountain twenty-three miles north of Kathmandu at an altitude of 11,500 feet and a ground speed of 300 nautical miles per hour, killing all ninety-nine passengers and fourteen crew members on board instantly.

[Relatives of seven of the passengers killed in the crash sued Thai Airways pursuant to the Warsaw Convention. The case was bifurcated for trial into liability and damages phases, by stipulation, then tried to the district court, sitting without a jury.] In the liability phase, applying U.S. federal law interpreting the term "wilful misconduct" under the Warsaw Convention, the court found that the crash of Flight TG-311 was the result of the crew's "wilful misconduct" in failing to monitor their navigational instruments which displayed a northerly course for the entire six minutes after the 360-degree turn and before impact. . . . [After ruling on various motions, the] court then proceeded to the damages phase. After a bench trial, the court awarded damages in an order dated July 10, 1996. . . . Thai Airways timely appealed, and the plaintiffs timely cross-appealed.

II

Among other provisions, the Warsaw Convention allows passengers injured or killed in an airplane crash to recover damages from the air carrier. . . . However, the liability of the carrier for each passenger so injured or killed is limited to $75,000. Warsaw Convention art. 22(1), *as modified by* Agreement Relating to Liability Limitations of the Warsaw Convention and the Hague Protocol, Agreement CAB 18900, approved by Civil Aeronautics Board Order E-23680, 31 Fed.Reg. 7302 (1966), *reprinted in* 49 U.S.C. § 40105 note (the "Montreal Agreement"). There is an exception to this limit where the damage has been caused by the carrier's "wilful misconduct": The carrier shall not be entitled to avail himself of the provisions of this convention which exclude or limit his liability, if the damage is caused by his wilful misconduct or by such default on his part as, in accordance with the law of the court to which the case is submitted, is considered to be equivalent to wilful misconduct. Warsaw Convention art. 25(1).

"Wilful misconduct under the Convention means the intentional performance of an act with knowledge that the ... act will probably result in injury or damage or the intentional performance of an act in such a manner as to imply reckless disregard of the probable consequences." *Johnson v. American Airlines, Inc.,* 834 F.2d 721, 724 (9th Cir. 1987). The intentional omission of an act may also support a finding of wilful misconduct. *Ospina v. Trans World Airlines, Inc.,* 975 F.2d 35, 37 (2d Cir.1992).

[A district court's finding of wilful misconduct under the Warsaw Convention is reviewed for clear error.] Under this standard, we must uphold the district court's decision unless, after reviewing the decision, we are left with a "definite and firm conviction that a mistake has been made." *David H. Tedder & Assocs., Inc. v. United States,* 77 F.3d 1166, 1169-70 (9th Cir. 1996).

The issue in this case is whether it was wilful misconduct for the crew to have failed to discern anytime during the six minutes after the 360-degree turn and before impact that the plane was heading north into known dangerous terrain instead of south. This was the rationale upon which the district court based its finding of wilful misconduct. We hold the district court did not clearly err in finding wilful misconduct under the circumstances of this case.

Although Thai Airways argues for a subjective standard in evaluating the flight crew's performance and the plaintiffs for an objective one, *Johnson* supplies the definition of wilful misconduct to be used in Warsaw Convention cases under the law of the Ninth Circuit: the crew must intentionally perform an act with knowledge that the act will probably result in injury or damage or intentionally perform an act in such a manner as to imply reckless disregard of the probable consequences.

Thai Airways argues *Berner v. British Commonwealth Pac. Airlines, Ltd.,* 346 F.2d 532 (2d Cir.1965) is on point and supports its position. In that case, the court held that if the plane crashed into a mountain because the pilot for some unknown reason became confused as to his actual position and began landing procedures at an improper time which he mistakenly thought was proper, "wilful misconduct would not have been established under any standard." Thai Airways argues there is no evidence the crew did not look at their instruments, no evidence that if they did fail to look at their instruments, they did so consciously, and no evidence that intentional misconduct is more likely than any other possible explanation for the crew's behavior, such as inadvertence or even negligence. Thai Airways insists that all the evidence shows that accumulated stress and workload from flying in dangerous territory and poor weather conditions, with an equipment failure, becoming preoccupied with their unsuccessful attempts to program the FMS, and with no ground radar and unhelpful air traffic controllers, rendered the crew incapable of recognizing that their navigational instruments indicated the aircraft was heading north rather than south. This is particularly true given that the desired course heading was 202 rather than 022, numbers which are easily transposed and confused, and which David McNair, the chief accident investigator for the Government of Nepal, in fact testified he and the other accident investigators transposed and confused in the calm of the flight simulator.

This might all very well be so. However, as stated in *Berner,* resolution of this case "depend[s] upon inferences to be drawn from essentially circumstantial evidence." Indeed, "subjective standards are nearly always satisfied by circumstantial proof." *Eastwood v. National Enquirer, Inc.,* 123 F.3d 1249, 1256 n.20 (9th Cir. 1997). Here, the district court judge could have determined from the evidence that frequently checking navigational instruments to verify heading is a task so fundamental to basic flying safety, the sheer fact the crew for nearly six minutes did not realize they were flying in the wrong direction indicates they must consciously have ignored this duty. Consciously ignoring this duty while flying in a notoriously mountainous area certainly "impl[ies a] reckless disregard of the probable consequences." *Johnson,* 834 F.2d at 724 (internal quotation marks omitted).

Captain Donald Lykins, an expert witness for the plaintiff, testified that "a flight crew looks at their instruments, just scans them; probably they're going by an instrument every few seconds." He opined that the flight crew's actions in this case were "completely substandard of any scheduled airlines in the world" because they ignored plainly visible compass readings indicating a wrong heading for a substantial amount of time. Another plaintiffs' expert, Captain Barry Schiff, stated that "[t]o think that a professional crew can go for six minutes without being aware where they were going is almost incomprehensible." He further testified [that he understood how a pilot could] "look away, do something, come back, and look at those instruments again, but to ignore them for six minutes, I can't understand how they could allow that to happen. . . ."

In view of the cumulative trial evidence, we cannot say the district court clearly erred in finding that the crew acted in conscious and reckless disregard of their duties, constituting wilful misconduct under the Warsaw Convention. *Compare In re Korean Air Lines Disaster of Sept. 1, 1983,* 156 F.R.D. 18, 24 (D.D.C.1994), *aff'd per curiam,* 52 F.3d 1122 (D.C.Cir.1995) (jury's finding of wilful misconduct supported because "the nature and extent of the deviation suggested that either the crew flew through Soviet airspace intentionally or that they repeatedly ignored fundamental and mandated navigational safety procedures which, if followed, would have alerted the crew to Flight 007's course deviation"). . . .

AFFIRMED.

Notes

1. In *Bayer Corp. v. British Airways, PLC,* 210 F.3d 236 (4th Cir. 2000), the court held that to establish willful misconduct, a plaintiff must prove that the carrier either intended to cause the damage or acted recklessly with subjective knowledge that the damage would probably result. In *Piamba Cortes v. American Airlines, Inc.*, 177 F.3d 1272 (11th Cir. 1999), the court held that the plaintiff must "prove that an air carrier subjectively knew its conduct would result in harm to its passengers." Under either of these formulations, would the carrier in *Koirala* have been found to have acted willfully?

2. In U.S. tort law, punitive damages are often available when the defendant has acted intentionally or recklessly. See 2 DAN B. DOBBS, THE LAW OF TORTS § 381, at 1064 (2001). In *Smith v. Wade*, 461 U.S. 30, 103 S.Ct. 1625, 75 L.Ed.2d 632 (1983), the Court said that most state courts "have adopted more or less the same rule, recognizing that punitive damages in tort cases may be awarded not only for actual intent to injure or evil motive, but also for recklessness, serious indifference to or disregard for the rights of others, or even gross negligence." Most other countries, however, do not allow punitive damages at all. The Warsaw Convention itself is silent on the issue, although the civil-law drafters could not have contemplated allowing punitive damages. Should punitive damages nonetheless be allowed in Warsaw Convention cases brought in the U.S. when the carrier has acted willfully? American courts have said no, often stressing a desire for Warsaw Convention uniformity. See *In re Korean Air Lines Disaster of September 1, 1983*, 932 F.2d 1475 (D.C. Cir. 1991); *In re Air Disaster at Lockerbie, Scotland on December 21, 1988*, 928 F.2d 1267 (2d Cir. 1991). Judge Abner Mikva, dissenting in the *KAL* case, argued that willful misconduct on the part of a carrier should waive any damages limitations, including any purported limitations on awarding punitive damages. 932 F.2d at 1490-94. What do you think?

Chapter 7

NONFEASANCE AND THE DUTY TO RESCUE

A. THE COMMON LAW APPROACH

SMITH v. LITTLEWOODS ORGANISATION LTD.

[1987] A.C. 241, 271; 1987 WL 492144 (HL); [1987] All E.R. 710

LORD GOFF.

. . . [T]he common law does not impose liability for what are called pure omissions. If authority is needed for this proposition, it is to be found in the speech of Lord Diplock in Dorset Yacht Co. Ltd. v. Home Office [1970] A.C. 1004, where he said, at p. 1060:

> "The very parable of the good Samaritan (Luke 10, v. 30) which was evoked by Lord Atkin in Donoghue v. Stevenson [1932] A.C. 562 illustrates, in the conduct of the priest and of the Levite who passed by on the other side, an omission which was likely to have as its reasonable and probable consequence damage to the health of the victim of the thieves, but for which the priest and Levite would have incurred no civil liability in English law."

Lord Diplock then proceeded to give examples which show that, carried to extremes, this proposition may be repugnant to modern thinking. It may therefore require one day to be reconsidered, especially as it is said to provoke an "invidious comparison with affirmative duties of good-neighbourliness in most countries outside the common law orbit" (see *Fleming, The Law of Torts,* 6th ed., p. 138). But it is of interest to observe that, even if we do follow the example of those countries, in all probability we will, like them, impose strict limits upon any such affirmative duty as may be recognised. . . .

Notes

1. This famous statement by Lord Goff sums up the common law approach to "omissions" or nonfeasance: there is no general affirmative duty to act for the protection of another person. Both English and American law recognize several duty-creating exceptions, however, which may come close to swallowing the rule. For example, where the defendant creates a risk of harm to the plaintiff, or harms the plaintiff, or has some pre-existing relationship to the plaintiff, a duty to assist or protect might well arise. But in the Biblical example cited by Lord Goff, those who passed by the injured man would owe him no duty to help him, since they did not cause his plight or have any pre-existing connection to him.

2. The classic example of the common law nonfeasance rule in action remains the absence of any duty to come to the assistance of someone in need of help. Lord Goff notes in his opinion that the rule may be "repugnant to modern thinking" in extreme cases, but it remains the rule. In a nutshell, the common law holds that "one is not required to rescue somebody who is in danger; one is not required to do so even when the potential rescuer can do so without risk for his or her own life." WALTER VAN GERVEN, JEREMY LEVER & PIERRE LAROUCHE, CASES, MATERIALS AND TEXT ON NATIONAL, SUPRANATIONAL AND INTERNATIONAL TORT LAW 295 (2000).

3. The Restatement (Second) of Torts uses this scenario to illustrate the majority rule in the United States:

> A sees B, a blind man, about to step into the street in front of an approaching automobile. A could prevent B from so doing by a word or touch without delaying his own progress. A does not do so, and B is run over and hurt. A is under no duty to prevent B from stepping into the street, and is not liable to B.

RESTATEMENT (SECOND) OF TORTS § 314, illus. 1. Nor would A be under any duty to assist B once he was injured. This rule carries over into the new Third Restatement. The Comment to § 37 says that "there is no duty of care when another is at risk for reasons other than the conduct of the actor, even though the actor may be in a position to help. . . . In the absence of duty, the actor cannot be held liable." RESTATEMENT (THIRD) OF TORTS: LIABILITY FOR PHYSICAL HARM § 37, comment *b* (P.F.D. No. 1, 2005).

4. Lawmakers in a small number of states in the U.S. have passed legislation making a failure to assist, under some circumstances at least, a criminal offense. These statutes are considered in more detail in section C below.

B. THE CIVIL LAW APPROACH

GERMAN PENAL CODE § 323c

Whoever fails to render assistance in case of accident, common danger or emergency, although such assistance was necessary and could have reasonably been expected from him under the circumstances, especially since he could have rendered it without placing himself in any significant danger and without violating any important conflicting commitments, shall be punished by up to one year's imprisonment or by fine.[1]

Notes

1. This provision has been rarely enforced, leading to the view that it "serves more of an 'educational function' than any real need in every day life." BASIL S. MARKESINIS & HANNES UNBERATH, THE GERMAN LAW OF TORTS 27 (4th Ed. 2002). Does this mean it has no value?

2. *Civil liability.* Notice that this is a criminal law, not a tort law; it is silent on the possibility of civil liability. One might think that German Civil Code paragraph 823(2), which allows for civil liability when a person "infringes a statute intended for the protection of others," would mean that a person harmed by

---

[1]Translated by Sabine Schlemmer- Schulte.

another's violation of Penal Code § 323c would have grounds for a tort suit. German courts, however, have rejected civil liability here on the ground that the statute is intended for the protection of society as a whole rather than particular persons, thus moving it outside of the scope of paragraph 823(2). See JEROEN KORTMANN, ALTRUISM IN PRIVATE LAW 42 (2005). And while it is theoretically possible that a willful refusal to rescue might give rise to civil liability under Civil Code paragraph 826 if such act was considered *contra bonos mores* (against good morals), cases have not so held. *Id.* at 43. At bottom, if the Biblical good Samaritan case "were to be considered now, it seems unlikely that German courts would have held the priest or the Levite liable for the harm that was caused by their inaction." *Id.* at 44.

3. Most other civil law European countries, including Austria, Belgium, Denmark, France, Greece, Italy, Portugal and Spain, have criminal statutes that allow for punishment for failure to assist. See 1 CHRISTIAN VON BAR, THE COMMON EUROPEAN LAW OF TORTS 624 n.315 (1998). Most Latin American countries have similar provisions. Alberto Cadoppi, *Failure to Rescue and the Continental Criminal Law*, in THE DUTY TO RESCUE: THE JURISPRUDENCE OF AID 93, 104 & 109-10 (Michael A. Menlowe & Alexander McCall Smith eds., 1993). In most of these countries, as in Germany, there is no civil liability for a violation. 2 CHRISTIAN VON BAR, THE COMMON EUROPEAN LAW OF TORTS 220 n.113 (1998). By contrast, in France any act that violates a criminal provision is considered a faulty act that will support civil liability under Civil Code articles 1382 and 1383 where harm is caused thereby. KORTMANN, *supra*, at 35.

4. These statutes may be called "bad Samaritan statutes," in that they penalize non-rescue. This is to distinguish them from "good Samaritan statutes," which insulate rescuers from civil liability for performing negligent rescues.

FRENCH PENAL CODE ARTICLE 223-6

Ordinance No. 2000-916

Anyone who, being able without risk to himself or third parties to prevent by immediate action a felony or a misdemeanor against the bodily integrity of a person, willfully abstains from doing so, is punished by a five years' imprisonment and a fine of €75,000.

The same penalties apply to anyone who willfully fails to render to a person in danger any assistance which, without risk to himself or to third parties, he could render him either by his own action, or by initiating rescue operations.[2]

Notes

1. The French statute appears on its face to require only rescues that are not particularly risky. Notice also that the statute allows people to escape liability either calling for assistance, or by assisting themselves. But, as one scholar has noted, "Rendering assistance is rarely risk-free, and merely reporting a peril may be, according to the courts, ineffective assistance. So line-drawing problems have arisen." Edward A. Tomlinson, *The French Experience With Duty to Rescue: A Dubious Case for Criminal Enforcement*, 20 N.Y.L. SCH. J. INT'L & COMP. L. 451, 461 (2000).

2. The French statute does not itself define "danger," and unlike some other European statutes, applies even where the defendant was not an eyewitness to this "danger." Further, there is no requirement that the plaintiff suffer harm from the lack of rescue, leading to the situation where "a defendant who abstains from rescuing a person in peril cannot raise as a defense that someone else rescued that person or that the person miraculously escaped any harm." *Id.* Notice, though, that the non-rescue must be "willful," meaning that a person who is incapable of rescuing another, or calling for help, will not be liable for failure to do so.

3. Most cases brought against non-rescuers under this statute fall into one of five categories: motorists who fail to help accident victims; doctors who fail to help sick people; parents who fail to call for assistance for sick children (sometimes on religious grounds); those who assist suicides; and "healers" who fail to advise their customers to seek expert medical advice. See Andrew Ashworth & Eva Steiner, *Criminal Omissions and Public Duties: The French Experience*, 10 J. LEGAL STUD. 153, 158-60 (1990).

4. A neophyte might guess that the French statute grew out of good-hearted motives and values, but the truth is more complicated. The French criminal code originally contained no duty to rescue provision. Only during the Nazi occupation of Vichy

---

[2]Translated in Legifrance (trans. Georges Rouhette & Anne Barton).

France in 1941 was such a provision introduced, aimed at requiring French citizens to "rescue" German troops attacked by the Resistance, or to act to prevent sabotage. Tomlinson, supra, at 462. Of course, France retained the duty to rescue after liberation from the Nazis and have continued to increase the penalties for violations, perhaps revealing a strong consensus that such an obligation is both manageable and morally desirable.

C. SHOULD WE ADOPT THE FRENCH APPROACH?

Edward A. Tomlinson
The French Experience with Duty to Rescue: A Dubious Case for Criminal Enforcement,
20 N.Y.L.SCH. J. INT'L & COMP. L. 451, 451-59 (2000).

The growing convergence between the common law and civil law traditions has been a favorite theme of comparativists in recent years. This overall pattern finds a striking exception in the duty to rescue. . . . [A] significant number [of common-law commentators] strongly believe that the civil law approach is superior. How can our legal system allow the strong swimmer who watches a small child drown escape any liability by claiming that as a stranger he or she had no duty to rescue?

. . . There are four principal arguments against bad Samaritan statutes enforcing criminally a duty to rescue. First, these statutes enforce a morality of benevolence by requiring one person to confer a benefit on another whose sole basis for claiming that benefit is the presence of some danger to the recipient's well being. Second, there is no principled way to draw the line between the aid which the law should require and the aid which the law should leave to the dictates of each individual's conscience. Third, the affirmative duties imposed by bad Samaritan statutes unduly interfere with individual liberty. Fourth, causing harm is a necessary condition for liability; the failure to rescue does not satisfy this condition because it merely allows harm to happen.

The most forceful of these objections is the line-drawing argument. The other objections . . . fade away when confronted with the hypotheticals presented by the proponents of easy rescue, hypotheticals in which the failure to rescue reflects an appalling indifference for human life. Proponents' writings are full of malicious persons who fail to warn blind persons of approaching manholes, who fail to lift the heads of sleeping drunks from puddles of water, who fail to throw ropes from bridges to save drowning bathers, or who fail to do anything to rescue small children wandering lost in the woods. There are also those selfish pool loungers who refuse to put down their drinks to grab drowning children by the trunks and pull them from the pool. These cases are easy cases for liability because the blameworthiness of the omission is clear, assuming the defendant was aware of what was happening and had the physical capacity to intervene.

In these cases, concerns about forced charity, interference with autonomy, and lack of causation seem misplaced, or at least unconvincing. However, these hypotheticals are contrived and skewer the issue because they are just that: hypothetical cases. In real life, cases rarely arise where the danger is so clear and the rescue is so easy. More importantly, when they do arise, rescue almost always occurs. Few people are likely to allow another to die or to suffer serious injury if they could prevent it with a flick of the wrist. In addition, the desirability of punishing inaction in these easy cases does not outweigh the line-drawing problems raised by applying duty to rescue statutes to more messy, but real world situations.

The most persuasive statement of the line-drawing objection appears in Lord Macaulay's Introductory Notes to the 1837 Indian Penal Code. . . . What was a good English gentleman in nineteenth century India to do when confronted by crowds of starving beggars whose immediate needs would quickly consume his available resources? With respect to this and many other fact situations, Macaulay hammered home the crucial question: How much money or how much exertion or, in other words, how many 'steps' must a person take to save a life when each extra step, considered by itself, is trivial? For Macaulay, there was no acceptable answer to that question; therefore, he rejected a general duty to rescue and limited the duty to act to assist another to situations where there was some special relationship between the potential rescuer and the person in peril. This latter category of cases was different because the criminal law could expect from persons with ties to the victim what it could not expect from strangers, such as exposure to inconvenience, pecuniary loss, and even personal danger. Macaulay's position has prevailed in most common law jurisdictions. . . .

The French experience provides some help in resolving this [line-drawing] debate. In France, the duty to rescue statute has remained largely unchanged for nearly six decades, and there is a large body of case law interpreting and applying its provisions. This large number of cases demonstrates that the duty to rescue is taken seriously in France; failure to rescue often results in a criminal prosecution, initiated either by the State or, as is possible in France, by the victim or the family of a deceased victim. These cases also demonstrate how one legal system has resolved the line-drawing and other interpretive problems raised by the duty to rescue. Similar problems are likely to arise in this country if we enact and seriously enforced duty to rescue statutes. More narrowly drafted statutes may alleviate some of the problems encountered in France, but no general duty to rescue statute can avoid delegating to the courts the responsibility for determining case by case what response the law expects from persons confronting a sudden or unexpected peril. In France, courts have performed that difficult task to produce results that are not "unacceptable" and perhaps even creditable. For those advocating a duty to rescue, the French experience may demonstrate that their proposal can work.

My appraisal of the French experience is less positive. To me, the French experience demonstrates that the critics of a general duty to rescue are correct when they argue that enforcing any such duty creates serious line-drawing problems and that those problems are likely to outweigh any benefit obtained by recognizing the duty. What convinces me is the fact patterns in the reported cases under the statute. . . . [T]he statute functions like a loose cannon; prosecutions have occurred in surprising situations never envisioned by most advocates of the duty to rescue. More importantly, the defendant's blameworthiness is not clear-cut in many of the prosecutions. In other words, in many cases . . ., it does not appear that a jury could find that it was "clear" beyond a reasonable doubt that the defendant confronted a person in grave peril and could have done more to assist that person without exposure to significant inconvenience, pecuniary loss, or personal injury. Granted, some of those prosecutions resulted in acquittals, but the State still put the defendant on trial and trial judges – jury trial is not available – reviewed the appropriateness of the defendant's response to what was most likely an emergency situation not of the defendant's choosing. That second guessing in the criminal courtroom of the defendant's borderline behavior strikes me as undesirable. In addition, in most of the cases where a convicted defendant's blameworthiness is clear, the defendant could have been convicted of some other offense in a common law jurisdiction not recognizing a general duty to rescue. We already punish the most culpable omissions by recognizing a duty to act where there is some special relationship between the defendant and the person in need of rescue or by enacting special statutes punishing inaction in discrete situations (e.g., hit and run statutes). Therefore, the French experience counsels against enforcing a general duty to rescue through the criminal law.

In addition, many cases where the defendant's culpability is clear are better handled under narrower duty to report statutes. . . . Duty to report statutes do not often raise the serious line-drawing problems inherent in duty to rescue statutes. . . . [I]n most cases, at least in the more technologically sophisticated twenty-first century, one can report a crime or other peril merely by calling 911 or some other emergency number. For example, the eyewitnesses to Kitty Genovese's murder[3] might have prevented it by telephoning the police. They were blameworthy because they failed to do so and not because they failed to leave the safety of their apartments to confront a knife-wielding murderer on a subway platform. Such cases show that line-drawing is much easier when the law only imposes a duty to report and not a duty of personal intervention. In the latter situation, what do we expect a layperson to do when confronted with a seriously ill or wounded stranger? What risks must the layperson take? Should the law take into account the layperson's perhaps irrational fear of contagion or legitimate concern over making the situation worse? The difficulty of these questions suggests that a narrow duty to report may be more palatable as a first step in reforming the common law than a broader duty to rescue. . . .

Notes

1. As suggested in this excerpt, common-law commentators have argued for a century that American jurisdictions should adopt a duty to rescue. See RESTATEMENT (THIRD) OF TORTS: LIABILITY FOR PHYSICAL HARM § 37, comment *e* (P.F.D. No. 1, 2005) (collecting articles and summarizing many arguments); Philip W. Romohr, *A Right/Duty Perspective on the Legal and*

---

[3]Kitty Genovese's murder was an infamous incident in New York City in the early 1960s in which 38 witnesses remained in their apartments listening to Genovese's screams for help as she was attacked and killed on a nearby subway platform. (Eds.)

Philosophical Foundations of the No-Duty-To-Rescue Rule, 55 DUKE L.J. 1025 (2006) (same).

2. A very small group of U.S. states – including Vermont, Rhode Island, Minnesota, Hawaii and Wisconsin, have adopted criminal statutes that require rescue, but each has qualifications, and prosecutions are not common. Vermont's statute (the "Duty to Aid the Endangered Act"), passed in 1967, was the first such statute in this country, and remains the broadest. It provides:

> A person who knows that another is exposed to grave physical harm shall, to the extent that the same can be rendered without danger or peril to himself or without interference with important duties owed to others, give reasonable assistance to the exposed person unless that assistance or care is being provided by others.

12 Vt. Stat. Ann. § 519 (a). A willful violation is punishable by a $100 fine. § 519 (c). Rhode Island's statute requires "any person at the scene of an emergency who knows that another person is exposed to, or has suffered, grave physical harm," to give "reasonable assistance" if "he or she can do so without danger or peril to himself or others." R.I. Gen. Laws § 11-56-1. Violation subjects the offender to a six month jail term and a $500 fine. *Id.* Minnesota's petty misdemeanor statute is similar to Rhode Island's, applying only to persons present at the scene of an emergency and requiring only non-perilous rescue attempts. Minn. Stat. Ann. § 604A.01. Minnesota's statute explicitly says that "reasonable assistance may include obtaining or attempting to obtain aid from law enforcement or medical personnel." *Id.*

Wisconsin's misdemeanor statute requires "any person who knows that a crime is being committed and that a victim is exposed to bodily harm" to summon law enforcement personnel or to "provide assistance to the victim," as long as compliance would not "place him or her in danger." Wis. Stat. Ann. § 940.34. Hawaii's misdemeanor statute is even narrower than Wisconsin's, requiring a non-perilous "attempt to obtain aid from law enforcement or medical personnel" from "any person at the scene of a crime who knows that the victim of the crime is suffering from serious physical harm." Haw. Rev. Stat. § 663-1.6.

3. Virtually all states in the U.S. have criminal statutes that require certain classes of people to report certain kinds of crimes. For example, in virtually all states, health care professionals and social workers have a duty to report child abuse. See Jessica

Givelber, Note, *Imposing Duties on Witnesses to Child Sex Abuse: A Futile Response to Bystander Indifference*, 65 FORD. L. REV. 3169 (1999). However, such statutes are frequently held not to create private civil causes of action or to set the standard of care in cases. See, e.g., *Perry v. S.N.*, 973 S.W.2d 301 (Tex. 1998) (child-abuse reporting statute given no effect in tort suit against a violator). Are reporting statutes a better idea than rescue statutes, do you think? Should tort liability be imposed under either?

4. A recent article concludes on the basis of empirical research that in the United States, "proven cases of non-rescues are extraordinarily rare, and proven cases of rescues are exceedingly common – often in hazardous circumstances, where a duty to rescue would not apply in the first instance. . . . [E]ven in the absence of a statutory duty, Americans appear to be too willing to undertake rescue if one judges by the number of injuries and deaths among rescuers." David A. Hyman, *Rescue Without Law: An Empirical Perspective on the Duty to Rescue*, 84 TEX. L. REV. 653, 656-57 (2006). If this information is accurate, how does this color your own view of whether adopting the French approach would be good in this country?

5. Not all civil-law commentators believe the European duty-to-rescue statutes are good things. After noting that "[t]he courts – at least in Italy – have shown a regrettable tendency to expand these statutes . . . and anyway to apply them in an inconsistent and expansionist way," one leading scholar asks whether civil law countries should continue to have them at all:

> One wonders, after all, how effective they are. Our cities are full of drunkards, drug-addicts and those whose suffering is manifested in other ways, but no one ever stops to help them: how many of these people are punished under a bad samaritan statute? Yet these statutes are well established and are unlikely to be abandoned. In these circumstances, perhaps the best approach is to attempt to reform these laws and to stop demanding too much from them. These statutes should be confined to the imposition of elementary duties to aid other people in danger, and they should also be as precise and limited as possible. In particular, they should be restricted to requiring that accidents should be reported to police or other authorities, a solution which is clearly more compatible with the nature of a modern, technologically sophisticated society. This is a limited to

> duty to rescue, a far cry from some of the broader claims of some examples of such legislation, but at least it makes for a realistic and enforceable law.

Alberto Cadoppi, *Failure to Rescue and the Continental Criminal Law*, in THE DUTY TO RESCUE: THE JURISPRUDENCE OF AID 93, 122-23 (Michael A. Menlowe & Alexander McCall Smith eds., 1993).

Chapter 8

MEDICAL MALPRACTICE: NON-DISCLOSURE AND INFORMED CONSENT

A. CONTRACT OR TORT?

In the United States, medical malpractice actions are the source of heated debate; they have motivated much of the tort reform legislation that has been enacted in numerous states. The common law rules governing malpractice actions originated in England and were consistent with rules governing other so-called common callings, such as innkeepers, common carriers and apothecaries. Physicians were legally bound to show that they had exercised a certain degree of care and skill or be found liable in tort. While a contract exists between physician and patient in most cases, the traditional remedy for malpractice in England, and subsequently in the United States, has been in tort. DIETER GIESEN, INTERNATIONAL MEDICAL MALPRACTICE LAW: A COMPARATIVE LAW STUDY OF CIVIL LIABILITY ARISING FROM MEDICAL CARE 4-7 (1988).

In civil law countries, actions for medical malpractice have historically been more likely to arise as actions for breach of a contract for services. This characterization can be traced back to Roman law. However, today most civil law countries (France being a major exception) will allow an action in tort *or* in contract. In many civil law countries, this distinction is not as significant as it would be in common law countries because the contractual obligation is one of reasonable care. However, in France and Belgium, courts must distinguish between an obligation to use reasonable care (*obligation de moyens*) and an obligation to achieve a specific result *(obligation de résultat)*. In these countries, if a contract for medical treatment is viewed as an *obligation de résultat,* the physician must prove he or she is not the cause of the failure or be held liable. *Id.* at 12.

In civil law countries that permit a plaintiff to proceed in contract or tort (delict), the choice tends to be more strategic than substantive. For example, in Germany, the damages rules are addressed in general sections of the law of obligations and apply to both contract and tort actions. While non-pecuniary (or non-material) damages were formerly limited to only a sub-group of tort claims, a 2002 revision of the BGB extended them to strict liability and contract claims. Harold Koch, *The Law of Torts, in* INTRODUCTION TO GERMAN LAW 205, 222-23 (Mathias Reimann and Joachim Zekoll eds., 2005). In Italy, the rule is that non-material damages would generally be unavailable in both contract and in delict; the Italian Civil Code Article 2059 makes them available "only in cases provided by law," the most important example of which is breach of the criminal code. Mauro Bussani, Barbara Pozzo, & Angelo Venchiarutti, *Tort Law, in* INTRODUCTION TO ITALIAN LAW 215, 226-27 (Jeffrey S. Lena & Ugo Mattei eds., 2002). Like the U.S., Greece is an example of a country where damages for non-material loss would be available in delict, but not in contract, GIESEN, *supra,* at 34.

Tort and contract are not the only sources of law protecting persons injured by malpractice. In addition to these theories, a person injured by malpractice in many civil law countries may also find recognition of important rights, such as that of autonomy, in the Constitution.* Criminal laws of various countries may also govern cases of medical error; this is increasingly true in Japan, as noted below. In addition, as most countries have national health insurance in place, certain types of claims (such as a dispute over availability of a particular type of treatment or repair of prior malpractice) may be governed by the comprehensive laws or guidelines that pertain to the system in place. *See,* GIESEN, *supra,* at 3-10, 33-37.

* For example, Article 1(1) of the German Federal Constitution of May 23, 1949, provides that human dignity is inviolable and to be preserved by the State. Article 20(1), stating that the Federal Republic of Germany is a democratic and socially responsible state, imposes the duty to provide for a dignified existence of its citizens. The Constitution recognizes the self-determination of individuals in Article 2. The Federal Constitutional Court has emphasized the constitutional mandate for an effective statutory healthcare system. Ursula Weide, *Health Care Reform and the Changing Standard of Care in the United States and Germany,* 20 N.Y.L.SCH. J. INT'L & COMP. L. 249, 291-92 (2000).

Generally, we think of malpractice as consisting of two basic types of errors: treatment errors, which encompass errors in diagnosis or execution of procedures, and non-disclosure malpractice. The latter arises when a person is treated without full disclosure of information that would affect the decision as to whether to pursue a particular course of treatment.

B. NON-DISCLOSURE MALPRACTICE

U.S. law uniformly recognizes that a patient is entitled to information about any proposed medical treatment. However, the scope of the required disclosure and the standard of care by which it is measured continue to be litigated. U.S. courts disagree as to whether the disclosure obligation should be measured by a standard that defers to medical custom, as established by expert testimony, or whether it should simply be that which a reasonable patient would consider material. The latter appears to be the emerging view. There are certain exceptions, such as "therapeutic privilege" which allows physicians to withhold some information if disclosure would harm the patient, but they are construed narrowly. U.S. law also requires that the plaintiff establish that the non-disclosure caused harm, that is, that the plaintiff would have withheld consent and avoided injury or had a different procedure that would not have caused harm. This is a significant hurdle in many cases.

Although informed consent as a basic tenet of a patient's rights has become well-recognized outside the U.S., differences exist among countries. England is known for the so-called *Bolam* test, *Bolam v. Friern Health Management Committee*, [1957] 1 W.L.R. 582; 2 All E.R. 118, in which Judge McNair stated that a doctor "is not guilty of negligence if he has acted in accordance with a practice accepted as proper by a responsible body of medical men skilled in that particular art." The House of Lords subsequently endorsed the standard in a non-disclosure context. Dieter Giesen & John Hayes, *The Patient's Right to Know – A Comparative View,* 21 ANGLO-AM L. REV. 101, 102-103 (1992). Australia and Canada follow an intermediate position, in which they view professional practice as relevant, but not necessarily dispositive. Thus, in Canada, evidence of medical custom will be heard, but supplemented with testimony from the patient or family members on issues of materiality and causation. *Id.* at 106-07. European civil law systems, such as France, Germany and Switzerland, are very strict about requiring disclosure and apply a standard which gives deference to patient autonomy rather than professional custom. *Id.* at 111-12.

Although the civil law of Japan was heavily based first on French, and later German, law, Japan's legal analysis of the concept of informed consent has been markedly different than the analyses discussed above. Although Japan recognized the concept sixty or more years ago, it has long resisted the concept of informed consent, at least in its Western iteration. Japanese courts and physicians still think about the issue differently from U.S. courts, although this is changing. The following excerpt describes Japanese law and examines the roots of the difference.

Robert B Leflar

Informed Consent and Patients' Rights in Japan

33 Hous. L. Rev. 1, 16-18, 20-22, 25-27, 45-54 (1996)

The Culture of Paternalism

. . . 1. *A Descriptive Model of Paternalist Medicine in Japan.* As former Prime Minister Masayoshi Ohira once said, "'Japan is a free society, but not an open society.'" The statement applies equally well to health care as to politics. Japanese are free to select the doctor of their choice. Once entered into the mysterious realm of medicine, however, traditionally patients have had little or no access to information about their condition or prospects; they have been expected to give themselves over to the physician's ministrations without question, in blind trust.

The power of this customary practice model is suggested by the variety and richness of expressions that have grown up to describe it, as well as by the vast range of situations in which it is put into practice. The creed of the feudal lords of the Tokugawa period in ruling their subjects – "Keep them ignorant and dependent" – is ironically often applied to doctors' methods of managing their patients. Frank dialogue is considered unnecessary, because the relationship of physicians with patients is one of "tacit understanding." The physician understands the patient's condition and needs from keen observation of "every breath the patient takes"; not a word need be said. Treatment decisions are left to the doctor. . . .

Further diminishing the likelihood of autonomous decision-making by the patient is the notion, elaborated by cultural anthropologists, that "personhood" in Japanese culture is a more group-dependent concept than the autonomous individuality celebrated in American culture and postulated at the core of Western liberal philosophical theory. . . .

2. *Cloaking the Diagnosis of Cancer.* Aversion to the concept of informed consent is perhaps most pronounced in the treatment of cancer, Japan's leading cause of death. Japanese physicians' "culturally prescribed pattern of behavior" has been to avoid revealing the diagnosis of cancer to the patient unless the prognosis for cure is excellent; physicians discharge their responsibility by discussing the matter with the patient's family instead. Even the Emperor Showa was never told he had cancer before his death in 1989, and a ranking official of the Imperial Household Agency stated that he would not have been told even if he had asked what his ailment was. As late as the mid-1980s, most hospitals had a firm policy of never disclosing cancer diagnoses to any patients. Physicians would disguise the truth even from patients who were fellow doctors. Though these practices are gradually changing, most physicians remain inveterately attached to the notion that an exception to informed consent must be made in the case of patients with intractable cancer.

Physicians discuss other life-threatening diseases such as congestive heart failure, cerebrovascular disease, and cirrhosis with their patients, so why is cancer an exception? One common explanation is that cancer has traditionally been viewed as "synonymous with the death sentence." A great many physicians are apparently convinced that to pronounce the verdict of cancer would cause patients to give up all hope, resign themselves to their fate in untimely fashion, and perhaps even commit suicide. To set in motion this train of consequences would be a breach of the profoundest ethical obligation of the traditional Japanese physician, that of keeping the patient alive. From this point of view, telling a patient "you have cancer" is an act of irresponsible cruelty. American physicians' custom of full disclosure is often viewed with disdain as an infliction of brutality on the patient, motivated by the selfish desire to disclaim responsibility for the patient's fate and to avoid malpractice lawsuits. . . .

In contrast to the circumlocutions employed with patients, physicians frankly discuss the patient's condition and prospects with one or more family members. The physician also tells the family what story was given the patient, so that the family can be enlisted in the deception. A cultural propensity to view the family, rather than the individual, as the relevant decisionmaking unit on matters affecting any of its members may account in part for the social acceptance of this manner of discharge of the physician's responsibility to explain the patient's condition and treatment. . . .

Culture-specific explanations such as those suggested above must not be pressed too far. Seriously ill patients' dependence on physicians for psychological sustenance has a universal aspect, and the ease with which that dependence can translate into physicians' custom of withholding bad news does not necessarily depend on any traits of national character. According to one survey, physicians in southern and eastern Europe tend not to reveal a cancer diagnosis to the patient; the same is reportedly true in Argentina. . . .

Nevertheless, the traditional paternalistic pattern of secrecy is not easily explicable by models of economic behavior or rational choice. More likely it is a reflection of a combination of physician-patient status and power differentials resulting from social hierarchy, from the patient's typically weakened physical and psychological state, from gender difference in some cases, and from the physician's superior command of medical knowledge and skills. . . .

Medical Paternalism and the Law

The legal system, which in the United States provided the chief impetus toward recognition and elaboration of informed consent rights, has not played a similar role in Japan. As a formal matter, the principle of informed consent is universally recognized by the Japanese judiciary, though exceptions to the doctrine are drawn more broadly than in American jurisprudence. The outstanding characteristic of Japanese case law concerning informed consent, however, is the ample deference accorded the medical profession regarding the scope, timing, and even necessity of communicating information to patients. In the absence of judicial initiative restricting physicians' discretion, reformers have turned to legislative endeavors, with only indirect success. The 1992 revision of the Medical Services Law appears to have wedged open the door for efforts to build momentum for gradual change through a consensus development process. . . .

2. *Judicial Deference to Medical Custom Concerning Communication with Patients.* The Japanese Supreme Court first recognized and elaborated the physician's duty of explanation in a 1981 case involving a boy who died of heart failure due to a massive hemorrhage during an operation to remove a bone

fragment from the brain. The Court stated that the physician's duty of disclosure encompassed the nature of the proposed operation and the risks involved. However, the Court construed the duty narrowly, holding that the physician had no obligation to explain such matters as the patient's current symptoms and their causes; the extent of improvement to be expected from the operation; the specific prognosis if the operation were not performed; and, in cases of uncertain risk, the extent to which the condition is understood.

The Supreme Court's constrained view of the scope of the duty of explanation has steered lower courts firmly in the direction of deference to the medical profession's existing practices concerning the proper extent and timing of risk disclosures. For example, the Tokyo High Court, in a 1985 decision rejecting a claim that the plaintiff should have been offered an informed choice between two alternative courses of measles prophylaxis, concluded:

> [W]e do not accept that the premise of the physician's duty of explanation is that the decision to adopt a course of medical treatment must be entrusted to the patient's "self-determination" or choice. Medical care is the physician's professional responsibility, requiring a high level of expertise. Physicians must follow standards of medical care, providing the care they believe proper. If they were required to follow the patient's choice of treatment, physicians would always have to ascertain patients' intentions, which would cause confusion; appropriate medical care, a specialized art, could scarcely be carried on. If patients desire an alternative, they have the freedom to change physicians. . . .

The Japanese cases stress that in various specified circumstances, the failure to disclose risks is excused or the duty of disclosure never arises. Some such circumstances are familiar to American medical jurisprudence: emergencies, unforeseeable or unknown risks, and cases in which the patient lacks the capacity to understand the physician's explanation. . . .

Courts have also excused physicians from the duty of disclosing risks that are commonly known, and they have held that patients need not be told of the availability of treatments that have not yet become standard medical practice. In some cases, a balancing test is employed: for example, patients need not be informed of risks associated with compulsory vaccinations, because the incidence of adverse effects is low and the public health benefits of vaccinations are significant.

A controversial line of cases holds that a tentative diagnosis, particularly of cancer, need not be accurately reported to the patient. In the internationally notorious Makino case, a nurse suffering abdominal pain was told by her physician, after an echogram and CT scan, that she had gallstones and required an immediate operation. In fact, the tests showed that although there was a possibility of nonmalignant gall bladder disease, the strong likelihood was of advanced cancer of the gall bladder. Believing that a gallstone operation could be put off, the nurse cancelled her appointment to enter the hospital, took an overseas trip, and sought no further medical attention for three months. She subsequently died from cancer, and her family brought an action claiming that timely disclosure of the cancer diagnosis would have impelled her to seek immediate treatment and could have saved her life.

Although the district court, departing at least in rhetoric from most previous decisions, stated that "patients have a right of self-determination," it held that the physician had not breached his duty to inform the patient. The doctor's "strong suspicion" of cancer was not a final diagnosis. Taking into account the psychological blow the patient would supposedly sustain upon being told of this suspicion, the prevailing medical practice of not informing patients of a diagnosis of cancer, and the fact that the doctor had twice warned the patient of the necessity of immediate hospitalization, the court found that the doctor's prevarication about gallstones and failure to communicate specifically the likely consequences of declining further treatment lacked legal significance. The decision was affirmed by both the Nagoya High Court and the Supreme Court of Japan.

The Supreme Court's 1995 decision focused on the fact that the physician, who had no knowledge of this first-time patient's personal ability to withstand the possible shock of hearing a pronounced cancer diagnosis, had acted in keeping with the general practice of physicians at the time the case arose. In so doing, the Supreme Court took a stance that simultaneously maintained the judiciary's traditional deference to the medical profession and implicitly recognized the possibility that the courts may well be swayed in the future by changes in social attitudes.

Notes

1. In addition to the cultural conditions that underlie Japan's version of informed consent, there are economic factors. Leflar mentions the price-controlled fee for service health care system in Japan. Fees are regulated and uniform nationwide, and the fee for a consultation is fairly low, giving physicians an incentive to see as many patients as possible in as short a time as possible. 33 HOUS. L. REV. at 38. In another interesting article, authors George J. Annas and Frances H. Miller assert that the Japanese law on informed consent "reflects the alternatives available in its health care system, which downplays the individual and de-emphasizes high-cost, low-yield technology." Physicians prescribe and sell drugs directly, and they thus have an entrepreneurial stake in the system that U.S. doctors do not. At the time the article was written, Krestin, an anti-cancer drug with no proven efficacy anywhere in the world, was one of the most popular drugs in Japan. "Physicians apparently feel less guilty about failing to inform patients that they have cancer when they can prescribe the ineffective Krestin, because it produces no debilitating side effects." George J. Annas & Frances H. Miller, *The Empire of Death: How Culture and Economics Affect Informed Consent in the U.S., the U.K., and Japan,* 20 AM. J. L. & MED. 357, 375-76 (1994).

2. What cultural values are reflected in the U.S. rules? While we might say patient autonomy or protection of the individual, Annas and Miller argue that Western law reflects the view that death is an unacceptable outcome. They state, "A society's cultural beliefs concerning death influence health resource allocation, and will be reflected in a country's informed consent laws. Where individualism is highly prized and medical care is seen as a market good, legal doctrine will place a high premium on information disclosure to facilitate patient/consumer choices, especially among treatment alternatives." *Id.* at 393. Do you agree that attitudes toward death likely affect a society's attitude toward disclosure of risks? Is that a bad thing?

3. Japan is moving toward a broader view of the informed consent obligation. There have been a variety of developments, including an opinion by the Japanese Supreme Court recognizing a right to accurate advance information about physicians' treatment intentions during life and death situations that arise

during surgery.* Although U.S. victims of malpractice are considerably more likely to bring a compensation claim than patients injured by malpractice in Japan, use of the criminal justice system to prosecute professional negligence makes Japanese law stronger than U.S. law in some respects. In Japan, people injured by malpractice turn to public authorities before seeking private counsel, and may ask prosecutors to pursue rehabilitation of the defendant by eliciting expressions of remorse before (or in conjunction with) making private compensation claims. Robert B Leflar & Futoshi Iwata, *Medical Error as Reportable Event, as Tort, as Crime: A Transpacific Comparison,* 12 WIDENER L. REV. 189 (2005).

4. The importance of cultural influences in understanding the impact – or irrelevance – of a legal standard is reinforced by the experience of Malaysia. Malaysian law has long followed the common law position that a physician has a duty to inform the patient of risks, but it follows the *Bolam* test, *supra,* which held that doctors' actions or non-actions should be judged by the practice of other doctors, whether in the context of diagnosis, treatment or disclosure. However, a case study of Malaysian law asserts that "[i]n a religious society such as Malaysia, to be afflicted with an illness is quite naturally accepted as one's fate." The authors state that the average Malaysian person, particularly one who practices Islam, believes affliction with disease is fate and a doctor's failure to inform a patient of risks would be viewed as an indication that an illness was pre-ordained. *See* John D. Blum, Norchaya Talib, Pieter Carstens, Muhammad Nasser, David Tomkin & Adam McAuley, *Rights of Patients: Comparative Perspectives from Five Countries,* 22 MED. & L. 451, 455 (2003).

5. In a country as ethnically diverse as the United States, there are great differences in the preferences of patients regarding disclosure of the diagnosis and prognosis of a serious illness. In a study about informed consent in a clinical setting, the authors found that Korean-Americans and Mexican-Americans were less

*The case is *Takeda v. State*, 54(2) MINSHŪ 582, 1710 HANREI JIHŌ 97, 1031 HANREI TAIMUZU 158 (Sup.Ct. 3d Petty Bench, Feb. 29, 2000. It is discussed in an epilogue prepared by Professor Leflar: Robert B Leflar, Nihon no Iryō to Hō: Infōmudo Konsent Runessansu [Law and Health Care in Japan: The Renaissance of Informed Consent] 125-146 (Tokyo: Keiso Shobo 2002 (Michiyuki Nagasawa, trans.) English version excerpted in Timothy Stolzfus Jost, READINGS IN COMPARATIVE HEALTH LAW AND BIOETHICS 154-159 (2d ed. 2007). It involved a Jehovah's Witness who was not informed that, despite her clear absence of consent for a blood transfusion during surgery for a liver malignancy, it was the custom of physicians to administer a transfusion to save human life. Reversing a Tokyo District Court judgment for defendants, the Supreme Court of Japan stated that the doctors were obliged to tell her of the hospital's policy to transfuse if it was necessary to save life. The patient lived five years, instead of the expected twelve months, but received an award for emotional distress for infringement of her personal rights.

likely than European-Americans and African-Americans to believe the patient should know the truth or make decisions about the use of life-support. The authors described the decision-making style of these patients as "family-centered." By this, they meant that it would be the sole responsibility of the family to hear bad news and to make the difficult decisions regarding life support. They found similar results regarding cancer diagnosis with ethic groups such as Italians, Greeks and Chinese. Leslie J. Blackhall et al., *Ethnicity and Attitudes Toward Patient Autonomy,* 274 J.AM.MED.ASS'N 820, 823-24 (1995). How should a physician react to these apparent differences in preference? What if the patient's family, but not the patient, communicate the desire that they be the only ones told? Will exceptions such as "waiver" of informed consent, or "therapeutic privilege" protect a physician who attempts to be culturally sensitive by steering the discussion around the patient from malpractice liability? Do you agree with the Japanese physicians who view disclosure motivated by a desire to protect oneself from liability as an ethical breach?

6. In the United States, the issue of which standard of care will govern in informed consent cases is important because if a standard of customary practice is adopted, the plaintiff must obtain an expert witness to testify specifically as to the custom regarding the disclosure in question. This can be difficult to obtain and adds to the cost of litigation because expert witnesses must be paid by the party using them. Many civil law jurisdictions that follow the inquisitorial model expect judges to play a much more active role in investigating the facts of the case, and allow judges to appoint experts to help the court. Are those experts less biased because they are not retained by the parties? The German Federal Supreme Court has noted that medical professionals tend to stick together to the disadvantage of plaintiffs. GIESEN, *supra* at 714-20.

Chapter 9

GOVERNMENTAL LIABILITY

A. COMPARATIVE OVERVIEW

The influence of governmental entities in modern society cannot be over-emphasized. Whether at a national, state, or local level, governmental entities and their agents interact with people daily and injuries inevitably result. The area of governmental liability may encompass a variety of wrongs, only some of which typically fall within the law of tort or delict. In the United States, limitations on the tort liability of governmental entities arise in two basic contexts: through exceptions to statutes waiving sovereign immunity or through judicially-recognized pockets of limited duty. With regard to the limited duty doctrines, it is common to see courts grappling with the question of whether a governmental decision should be sheltered from review because it is a "discretionary function," or because it falls within the well-established "public duty" rule, which provides that police and similar public entities do not owe a legally enforceable duty to members of the general public.

Although the discussion takes a somewhat different form in many other countries, they, like U.S. courts, have had to struggle with the following questions: 1) what purpose does governmental accountability serve and what policy considerations shape its contours? 2) in what forum should disputes between citizens and state or local entities be heard? 3) what types of injuries should be redressed? Civil and common law jurisdictions approach these questions quite differently in many respects. The following excerpt explains the fundamental structural differences that differentiate the judicial systems in civil law countries from common law systems. These systemic differences help explain the dramatically different attitudes toward certain types of government liability.

John Henry Merryman & Rogelio Pérez-Perdomo
**THE CIVIL LAW TRADITION:
AN INTRODUCTION TO THE LEGAL SYSTEMS
OF EUROPE AND LATIN AMERICA**
pp. 86, 88, 134-135 (3d ed. 2007)

The Division of Jurisdiction

The typical common law country has a unified court system that might be represented as a pyramid with a single supreme court at the apex. Regardless of the number of different kinds of courts and of the way jurisdiction is divided among them in lower parts of the pyramid, every case is at last potentially subject to final scrutiny by one supreme court. . . . It seems entirely natural to us that the ultimate power to review the legality of administrative action and the constitutionality of legislative action, as well as to hear and finally decide the great range of appeals in civil and criminal disputes, should be lodged in a supreme court.

Matters are typically quite different in the civil law world. There it is usual to find two or more separate sets of courts, each with its own jurisdiction, its own hierarchy of tribunals, its own judiciary, and its own procedure, all existing within the same nation. A case falling within one jurisdiction will be immune from consideration, whether at the trial or at the appellate level, in the others. If the typical common law judicial system can be represented as a pyramid, the typical civil law judicial system must be visualized as a set of two or more distinct structures. . . .

A typical civil law nation will also have a set of administrative courts, entirely separate and exercising an independent jurisdiction. The basic reason is . . . the revolutionary doctrine of separation of powers. One of the complaints against the judiciary (i.e., the ordinary judiciary) in pre-revolutionary France was that the judges wrongly interfered with the administrative work of the government in a variety of ways. In England the courts had the powers of *mandamus* (to compel an official to perform a duty) and *quo warranto* (to question the legality of an act performed by a public official). In France, by contrast, one objective of the revolutionary reforms was to deprive ordinary judges of any power to determine the legality of administrative action or to control the conduct of government officials. Just as the separation of the legislative and judicial powers denied judges any opportunity to interfere in the legislative process, so the separation of the administrative and judicial powers denied them that opportunity in the administrative process. . . .

The widespread distrust of the judiciary, the traditional image of the judge and the judicial function, and the principle of separation of powers made such review [of the legality of administrative action] by the ordinary judiciary an unacceptable solution. In addition, the insistence that ordinary judges not be lawmakers in any sense led to rejection of the idea that prior judicial decisions should control future judicial action, even with respect to the same administrative act. . . .

[T]he solution adopted in France, and subsequently in much of the civil law world, was to establish a separate tribunal within the administration. In other nations, including Germany, the same result was achieved by setting up a system of administrative courts. Although there are many important differences between the two approaches typified by the French and German solutions, both met the same basic requirements. First, review of the legality of administrative action was kept out of the hands of the ordinary judiciary, and the principle of separation of powers was preserved. Second, a decision that an administrative act was illegal, and therefore void, could be given . . .effect without introducing the principle of *stare decisis* into the system of justice administered by the ordinary courts. Although there is great variety in the ways in which individual nations following the civil law tradition have worked out their systems for reviewing administrative legality, the basic pattern described here is the dominant one.

Note

The excerpt above answers the question of where legal disputes stemming from governmental activity may be heard and provides an explanation of why civil law countries established special tribunals. Apart from administrative tribunals, many civil law countries have constitutional courts. Power to declare legislation unconstitutional is concentrated in these courts. France differs from the norm in that it has a Constitutional council that has traditionally been more political than judicial.[1] In the United States, the power to adjudicate constitutionality of legislation is diffused through the court system. *Id.* at 137-38. Many tort-like actions local governmental entities may be litigated under a federal civil rights statute, 42 U.S.C. § 1983. There are many substantive hurdles to recovery in these civil rights actions.

Having identified the fundamental structural differences in how civil code countries approach governmental liability, the following excerpt takes up the issue of how France and England differ in philosophy and substance. U.S. law is, predictably, much closer to English law.

James E. Pfander

Government Accountability in Europe: A Comparative Assessment*

35 Geo. Wash. Int'l L. Rev. 611, 615-616, 623-624 (2003)

Damages in Tort for Government Wrongs

England has long permitted individuals to file suit against government officials whose actions, unless justified in law, would have been tortious at common law. These officer suits often seek damages in accordance with common law precepts, and liability often turns on whether the official can statutorily justify the tortious conduct. Thus, one could say that a constable on the street corner committed the tort of trespass and false imprisonment if he entered onto private land to make an arrest without legal justification. Similarly, actions against governmental agents may allege simple negligence or the commission of a nuisance and resulting damages.

---

[1] The Constitutional Council is composed of all former Presidents of France and nine additional persons. Before certain laws become effective, they must or may (depending on the circumstances) be sent to this council for a decision on constitutionality. A decision is made without benefit of oral hearings, parties or any attributes of a judicial hearing. If the legislation is found unconstitutional, it cannot become effective unless the Constitution is amended.

For many years, English law imposed important restrictions on the scope of such remedies. First, the central government enjoyed sovereign immunity from suit in tort; plaintiffs could only sue government officers as natural persons and name local government entities as defendants in such actions. Second, vicarious liability followed the rules of sovereign immunity so courts could hold local, but not central governments vicariously liable for the torts. Under English law, the constable worked for the public as a whole, which meant that public funds were unavailable to compensate individuals for harm done by police officers. The constable, needless to say, often lacked funds to provide a complete remedy.

Parliament has in recent years set aside many of the rules that restrict liability in tort. The Crown Proceedings Act of 1947 abrogated the central government's sovereign immunity from suit in tort, making it clear that the Crown bore the same liability as a private party for damages resulting from its actions. Since 1964, moreover, England has provided public funds to compensate victims of police misconduct. As a result, today one can, in principle, bring suit for damages resulting from the tortious acts of any public agent or officer, subject to a few remaining immunities.

If the availability of suit now seems clear, the question of the scope of liability and the proper measure of damages remains in dispute. In general, England has been reluctant to recognize government liability for omissions.[33] . . .

Liability in Tort [in France]

French law distinguishes between suits against government officials who bear personal responsibility for the injury (*faute personelle*) and suits against the government for actions taken in the scope of official duties (*faute de service*). Suits against officials in their personal capacity go forward in the ordinary civil courts, whereas actions against the government for course-of-employment torts go forward in the administrative courts. Often, litigants will strain, with some assistance from the *Conseil d'Etat*, to bring their claims within the bounds of *faute de service* in order to

[33] *See e.g., Osman v. U.K.*, 95 Eur. Ct. H. R. 3125, 3126-3127 (1998)(finding a violation of the Convention's guarantee of access to court where English courts affirmed a dismissal on the pleadings of an action to impose liability on the police for failure to prevent the commission of a crime).

secure a recovery that the government, rather than a possibly impecunious official, must pay.

French law takes a relatively expansive view of the sorts of administrative faults that give rise to liability. For one thing, simple fault standing alone will often result in liability. Additionally, unlike its U.S. counterpart, French law holds that gross fault or negligence will suffice for the imposition of liability even in the most sensitive areas of policy formation. Finally, and in some ways most interestingly, French administrative law imposes no-fault liability in cases where the state has engaged in conduct that creates a risk of injury; where the predictable injury occurs, the state must compensate the injured.

French liability without fault provides a striking example of the principle that the public must pay the cost of government conduct, and that an unequal burden should not fall upon any particular individual citizen of the nation. The same principle underlies the idea of even-handed taxation and the payment of compensation for governmental takings of private property, ideas that find an expression in Anglo-American public law, but French administrative law presses this notion of equity of burdens well beyond its English counterparts. Thus, the *Conseil d'Etat* (1) permitted a bank to recover compensation from the Minister of Justice for money lost as a result of a bank robbery conducted by three criminals on parole-like releases from prison; (2) allowed an injured party to recover against a local child care agency for injuries inflicted by a child in foster care; and (3) granted the child of a schoolteacher exposed in utero to German measles recovery for injuries from the public school. All of these instances of liability go well beyond what one could imagine in the United States.[84]

Notes

1. Professor Pfander mentions the *Consèil d'Etat*, a unique body that fashions French administrative law. It arose after the French Revolution and performs both a consultative and a judicial

---

[84] *Cf. DeShaney v. Winnebago County*, 495 U.S. 189 (1998) (holding that the state owes no duty under the Constitution to protect its citizens against invasions by private actors). If the occasions for liability in France extend beyond those in England and the United States, however, the measure of damages may be somewhat less. Until comparatively recently, French law did not recognize public liability for resulting mental loss or anguish.

role. A litigation section hears challenges to administrative action. The *Consèil d'Etat* decisions examine sources such as the constitution, international treaties, statutes and regulations. The *Consèil d'Etat* also is able to develop general principles of law that are constrained neither by precedent nor statutory law. Administrative agencies do not regard these general principles as precedential, but rather as interpretation that provides a backdrop for principles of administrative action. Respect for prior adjudications by the administrative tribunals is demonstrated by giving their decisions an effect that is like issue preclusion. *Id.* at 622-23.

2. Look again at the examples of French rulings permitting recovery at the end of thc Pfander excerpt. He is surely correct in describing them as well beyond what U.S. courts would recognize as an acceptable basis for governmental responsibility. The *Conseil d'Etat* would not impose liability for administrative acts that affect or annoy all citizens; it recognizes this is an inevitable byproduct of the lawful exercise of government functions. But no-fault liability is acceptable as an application of the French commitment to equality when a burden falls on a particular individual or group. TIM KOOPMANS, COURTS AND POLITICAL INSTITUTIONS, A COMPARATIVE VIEW 142-43 (2005).

3. France is not unique in recognizing governmental accountability in situations that would seem far outside the mainstream of U.S. law. The French philosophy and model of accountability has had a huge impact in many European countries such as Italy, Greece, Spain and the Netherlands. Rolf Stürner, *Suing the Sovereign in Europe and Germany,* 35 GEO. WASH. INT'L L. REV. 663, 667 (2003). Even beyond Europe, the French vision of separation of powers through the creation of administrative courts or special courts has been enormously influential in the rest of the world.

4. One downside to the English & U.S. view of limited governmental liability is that certain types of negligence remain unredressed because of the sensitivity of allowing a court to rule on them. For example, the discretionary function limitation on duty sacrifices negligence liability to permit protection of public decision-making processes and to promote their independence. The hierarchy of U.S. courts and the precedential effect given to decisions of higher courts prevents power struggles over these decisions.

A Spanish case illustrates how differently things work out when attributes of the judicial system and the rules on governmental accountability are changed. Spain has a system of separate courts, including an Administrative Division of the *Tribunal Supremo* (TS), and a *Tribunal Constitucional* (Constitutional Court) (TC). A litigant brought a case in the TS accusing members of the TC of violating the law by selecting its law clerks privately (or through connections) rather than as a result of a civil service examination. The TS dismissed his case, and the litigant then filed an appeal with the TC. When the TC dismissed his appeal, he sued the judges of the TC in the TS. The TS held that eleven of the twelve members of the TC had committed gross professional negligence by dismissing an appeal without adequate legal reasoning, thus violating plaintiff's right to effective judicial protection, and "harming his faith in a social and democratic State, subject to the rule of law." The judges were ordered to pay damages of 500 Euros each. Professor Jordi Ribot describes the situation as not uncommon among jurisdictions that have some fluidity in the types of cases that may be heard by Constitutional as opposed to ordinary courts. While it permits accountability, the system has allowed an unfortunate power struggle. Jordi Ribot, *Spain, in* EUROPEAN TORT LAW 2004, TORT AND INSURANCE LAW YEARBOOK 539, 550-51 (Helmut Koziol & Barbara C. Steinger, eds., 2004)(discussing *Tribunal Supremo* (Civil Chamber) 23 January 2004; RJ 2004).

B. GOVERNMENTAL ACCOUNTABILITY FOR FAILURE TO REGULATE OR PROTECT

In the United States and in much of Europe, there is great reluctance to impose liability on government entities for failure to take actions to protect their citizens. Whether citizens are arguing that there was an affirmative obligation to enact regulations that would protect them or a failure to enforce existing regulatory standards in a given case, the result is usually no liability. The view is that duty is owed to the public generally but not enforceable by specific individuals. In the United States, duty is found only when the plaintiff falls within the scope of a narrow exception, such as a special relationship with the governmental entity. Although most civil law systems do not use the concept of lack of duty to limit liability, many agree that the discretion of government agencies to prioritize among competing policy objectives must be protected. As might be expected, based on the section above, the French are much more likely to impose liability than other countries. See generally Willem H. van Boom and Andrea Pinna, *Liability for Failure to Regulate Health and Safety Risks, in* EUROPEAN TORT LAW 2005, TORT AND INSURANCE LAW YEARBOOK,2, 7-14 ((Helmut Koziol & Barbara C. Steinger eds, 2005).

The French are not alone in their willingness to second-guess governmental decisions, as the following decision from the Supreme Court of Costa Rica reveals. Before reading that decision, it is helpful to know something about the development of governmental tort liability in Latin America. As would be expected, the countries of Latin America are civil law systems. Civil Codes in Latin America drew inspiration from a variety of European Codes, as interpreted and elaborated by influential Latin American jurists. But, as in Europe, the sparse wording of the Civil Codes coupled with a reluctance to amend them as one would a statute has placed much responsibility for their interpretation on courts. In addition relying on courts to determine the scope of governmental responsibility, Costa Rica and other Latin American countries responded to the threat of authoritarian governments by placing the right of redress against the sovereign in their constitutions.

In addition to the extensive constitutional protections that exist in some Latin American constitutions, the Inter-American system of protecting human rights has been influential in reining in governmental power. The American Convention on Human Rights and a wide variety of treaties that protect vulnerable groups provide extensive protection against torture, forced disappearances of persons, and discrimination. The Inter-American Commission of Human Rights and the Inter-American Court of Human Rights supervise compliance with the treaties. The Inter-American Court required that states have a legal system that guarantees that individuals can sue the sovereign when rights protected by the treaties are violated. Many of the international norms guaranteeing fair trial and procedural protection have been incorporated into domestic laws. See Claudio Grossman, *Suing the Sovereign from the Latin American Perspective*, 35 GEO. WASH. INT'L L. REV. 653, 656-660 (2003).*

With regard to suing governmental entities in tort, Professor Grossman explains:

> Suing the sovereign in tort in domestic courts is not a child of statutory law. In the Latin American region, tort liability for governmental acts . . . was generally-speaking and certainly up until the 1950s, shaped by judges themselves. . . . Difficulties in legislative reform stress the importance of reinterpreting Civil Code provisions in order to adapt them to the realities of a modern society. Specifically, this applies to the law of torts, as the legal provisions developed in the twentieth century were insufficient insofar as they did not allow individuals to sue the sovereign. Through interpretation, the judiciary started to allow for cases where civil servants acted with malice or negligence. . . . [E]ven though this was a step forward in the attempts to allow individuals to sue the sovereign, the requirements of malice and negligence restricted state responsibility to cases against civil servants who were responsible for acting "irresponsibly." Serious problems of proof, sometimes insurmountable, were a serious hurdle for success in litigation.
>
> During the wave of democratization from . . . the rejection of authoritarianism in the region and the ensuing possibilities for the expansion of human freedom in Latin America, statutory developments in the area of state responsibility commenced, expanding the scope of liability beyond the strait jacket of the Civil Code. Many Latin American countries seek to constitutionalize all provisions relating to suing the sovereign. An example of this is the Chilean Organic or Basic Law of the Administration.[39] Article 44 of this statute (in line with the French tradition) allowed for state responsibility for the tort of "lack of service." This type of liability does not require proof of "guilt or malice;" instead, the failure of the state to provide "needed" services must be established. These developments, however, have not been homogeneous.

---

[39] Ley Orgánica Constitucional de Bases Generales de la Administración del Estado, No. 18.575, art. 44 (2000) (Chile).

> For example, the same law in Chile that established "lack of service" as a basis for liability also immunized the armed forces and the police from such liability.

Id. at 660-661.

ESTATE OF PICADO GONZÁLEZ v. STATE

Resolution 584; No. 97-00072-1063-CA
First Chamber, Supreme Court (Costa Rica)
August 11, 2005*

[The action was brought by the widow of Carlos Picado González against the State in the Administrative and Civil Court of the Treasury Ministry. Picado González was killed in 1997 when he was struck by a car while trying to cross the General Highway close to the the development of Los Arcos. He was extremely drunk at the time and the individual who struck him was exonerated of manslaughter charges. In 1986, the Neighborhood Association of Los Arcos had asked the Ministry of Public Works and Transportation to build a pedestrian bridge across the highway, but this had never been done. The widow requested compensation on the theory that the government had negligently failed to build a pedestrian bridge over the highway, and she argued that they government should be strictly liable as well. She lost at trial and in the appellate tribunal.]

III. Evolution and Independence of the Regime of Public Liability

Upon becoming itself a subject of the law and an essential part of the democratic framework, the state came to take *responsibility* for its acts. This development led to the abandonment of the notion that those who exercised power enjoy absolute immunity. . . . The state and the administration now have an obligation to repair any harm they cause, as an inalienable principle of any constitutional order. Of course, the elaboration of this idea required drawing on our common legal regime, the Civil Code. However, in this century, the obligation

---

** This case is identified and translated in ÁNGEL R. OQUENDO, LATIN AMERICAN LAW 588-593 (2006). Additions to the text of the opinion that extend beyond the Oquendo excerpt translated by Julie Davies.

that today is imposed on the State and the Administration for the harms they cause is a principle of any constitutional structure.

IV. Strict Liability

Extracontractual civil responsibility of the Public Administration is characterized by a theory of strict liability that encompasses at its base the theory of risk and the theory of equilibrium. With this, reparation can be paid to someone who has suffered harm attributable to a public organization as the center of authority.

V. Constitutional Foundation of Strict Liability

The evolution of the regime at issue, which imposes strict liability, finds full support in our constitutional jurisprudence, which establishes clear rules and principles regarding the so-called *right to full compensation for damages.*

VII. Extraordinary and Illicit Omissions

Compulsory Compensation for Harm Resulting from Inaction. In actuality, it is accepted that administrative conduct includes not only active conduct by the Administration (and with that, the administrative act) but also omissions, this "do nothing" which is called Administrative inactivity. . . . It may be said that administrative indolence can produce (and produces) worse harms than actions of the public entity. It is from there it must be affirmed that the Public Administration is also responsible for harms and injuries occasioned by its administrative inactivity. . . .

VIII. The Causal Link as a Prerequisite for Liability

. . . In the present case, it is evident that the non-existence of a pedestrian bridge required Don Carlos, like any other pedestrian, to cross the highway without any means to regulate traffic, even though on a highway, vehicles normally travel with high speed. The non-existence of a means or instrument to cross the highway left Mr. Picado González in a situation of risk that, without doubt, was a direct and proximate cause of his death. . . .

Notes

1. The court ultimately reduced the amount of the recovery because Picado González was drunk while crossing the highway.

2. The use of strict liability (*responsabilidad objectiva*) is a very interesting aspect of this case, particularly for a student of U.S. tort law. A strikingly similar U.S. case involved a pedestrian who was struck by a car while walking on a highway. He alleged that the county should have built a walkway along that shoulder of the road. The court stated,

> For there to be governmental tort liability, there must be an underlying common law or statutory duty of care. There is no liability for the failure of a government entity to build, expand or modernize capital improvements such as buildings and roads. A governmental entity's decision not to build or modernize a particular improvement is a discretionary function with which our supreme court has held courts cannot interfere. There was no statutory or common law duty to provide a walkway for pedestrians like the Nehmads. A road shoulder for vehicles was maintained but the county never assumed the duty of providing a walkway when it created and maintained the shoulder.

Nehmad v. Metropolitan Dade County, 545 So.2d. 300 (Fla. App. 1989).

3. By deciding that the state must be treated in the same way as an individual in a torts case and then proceeding to impose strict liability, the Costa Rican Supreme Court appears to be paving the way for much greater governmental accountability. It remains to be seen whether the other branches of government will feel the need to rein in the Court. Possibly the difficulties individuals experience in obtaining access to justice will prevent excessive litigation.

C. GOVERNMENTAL ACCOUNTABILITY IN A STATE-DOMINATED SYSTEM

The experience in Latin America described above underscores the importance of accountability to the legitimacy of governments, both in the eyes of their own people and in the eyes of the outside world. In a country like China, where the State is involved in enterprises at every governmental level, encounters between citizens and representatives of the government are unavoidable. Since state functionaries exert a dominant presence everywhere, including in judicial tribunals, there is a risk that they will not be fair or objective in responding to claims against the government.

The Chinese Constitution of 1982 did not adopt a division of powers in the style of the U.S. Constitution. It adopted the National People's Congress System, in which people's congresses are the sources of state power at the national and sub-national levels. Executive and judicial powers stem from the People's Congress and are subject to their control. The Constitution declares that courts will be independent, but because the People's Congress or its standing Committee select the judges and may remove them from office, there is both political and financial control over them.

Although the Chinese Constitution provided that individuals might bring a tort action in court, as a practical matter, it was very difficult until 1989. In 1989, China, following a continental model, adopted an Administrative Litigation Law (ALL). It established a system of judicial review over all agency actions and created a right to compensation. The State Compensation Law of 1994, enacted by the National People's Congress, further defined the scope of compensation, principles of sovereign immunity that would apply, and procedures for making claims. See XiXin Wang, *Suing the Sovereign Observed from the Chinese Perspective: The Idea and Practice of State Compensation in China*, 35 GEO.WASH. INT'L L. REV 681, 681-684 (2003). Professor Wang praises this legislation as a step forward, though he characterizes the government's attitude toward it as ambivalent.

Even though the system seems to resemble the French model of public law, the devil is in the details. China scholars are dubious about the Chinese government's commitment to creating a robust system for citizens to utilize in addressing governmental abuses. Michael Palmer writes:

> The ALL is generally considered both within and outside China to have been only a limited success in affording aggrieved citizens access to administrative justice and in controlling administrative conduct. One of its most important limitations is that it permits review by the court only of specific administrative conduct, with

> neither administrative rules nor "abstract administrative acts" falling within the court's jurisdiction. In addition, under China's system of legislative interpretation of law, it is the enacting body that enjoys the authority to interpret an item of legislation. In addition, it is only personal and property rights that ALL protects, with important political issues and rights excluded from the jurisdiction of the administrative chambers. Perhaps just as importantly, the court may examine only the legality of the conduct challenged and is not empowered to consider the appropriateness or reasonableness of conduct within the discretion of administrative decision-makers. This is a particular problem in the China context, because the often broad and ambiguous wording of Chinese legislation allows administrators and administrative agencies a wide degree of discretion.

Michael Palmer, *Controlling the State? Mediation in Administrative Litigation in The People's Republic of China*, 16 TRANSNAT'L L. & CONTEMP. PROBS. 165, 178-79 (2006).

Even with a legal structure in place that would permit governmental accountability in some cases, the consolidation of power in the state and the relationship between local entities and the Party can make recovery difficult. Kevin O'Brian and Lianjiang Li write that local Party committees control the appointment of judges and the budget of local courts. Local governments have hindered litigants by blocking access to official documents, detaining lawyers who agree to help villagers, and detaining the litigant or family members of the litigant, pressuring judges to resolve a case favorably for the government, or unduly delaying cases. The Party itself is immune from suit, and some local officials have asked the Party to issue an order to a court not to accept a case because it involves a sensitive matter. Even if a litigant ultimately prevails, the government may refuse to pay the judgment or threaten retaliation. Kevin O'Brian and Lianjiang Li, *Suing the Local State: Administrating Litigation in Rural China, in* ENGAGING THE LAW IN CHINA, STATE, SOCIETY AND POSSIBILITIES FOR JUSTICE 31, 31-41 (Neil J. Diamant, Stanley B. Lubman & Kevin J. O'Brien eds., 2005). Randall Peerenboom explains that independence of the judiciary is further undermined because trial judges must often obtain approval from more senior judges before issuing a final judgment in difficult cases. RANDALL PEERENBOOM, CHINA'S LONG MARCH TOWARD RULE OF LAW 286 (2002).

As evidenced by the following case it *is* possible to recover against the government under some circumstances. The case involved local functionaries of the Police Patrol Platoon who had lost or ignored a claim for compensation that plaintiff was attempting to assert against a private party who had injured him in a fight. After two years at the Platoon office, the file was passed to the Defendant Xinfu District Branch of the Public Security Bureau of Fushun City. Another year passed with no resolution.

QIAO FENZGHU (PLAINTIFF) AND XINFU DISTRICT BRANCH OF THE PUBLIC SECURITY BUREAU OF FUSHUN CITY (DEFENDANT),

Administrative No. 10-11 of 1997, 1997-09-29.

The Court of First Instance analyzed the case as follows: . . .

PART IV GROUNDS OF JUDGMENT AT THE FIRST INSTANCE TRIAL

The People's Court of Xinfu District, Fushun City of Liaoning Province considered that:

The Public Security Bureau was the statutory enforcement authority under the Regulations of the People's Republic of China on Administrative Penalties for Public Security ("the Regulations"). The Public Security Bureau shouldered the statutory duties of protecting the lawful rights of citizens from illegal and violent infringements. The Police Patrol Platoon and the Branch should have found out the true facts of this minor assault case . . . and disposed of it impartially. In light of the facts that the Police Patrol Platoon and the Branch had delayed the Case for 3 years and refused to handle the case any further, their acts obviously violated the applicable law. Although there was no time limit prescribed in the Regulations on handling a case, in view of the enforcement implementation and the effective implementation of the Administrative Law, administrative security cases should generally be disposed of and concluded within 6 months or up to a maximum of 12 months in exceptional circumstances. However, this Case had been delayed for 3 years. Therefore, there was no doubt in the ruling by the Court that the Defendant had failed to exercise its statutory duties. . . .

Generally speaking, in relation to administrative cases on personal injuries, compensations should be borne by the persons committing the infringing acts. However, in this case, the Police Patrol Platoon collected the original invoices from the Plaintiff and then delayed the case; the Police Patrol Platoon failed to return the evidence and finally lost it. . . . The Defendant entirely had the authority to re-investigate the Case and to gather other evidence based on what the Plaintiff had submitted. . . . Therefore, the Public Service Security Bureau should be liable for the loss of the Case file.

Notes

1. Notwithstanding the limitations on government accountability discussed above, this case represented a victory for the plaintiff over administrative incompetence. Although our own legal system allows much greater accountability than the Chinese system, it is interesting to consider whether such a case would be actionable in the United States. The answer is very complicated. Since the plaintiff was claiming that the administrative tribunals botched his case, lost his proof, and prevented him from recovering from the man who beat him up, presumably this would not constitute a "discretionary act." But if, as the court states, there were no strict time limits on agency action, perhaps the action for damages against the agency would not go forward.

2. Attempts to frame the same type of claim as a constitutional tort would run into serious obstacles. Judges, including those in administrative agencies, are immune from individual suits for damages. Local governmental entities are not held liable on a *respondeat superior* basis for the occasional slip by an employee, and at the state level, there may be sovereign immunity. In one well known case, an action was filed against the state and local public aid officials for administering the federal-state programs of Aid to the Blind and Disabled (AABD) in a manner inconsistent with federal regulations and the Constitution. Eligibility determinations were to have been made within 30 or 45 days of receipt of an application, but were not processed within the applicable time period. The plaintiffs, who were unlawfully deprived of benefits by the delay, sought to enjoin compliance in the future and payment of those benefits that were improperly withheld. The Court refused to order the payment, deeming it a retroactive award to be paid from the state treasury. *Edelman v. Jordan*, 415 U.S. 651, 94 S.Ct. 1347, 39 L.Ed.2d 662 (1974).

3. The experience in Romania, which emerged from Communist rule only in 1991, is quite similar to that in China. Romania adopted a Civil Code and Constitution modeled on the French system. Nonetheless, concerns about corruption of the judiciary and collusion between the government ministries and the judges persist. It is apparent that many of the government agencies have no intention of responding to complaints, even when forwarded by a Government Ombudsman. See Pfander, *supra*, at 626-631.

Chapter 10

DOMESTIC TORT CLAIMS AGAINST FOREIGN NATIONS: THE FOREIGN SOVEREIGN IMMUNITIES ACT

Any tort suit brought in a U.S. court against a foreign government must comply with the restrictions imposed by the Foreign Sovereign Immunities Act, a statute passed by Congress and signed into law in 1976. The FSIA is roughly analogous to the Federal Tort Claims Act, which represents a conditional waiver of the United States government's immunity from tort suits and which applies to any tort suit against the U.S. government. Under the FSIA, foreign governments are immune from suits in U.S. courts, unless a particular exception applies. This chapter explores the two FSIA exceptions of greatest relevance to our study of global torts: the "tortious conduct" exception, and the more recent "state-sponsored terrorism" exception.

A. THE TORTIOUS CONDUCT EXCEPTION

O'BRYAN v. HOLY SEE

471 F.Supp.2d 784 (W.D. Ky. 2007)

HEYBURN, Chief Judge.

Plaintiffs James O'Bryan, Donald Poppe, and Michael Turner ("Plaintiffs") filed this putative class action against the Holy See ("Defendant") in its Capacity as a foreign state and in its capacity as an unincorporated association and head of an international religious organization, alleging claims for liability under the doctrines of *respondeat superior* for acts of bishops and priests, violations of customary international law of human rights, negligence, breach of fiduciary duty, infliction of emotional distress, deceit, and misrepresentation. Plaintiffs' claims arise from sexual abuse by local Catholic priests many years ago. They seek monetary and injunctive relief.

This Court has previously ruled that the Holy See is considered a foreign state, and, therefore the Foreign Sovereign Immunity Act ("FSIA") governs any claims against it. Defendant now challenges the Court's subject matter jurisdiction under FSIA. Applying FSIA and its various exceptions present a number of novel, complex, and intertwined questions. The Court ultimately concludes that some of Plaintiffs' claims premised upon the acts and omissions of Holy See officials and employees within the United States fit within the federal court jurisdiction under FSIA.

I.

Plaintiffs' factual and legal allegations are critical to the subsequent FSIA analysis. Their central thrust is that the "root [of the childhood sexual abuse] problem" is "the deliberate failure of the Holy See to take effective action to prevent childhood sexual abuse by its priests, clerics, bishops, archbishops, cardinals, agents, and employees." Plaintiffs say that the Holy See imposed a policy of secrecy surrounding incidents of childhood sexual abuse and failed to take steps to prevent abuse, punish offenders, or avoid recidivism by prior offenders. Plaintiffs make four specific allegations.

Plaintiffs allege first that the Holy See violated its international law obligations under the Universal Declaration of Human Rights and the Convention on the Rights of the Child. Second, Plaintiffs allege that Defendant, "by and through its agents, servants and employees," breached duties owed to Plaintiffs. Those duties included the duty to provide safe care, custody, and control to the minor children entrusted to Roman Catholic; the duty to warn parents of those children that the priests and other clerics to whom they entrusted their children were known perpetrators of childhood sexual abuse; and the duty to report known or suspected perpetrators of childhood sexual abuse to the appropriate authorities. Third, Plaintiffs allege that the Holy See breached fiduciary duties owed to Plaintiffs, including but not limited the duty to warn parents of children placed in the care, custody, and control of known perpetrators of childhood sexual abuse and the duty to report known or suspected perpetrators of child sexual abuse to the appropriate authorities. Fourth, Plaintiffs allege that Defendant's conduct constitutes an outrage and infliction of emotional distress. Fifth and sixth, in claims solely against the Holy See in its capacity as an incorporated association and head of an international religious organization, Plaintiffs allege torts of deceit and misrepresentation. Plaintiffs also seek a variety of injunctive relief. . . .

II.

For most of our nation's history, it was our national policy to grant foreign states complete immunity from civil suits in United States courts. Beginning in 1952, this view began to change. Gradually, a view evolved that one could sue foreign states in United States courts under certain limited exceptions. The specific determinations were generally left to the State Department until 1976 when Congress enacted FSIA, which sought to codify the existing exceptions. Now, FSIA provides the sole basis for obtaining jurisdiction over a foreign state in United States courts. *Argentine Republic v. Amerada Hess Shipping Corporation,* 488 U.S. 428, 434, 109 S.Ct. 683, 102 L.Ed.2d 818 (1989).

Under FSIA, foreign sovereigns are presumptively immune from the jurisdiction of the United States courts. To assert subject matter jurisdiction over a foreign sovereign, a court must meet one of FSIA's exceptions. Plaintiffs have alleged that several exceptions to the FSIA apply: the waiver exception, the commercial activity exception, and the tortious conduct exception. [The waiver exception does not apply here because there is no evidence the Holy See has either implicitly or explicitly agreed to waive its sovereign immunity. The commercial activity exception does not apply because the "true essence" of the claim here is not commercial, but rather clearly sounds in tort.] The tortious conduct exception requires a more lengthy discussion . . .

III.

Section 1605(a) of the FSIA also provides an exception to foreign sovereign immunity for tortious acts of a foreign state or its agents. The tort exception provides:

> A foreign state shall not be immune from the jurisdiction of courts of the United States or of the States in any case not otherwise encompassed [by the commercial activity exception], in which money damages are sought against a foreign state for personal injury or death, or damage to or loss of property, occurring in the United States and caused by the tortious act or omission of that foreign state or of any official or employee of that foreign state while acting within the scope of his office or employment.

28 U.S.C. § 1605(a)(5). A related subpart provides that the tort exception itself shall not apply to "any claim based upon the exercise or performance or the failure to exercise or perform a discretionary function regardless of whether the discretion be abused." 28 U.S.C. § 1605(a)(5)(A). The Court will discuss this "exception to the exception" in Section IV.

First, however, the Court must answer a number of questions to determine whether the tortious activity exception even applies. Does FSIA's geographic limitation restrict any claims in this case? Are the individual actors actually officials or employees of the Holy See as the tortious activity exception requires? And, if so, were those officials acting within the scope of their employment? The Court will address each question in turn.

A.

No one disputes that the tortious activity exception is restricted to cases in which the personal injury, death, or damage to or loss of property occurs in the United States. The actual personal injuries complained of in this suit – the sexual abuse of Plaintiffs and purported Class Members – meet that requirement. However, the analysis does not end here. The Seventh and D.C. Circuits have added the requirement that the tortious act or omission (in addition to the actual personal injury) must occur in the United States. *See Frolova v. Union of Soviet Socialist Republics,* 761 F.2d 370, 379 (7th Cir.1985); *Asociacion de Reclamantes v. United Mexican States,* 735 F.2d 1517, 1524 (D.C.Cir.1984). The Ninth Circuit has a slightly different rule, holding that "if plaintiffs allege *at least one entire tort* occurring in the United States, they may claim under § 1605(a)(5)." *Olsen v. Government of Mexico,* 729 F.2d 641, 646 (9th Cir.1984) (emphasis added). The Sixth Circuit has not considered this additional requirement.

Subsequently, Chief Justice Rehnquist, speaking for a unanimous Supreme Court, discussed the issue in *Argentine Republic v. Amerada Hess Shipping Corp., supra.* The Court did hold that § 1605(a)(5) is "limited by its terms ... to those cases in which the damage to or loss of property occurs *in the United States.*" The Court then concluded that "[b]ecause respondents' *injury* unquestionably occurred well outside [the United States], the exception for noncommercial torts cannot apply." The Court then discussed the fact that a tort may have had effects in the United States, drawing a distinction between § 1605(a)(5) and § 1605(a)(2), under which a foreign state may be liable for commercial activities "outside the territory of the United States" that have a "direct effect" inside the United States. It said that "Congress' decision to use explicit language in § 1605(a)(2), and not to do so in § 1605(a)(5), indicates that the exception in § 1605(a)(5) covers only torts occurring within the territorial jurisdiction of the United States." While the Supreme Court's conclusions are not completely clear, its language suggests a view that both the injury and the tortious act or omission must occur in the United States. This is strong enough language for this Court to adopt the same view.

Here, Plaintiffs allege torts that occurred both outside and inside the United States. Plaintiffs concede that the *acts* of *Defendant itself* were all "committed outside the United States." Moreover, any omissions committed by the Holy See itself clearly occurred outside of the United States. Therefore, under FSIA's territorial requirements, the Holy See cannot be held liable for "its own" alleged torts (as opposed to those committed by its officials or employees), because those alleged torts all occurred outside of the United States. Holding otherwise would constitute a dramatic expansion of FSIA.

On the other hand, Plaintiffs allege that acts and omissions by agents of the Holy See inside the United States caused personal injuries. Specifically, Plaintiffs allege that Defendant's agents, officials, and employees failed to report known or suspected child abuse, failed to warn parishioners about known or suspected pedophiles in child-care positions, failed to provide adequate care to children entrusted to its churches and school, failed to maintain the premises of churches and schools in a reasonably safe condition, and failed to adequately supervise or control known or suspected sexual predators. These torts – both acts and omissions – alleged to have been committed by the "Defendant's agents, officials, and employees" *in the United States* all certainly occurred within the United States, and thus squarely fall under the tortious activity exception of FSIA.

B.

The critical question then becomes whether the agents discussed above – the United States-based archbishops, bishops, and other clergy of the Roman Catholic Church – are officials or employees of the Holy See as defined in FSIA. This is not an easy question to answer. FSIA allows actions against foreign sovereigns only where "money damages are sought against a foreign state for personal injury ... occurring in the United States and caused by the tortious act or omission of that foreign state or of *any official or employee* of that foreign state while acting within the scope of his office or employment."

The FSIA provides no definition of "official" or "employee." Whether the American Catholic archbishops, bishops, and other clergy are employees of the Holy See would appear to be a question of Kentucky state law. *See, e.g., Randolph v. Budget Rent-A-Car,* 97 F.3d 319, 325 (9th Cir.1996) (holding that the "question of whether Maghrabi was a Saudia employee is governed by California law"). *See also First Nat. City Bank v. Banco Para El Comercio Exterior De Cuba,* 462 U.S. 611, 622 n. 11, 103 S.Ct. 2591, 77 L.Ed.2d 46 (1983) ("Banco") ("where state law provides a rule of liability governing private individuals, the FSIA requires the application of that rule to foreign states in like circumstances"). "Under Kentucky law the right to control is considered to be the most critical element in determining whether an agency relationship exists." *Grant v. Bill Walker Pontiac-GMC, Inc.,* 523 F.2d 1301, 1305 (6th Cir.1975).

Under FSIA's burden-shifting structure, once a foreign state has made a prima facie showing of immunity, the plaintiff then bears the burden of coming forward with facts showing that one of the statutory exceptions to immunity applies. However, once the *asserted allegations* bring claims within the statutory exceptions to FSIA, the burden then shifts to the party asserting immunity to prove that the exceptions do not apply. The ultimate burden of persuasion remains with the foreign sovereign at all times.

Here, Plaintiffs have alleged that the Holy See exercises substantial control over the Catholic archbishops, bishops, and other clergy based in the United States. . . . Therefore, the burden shifts to the Holy See to prove that the exception does not apply. The Holy See has declined to provide such evidence at this time, and therefore the Court concludes at this time that the Holy See does exercise control substantial enough to justify a conclusion that those persons are "employees" of the Holy See for the purposes of FSIA. However, facts may emerge during the litigation that allow the Holy See to meet its burden, and thus the Court is willing to reexamine its ruling on this issue at an appropriate time.

C.

Even if the bishops and clergy of the Roman Catholic Church are ultimately deemed to be officials or employees of the Holy See, the Court must address a final issue: whether those employees or officials were acting within the scope of their office or employment when they engaged in the conduct alleged here. For conduct to be within the scope of employment, the conduct must be "of the same general nature as that authorized or incidental to the conduct authorized." *Wood v. Southeastern Greyhound Lines,* 302 Ky. 110, 194 S.W.2d 81, 83 (1946).

To be sure, under Kentucky law, a priest's sexual misconduct is outside the scope of employment and thus his employer cannot be held liable for that misconduct. *Osborne v. Payne,* 31 S.W.3d 911, 915 (Ky.2000). Plaintiffs' claims, however, are more nuanced than those in *Osborne.* Plaintiffs allege that Defendant's agents in the United States, pursuant to directives from Defendant Holy See, committed various acts and omissions in covering up and otherwise failing to properly address the issue of childhood sexual abuse in the Catholic Church and its entities. Those policies, Plaintiffs allege, led to their injuries. If, as Plaintiffs allege, these bishops, archbishops, and other clergy followed a written or unwritten policy established by the Holy See, they certainly acted within the scope of their office or employment.

Plaintiffs' allegations seem to fit squarely within the *Wood* test: the negligent conduct asserted here is alleged to be not only "of the same general nature as that authorized," but in fact the actual authorized – indeed, the allegedly mandated – conduct. Following the mandates of the Holy See is certainly conduct within the scope of the archbishops', bishops', and other clergy-members' employment. It is unclear whether Plaintiffs allege other acts or omissions that were not part of an alleged Holy See policy.

D.

In summary, the Court finds that the tortious activity exception does apply to claims arising from certain acts or omissions of archbishops, bishops and clergy of the Catholic Church that occurred inside the United States. At least to the extent these persons acted pursuant to a Holy See policy, these persons were acting within the scope of their employment. Subsequent evidence may require the Court to revisit these conclusions and refine the precise acts or omissions subject to jurisdiction under FSIA. However, the claims against the Holy See directly (i.e. as opposed to via its officials or employees) cannot be sustained because these actions or omissions occurred outside of the United States.

IV.

Having concluded that some of Plaintiffs' claims meet the tortious conduct exception to FSIA's general rule of immunity, the Court must now consider a final issue. This concerns "the exception within the exception." FSIA will not allow a tort claim, even against officials or employees of the Holy See whose acts and injuries occur in the United States where those officials were exercising their discretionary function. Called the discretionary function exception, it exempts claims "based upon the exercise or performance or the failure to exercise or perform a discretionary function regardless of whether the discretion be abused." 28 U.S.C. § 1605(a)(5)(A).

The discretionary function exception of the FSIA is modeled after the corresponding exception in the Federal Tort Claims Act ("FTCA") and is interpreted and applied consistent with FTCA law. This exception appears based upon the policy view that foreign states should be immune from the consequences of discretionary acts of employees, even within the scope of their employment. Courts have found that both the FTCA and FSIA exceptions are intended to preserve immunity "for decisions grounded in social, economic, and political policy." *In re Terrorist Attacks of September 11, 2001,* 349 F.Supp.2d 765, 794 (S.D.N.Y.2005). Consequently, the discretionary function exception preserves immunity for planning-level decisions, as opposed to operational-level decisions. *Id.*

Defendant must satisfy two elements to avail itself of FSIA immunity under the discretionary function exception. First, the challenged action must be discretionary; that is, it must involve "an element of judgment or choice." *Berkovitz v. United States,* 486 U.S. 531, 536, 108 S.Ct. 1954, 100 L.Ed.2d 531 (1988); *United States v. Gaubert,* 499 U.S. 315, 322, 111 S.Ct. 1267, 113 L.Ed.2d 335 (1991). In the FTCA context, this prong means that if a "federal statute, regulation, or policy specifically prescribes a course of action for an employee to follow," the discretionary function exception does not apply. Second, and even if the challenged action did involve an element of judgment or choice, "a court must determine whether that judgment is of the kind the discretionary function exception was designed to shield." The Supreme Court explained this prong in *Berkovitz* in the following manner:

> The basis for the discretionary function exception was Congress' desire to "prevent judicial 'second-guessing' of legislative and administrative decisions grounded in social, economic, and political policy through the medium of an action in tort." The exception, properly construed, therefore protects only governmental actions and decisions based on considerations of public policy.

To answer the questions posted by the two *Berkovitz* elements, the Court must define Plaintiffs' negligence claims by their constituent elements. These claims can be distilled into three principal omissions, as laid out in the Complaint: that (1) Defendants failed to *provide safe care* to children entrusted to their care; that (2) Defendants *failed to warn* parishioners that their children would be under the care of known or suspected pedophiles; and that (3) Defendants *failed to report* known or suspected child abuse to the appropriate authorities. For the reasons that follow, only the first group of claims meets the discretionary function test and are exempt from suit.

The first claim seems to be essentially a negligent hiring claim: that the Defendant hired persons whom it knew or suspected were child sexual abusers and place them in positions where they could sexually abuse children. Applying the first prong of the *Berkovitz* test, such personnel decisions appear to involve a discretionary activity. Not surprisingly, courts have generally held that negligent hiring decisions are protected by the discretionary function exception. Although Defendant's hiring decisions may have indeed been negligent, the discretionary function exception to the FSIA protects such decisions. Therefore, Plaintiffs' negligence claim based upon the "duty to provide safe care, custody, and control" of minor children in Catholic schools and churches cannot proceed.

The second negligence claim is that Defendant failed to warn parishioners that their children would be under the care of known or suspected pedophiles, allegedly pursuant to a policy promulgated by the Holy See itself. Under the tests laid out in *Berkovitz* and *Gaubert,* the decision by the bishops, archbishops, and other clergy not to warn parishioners would appear to be a decision specifically prescribed by that policy. Therefore, their decisions do not satisfy the first prong of the *Berkovitz* test, because they did not involve "an element of judgment or choice." Therefore, the alleged failure of the Holy See's officials and employees to warn parishioners that their children would be under the care of known or suspected pedophiles is not a decision protected by the discretionary function exception.

Finally, Plaintiffs' claim that Defendant's officials and employees failed to report known or suspected perpetrators of child sexual abuse to the relevant state and local authorities. Like the failure to warn claim, Plaintiffs claim that the Holy See's employees and officials failed to report child sexual abuse to the appropriate authorities pursuant to a policy promulgated by the Holy See. Again, as alleged, this decision did not involve an "an element of judgment or choice" because an established policy required the action. Thus, liability for such decision is not barred by the discretionary function exception.

V.

. . . Defendant asserts that the doctrine of international comity bars Plaintiffs' claims. The FSIA represents the position of the United States government on the doctrine of international comity. The FSIA is an exercise of Congress' "undisputed power to decide, as a matter of federal law, *whether and under what circumstances* foreign nations should be amenable to suit in the United States." *Universal Consol. Companies, Inc. v. Bank of China,* 35 F.3d 243, 246 (6th Cir.1994) The FSIA represents Congress' determination as to "whether and how foreign states may be sued in American courts." *Id.* The doctrine of international comity is indeed an important one, but the FSIA is the proper framework for American courts to apply in cases where the doctrine is asserted. This Court has already addressed the FSIA, and thus any further discussion of the doctrine of international comity is unnecessary.

[Finally,] Defendant asserts that the FSIA bars Plaintiff's fraud and misrepresentation claims. Defendant asserts this is the case based on the statutory language of the FSIA, which bars any claims under the FSIA "arising out of ... misrepresentation [or] deceit." Fraud or misrepresentation claims *may* be made under the commercial activity exception. However, this Court has already determined that the commercial activity exception does not apply, and thus the language of section 1605(a)(5)(B) applies here. Thus, the plain language of FSIA bars Plaintiffs' misrepresentation and fraud claims. . . .

Notes

1. As the *O'Bryan* case makes clear, the FSIA parallels the Federal Tort Claims Act in a number of particulars. For example, many of the exceptions to liability – or, more properly, retentions of sovereign immunity – are identical. One especially noteworthy parallel is both statutes' "discretionary function" provision, which the probably the most litigated issue in FTCA cases. See generally 1 DAN B. DOBBS, THE LAW OF TORTS § 262 (2001). Notice that courts draw directly on FTCA case law on that clause to interpret the FSIA's similar provision. Is the policy behind the discretionary function immunity identical in both the domestic and foreign contexts?

2. In order for a foreign government to be liable under the tortious conduct exception to the FSIA, an employee or agent of the foreign state must have committed the tort "within the scope of employment." In making that determination in cases, courts can and do look to a vast body of case law on vicarious liability of employers for the torts of their employees. "Under the traditional rules, a servant's conduct is not within the scope of employment unless it is of the same general kind as authorized or expected, or incidental to such conduct, and the servant was acting within the authorized time and space limits." 2 DAN B. DOBBS, THE LAW OF TORTS § 335, at 910 (2001). Workers' compensation law also contains a virtually identical concept – under most states workers' comp law, an employee is entitled to payment from the workers' compensation fund only when the injury occurred on the job and within the scope of employment. See generally *Id.*, § 393, at 1100-01.

3. Another requirement for liability under the tortious conduct exception is that the tort must have been committed inside the United States. The FSIA defines "United States" as including "all territory and waters, continental and insular, subject to the jurisdiction of the United States." The Supreme Court has held that this means "the continental United States and those islands that are part of the United States or its possessions." *Argentine*

Republic v. Amerada Hess Shipping Corp., 488 U.S. 428, 109 S.Ct. 683, 102 L.Ed.2d 818 (1989). Why this requirement? The *Amerada Hess* Court explained that "Congress' primary purpose in enacting 1605(a)(5) was to eliminate a foreign state's immunity for traffic accidents and other torts committed in the United States, for which liability is imposed under domestic tort law." *Id.* at 439-40. Further, "In enacting the FSIA, Congress intended to bring U.S. practice into conformity with that of most other nations. . . . [C]odifications by other nation-states and international organizations – with which Congress sought to be consistent – have provided that a state loses its sovereign immunity for tortious acts only where they occur in the territory of the forum state." *Persinger v. Islamic Republic of Iran*, 729 F.2d 835 (D.C. Cir. 1984). Going beyond this and removing sovereign immunity "for governments acting on their own territory" creates "the potential for international discord and for foreign government retaliation." *Id.* at 841.

B. THE TERRORISM EXCEPTION

WEINSTEIN v. ISLAMIC REPUBLIC OF IRAN

184 F.Supp.2d (D.D.C. 2002).

LAMBERTH, District Judge.

This wrongful death action against the Islamic Republic of Iran, the Iranian Ministry of Information and Security, and three senior officials of the Iranian government arises from an act of state-sponsored terrorism. The decedent, a United States citizen named Ira Weinstein, was killed in the terrorist bombing of the Number 18 Egged passenger bus in Jerusalem, Israel on February 25, 1996. The plaintiffs, who are family members and administrators of Ira Weinstein's estate, have brought this action pursuant to the Foreign Sovereign Immunities Act ("FSIA") of 1976, 28 U.S.C. § 1602-1611.

The FSIA grants federal courts jurisdiction over suits involving foreign states and their officials, agents, and employees in certain enumerated instances. In particular, the FSIA creates a federal cause of action for personal injury or wrongful death resulting from acts of state-sponsored terrorism. 28 U.S.C. § 1608(e) (giving federal courts jurisdiction over suits "in which money damages are sought against a foreign state for personal injury or death that was caused by an act of torture, extrajudicial killing, aircraft sabotage, hostage taking, or the provision of material support or resources ... for such an act if such act or provision of material support is engaged in by an official, employee, or agent of such foreign state while acting within the scope of his or her office, employment, or agency[.]"). The statute explicitly eliminates foreign governments' sovereign immunity in suits for money damages based on extrajudicial killings and provides that "[a]n official, employee, or agent of a foreign state designated as a state sponsor of terrorism ... shall be liable to a United States national or the national's legal representatives for personal injury or death caused by acts ... for which the courts of the United States may maintain jurisdiction [.]" 28 U.S.C. § 1605(a)(7); 28 U.S.C. § 1605 note, Civil Liability for Acts of State Sponsored Terrorism. . . .

[Defendants were served with process but did not enter an appearance.] Notwithstanding indicia of the defendants' willful default, however, the Court is compelled to make further inquiry prior to entering a judgment by default against them. As with actions against the federal government, the FSIA requires that a default judgment against a foreign state be entered only after a plaintiff "establishes his claim or right to relief that is satisfactory to the Court." 28 U.S.C. § 1608(e). . . .

I. FINDINGS OF FACT

The Court heard testimony in this matter on December 6 and 7, 2001. The plaintiffs proceeded in the manner of a bench trial and the following findings of fact are based upon the sworn testimony and documents entered into evidence in accordance with the Federal Rules of Evidence. Plaintiffs have "established [their] claim or right to relief by evidence that is satisfactory to the Court," as required by 28 U.S.C. § 1608(e). The Court finds the following facts to be established by clear and convincing evidence, which would have been sufficient to establish a prima facie case in a contested proceeding.

[Findings (1) through (6): All plaintiffs, including decedent, are United States citizens.]

[Findings (7) through (21): Ira Weinstein was a butcher for an Israeli supermarket chain at the time of his death. On February 25, 1996, he boarded the Number 18 Egged bus in Jerusalem to go to work. At about 6:45 a.m., Magid Wardah, another passenger, detonated an explosive charge which, at the direction of HAMAS, he had carried onto the bus concealed in a travel bag. The ensuing explosion caused the complete destruction of the bus, resulted in debris being hurled in excess of 100 meters, and led to the injury and death of numerous individuals, including Ira Weinstein. Weinstein was taken to a Jerusalem hospital, where he remained until his death on April 13, 1996. Despite all of his injuries, Weinstein was conscious when he arrived at the hospital and was at least semi-conscious for the majority of his time at the hospital. Dr. Charles Sprung, one of the world's foremost experts on severe trauma injuries, was in charge of his medical care. Weinstein endured extreme and conscious pain and suffering for forty-nine days, from the time of the explosion on February 25, 1996, until his death on April 13, 1996. Dr. Sprung met with the family on a daily basis and kept them updated as to Ira Weinstein's condition, testifying that Ira Weinstein's family appeared devastated during his stay at Hadassah Hospital.

[Findings 22 through (27): HAMAS publicly claimed credit for this bombing shortly after it occurred. Statements made by Hassan Salamah, the HAMAS member who planned the attack, to Israeli police verified this claim. Salamah later corroborated HAMAS' responsibility for the bombing in an interview with the CBS Television news program *60 Minutes*. HAMAS, the popular name for the Islamic Resistance Movement, is an organization supported by The Islamic Republic of Iran, dedicated to the waging of Jihad, or a holy war employing terrorism. The defendants knew of the destructive purposes and objectives of HAMAS, which were set forth in detail in the organization's charter introduced into evidence. Notwithstanding the destructive purposes and objectives of HAMAS, the Islamic Republic of Iran gave the organization at least $25-$50 million in 1995 and 1996, and also provided other groups with tens of millions of dollars to engage in terrorist activities. In total, Iran gave terrorist organizations, such as HAMAS, between $100 and $200 million per year during this period.

[Findings (28) through (33): Defendant the Islamic Republic of Iran is a foreign state and has been designated as a state sponsor of terrorism pursuant to section 6(j) of the Export Administration Act of 1979, 50 U.S.C.App. § 2405(j) continuously since January 19, 1984. Defendants Ayatollah Ali Hoseini Khamenei, Ali Akbar Hashemi-Rafsanjani, and Ali Fallahian-Kuzestani were high officials of the Islamic Republic of Iran on February 25, 1996. They were aware of, consented to, and were involved in Iran's support for HAMAS during the performance of their official duties. In particular, their approval would have been necessary to carry out the economic and other commitment of Iran to HAMAS, including the training of HAMAS terrorists in Iran. Defendant the Iranian Ministry of Information and Security is the Iranian intelligence service, functioning both within and beyond the territorial borders of Iran. Acting as an agent of the Islamic Republic of Iran, the Iranian Ministry of Information and Security performed acts within the scope of its agency, within the meaning of 28 U.S.C. § 1605(a)(7) and 28 U.S.C. § 1605 note, which caused the death of Ira Weinstein. The Iranian Ministry of Information and Security acted as a conduit for the Islamic Republic of Iran's provision of funds to HAMAS and training to the terrorists under the direction of HAMAS, including Hassan Salamah. Ira Weinstein's death was caused by a willful and deliberate act of extrajudicial killing. He and his family suffered legally-cognizable damages therefrom, as enumerated below.]

II. CONCLUSIONS OF LAW

A. *Subject Matter Jurisdiction – The FSIA Controls This Action*

. . . [A]n action brought against a foreign state, its intelligence service acting as its agent, and three of its officials, acting in their official capacities, must be brought under the FSIA. Indeed, the FSIA must be applied in every action involving a foreign state defendant. Verlinden B.V. v. Central Bank of Nigeria, 461 U.S. 480, 489, 103 S.Ct. 1962, 76 L.Ed.2d 81 (1983); 28 U.S.C. § 1330. That is, the sole bases for subject matter jurisdiction in an action against a foreign state defendant are the FSIA's enumerated exceptions to immunity. *Argentine Republic v. Amerada Hess Shipping Corp.,* 488 U.S. 428, 109 S.Ct. 683, 102 L.Ed.2d 818 (1989). Accordingly, this Court lacks jurisdiction over this matter unless it falls within one of the FSIA's enumerated exceptions to foreign sovereign immunity.

The FSIA has been construed to apply to individuals for acts performed in their official capacity on behalf of either a foreign state or its agency or instrumentality. In 1996, Congress enacted the Antiterrorism and Effective Death Penalty Act of 1996, which abrogates the immunity of foreign states for their sponsorship of terrorist acts. 28 U.S.C. § 1605. Specifically, Congress amended the FSIA to eliminate the immunity of those foreign states officially designated as state sponsors of terrorism by the Department of State, if the foreign state so designated commits a terrorist act, or provides material support and resources to an individual or entity that commits such a terrorist act, which results in the death or personal injury of a United States citizen.

28 U.S.C. § 1605(a)(7). Based on the foregoing authority, the Court concludes that it has jurisdiction over the subject matter of this action.

B. *Personal Jurisdiction*

This Court has *in personam* jurisdiction over foreign state sponsors of terrorism under 28 U.S.C § 1605(a)(7). . . . [T]he FSIA provides that personal jurisdiction over defendants will exist where a plaintiff establishes the applicability of an exception to immunity pursuant to 28 U.S.C. § 1604, § 1605, or § 1607, and service of process has been accomplished pursuant to 28 U.S.C. § 1608. Plaintiffs have demonstrated by clear and convincing evidence that § 1605(a)(7) of the FSIA applies in this action, and that service of process was properly accomplished pursuant to 28 U.S.C. § 1608.

C. *The Actions of the Defendants*

A foreign state may be liable under the FSIA when there is injury from a terrorist act, that act was perpetrated by the designated state or an agent receiving material support from the designated state, the provision of support was an act authorized by the foreign state, the foreign state has been designated as one providing material support to terrorism, either the victim or the plaintiff was a United States national at the time of the terrorist act, and similar conduct by the United States, its agents, officials or employees within the United States would be actionable. In this case, all of these elements have been demonstrated by clear and convincing evidence.

The action of the HAMAS agent in detonating an explosive charge on the Number 18 Egged bus on February 25, 1996 falls within the scope of the Torture Victim Protection Act of 1991. The Court finds that it was a "deliberated killing not authorized by a previous judgment pronounced by a regularly constituted court affording all judicial guarantees which are recognized as indispensable by civilized peoples."

There is no question that HAMAS and its agents received massive material and technical support from the Islamic Republic of Iran. The sophistication demonstrated in the use of a relatively small explosive charge with such devastating effect indicates that it is unlikely that this attack could have resulted in such loss of life without the assistance of regular military forces, such as those of Iran. Thus, the defendants not only provided the terrorists with the technical knowledge required to carry out the February 25, 1996 attack on the Number 18 Egged bus, but also gave HAMAS the funding necessary to do so. Further, as of February 25, 1996, Iran was a nation designated by the United States Department of State as providing material support for terrorism and Ira Weinstein was an American national.

Finally, it is beyond question that if officials of the United States, acting in their official capacities, provided material support to a terrorist group to carry out an attack of this type, they would be civilly liable and would have no defense of immunity. *Bivens v. Six Unknown Named Agents of the Federal Bureau of Narcotics,* 403 U.S. 388, 91 S.Ct. 1999, 29 L.Ed.2d 619 (1971).

D. *Damages*

(1) *Wrongful Death.* The plaintiffs produced comprehensive affidavit testimony from Professor Adrian Ziderman detailing the loss of accretions to the Estate of Ira Weinstein. These calculations were based on conservative procedures and assumptions. In accordance with Professor Ziderman's affidavit and the report attached thereto, the Court concludes that judgment should be entered for this element of damages for the Estate of Ira Weinstein in the amount of $248,164.00.

(2) *Survival Action -- Pain and Suffering.* The Court has no difficulty, based on the testimony of Dr. Sprung, finding that Ira Weinstein endured extreme pain and that he suffered greatly from the time of the explosion on February 25, 1996, until his death on April 13, 1996. As Dr. Sprung noted, during his seven-week stay at Hadassah Hospital, Ira Weinstein underwent several surgical procedures which were very painful, including the amputation of both legs, and he suffered immense pain as a result of extensive bum and blast injuries. . . . Notwithstanding the inherent difficulty and subjectivity involved in awarding damages based on the pain and suffering of a claimant, compensation is required once liability has been determined and in this case such compensatory damages are certainly warranted. . . . [I]n deciding the amount of damages to award in this case, the Court will look at damage awards for pain and suffering in other cases brought under the FSIA and also in personal injury lawsuits arising under a variety of circumstances. *See e.g., Eisenfeld,* 172 F.Supp.2d at 8 (awarding $1,000,000 to plaintiffs that suffered extreme pain for several minutes after being injured in the bombing of the Number 18 Egged bus); *Flatow,* 999 F.Supp. at 29 (awarding $1,000,000 for

3 to 5 hours of pain and suffering to plaintiff injured in another bus bombing); *Mousa,* Civil Action Number 00-2096 at 21 (awarding $12,000,000 for both past and future pain and suffering of plaintiff injured extensively in Number 18 Egged bus bombing). . . . Based on these and other similar cases, the Court finds that $10,000,000 is an appropriate amount of compensatory damages for the pain and suffering of Ira Weinstein.

(3) *Solatium.* The FSIA provides for an award for solatium where physical injury results in death. . . . [D]amages for solatium belong to the individual heir personally for injury to the feelings and loss of decedent's comfort and society. The unexpected quality of a death may be taken into consideration in gauging the emotional impact to those left behind. In this case, the impact upon Ira Weinstein's wife and three children was devastating. Their testimony established conclusively that they each loved Ira Weinstein dearly and that they have experienced a tremendous amount of mental anguish as a result of his death. Thus, the Court finds that the following amounts are appropriate compensation for this element of damages: Susan Weinstein: $8,000,000; Joseph Weinstein: $5,000,000; Jennifer Weinstein Hazi: $5,000,000; David Weinstein: $5,000,000.

(4) *Punitive Damages:* Punitive damages are awarded to punish a defendant for particularly egregious conduct, and to serve as a deterrent to future conduct of the same type. Restatement (Second) Torts, § 908 (defining punitive damages as "damages, other than compensatory or nominal damages, awarded against a person to punish him for his outrageous conduct and to deter him and others like him from similar conduct in the future."). As an initial matter, the Court must determine whether it can award punitive damages under the FSIA. Based on the language of the statute and in accordance with the corresponding caselaw, the Court finds that it can levy punitive damages against the Iranian Ministry of Information and Security.[1]FN1 The FSIA specifically provides courts with the power to award punitive damages against an agency or instrumentality of a foreign state in a case brought under section 1605(a)(7). 28 U.S.C. § 1606. In this

---

[1] The plaintiffs also seek punitive damages against the Islamic Republic of Iran itself. As the Court noted in *Elahi,* however, punitive damages may not be awarded against the Islamic Republic of Iran because "Congress recently repealed legislation that would have permitted punitive damages against a foreign state in cases, such as this one, brought under 28 U.S.C. § 1605(a)(7)." *See* P.L. No. 106-386, § 2002(f)(2) [October 28, 2000]. . . .

case, the Court finds that both of these requirements are easily satisfied. . . .

Having found that the FSIA authorizes it to award punitive damages, the Court still must determine whether such damages should be awarded in this case. According to the Restatement (Second) of Torts, punitive damages are merited in cases involving "outrageous conduct." . . . Under even the most restrictive interpretation of the term, the defendant's actions in this matter are clearly outrageous and warrant the imposition of punitive damages.

. . . In determining the amount of punitive damages to award, courts should consider several factors, including: "[1] the character of the defendant's act, [2] the nature and extent of the harm to the plaintiff that the defendant caused or intended to cause and [3] the wealth of the defendant." Restatement (Second) Torts § 908. The Restatement (Second) of Torts provides that a fourth "factor that may affect the amount of punitive damages is the existence of multiple claims by numerous persons affected by the wrongdoer's conduct. It seems appropriate to take into consideration both the punitive damages that have been awarded in prior suits and those that may be granted in the future, with greater weight being given to the prior awards." [After examining each of these factors,] the Court finds that $150,000,000 in punitive damages is an appropriate award in this case.

Notes

1. Prior to the passage of the state-sponsored terrorism exception to the FSIA in 1996, a U.S. national who wished to sue a foreign government for what we would now call an act of terrorism (torture, assassination, bombing, and the like) had to use the tortious conduct exception discussed in Section A above – meaning that if the act took place in the United States, the claim could succeed, but if the act took place overseas, it would not. See, e.g., *Smith v. Socialist People's Libyan Arab Jamahiriya,* 101 F.3d 239 (2d Cir. 1996) (tort claim against Libya arising from the bombing of Pan Am flight 103 over Lockerbie, Scotland not actionable since the tort did not occur in the U.S.); *Persinger v. Islamic Republic of Iran,* 729 F.2d 835 (D.C. Cir. 1984) (Court lacked jurisdiction to adjudicate a tort claim arising from Iran's seizure of American hostages at the U.S. embassy in Tehran since the tort did not occur in U.S.). The FSIA's terrorism exception changes all of that – a foreign country can now be sued by a U.S. national even if the terrorist act occurred in a foreign country.

2. How does the FSIA relate to the Alien Tort Statute, covered in Chapter 3? Remember first that the Alien Tort Statute does not apply at all to U.S. nationals who have been injured – the statute gives U.S. courts jurisdiction over tort claims brought *by aliens* where the tortious conduct violates "the law of nations." But which statute applies to a case brought in a U.S. court by an alien against another foreign *government*? The answer is "both." See *Argentine Republic v. Amerada Hess Shipping Corp.*, 488 U.S. 428, 109 S.Ct. 683, 102 L.Ed.2d 818 (1989) (holding, in a case brought under the ATS, that "[t]he FSIA's text and structure demonstrate Congress' intention that the FSIA be the sole basis for obtaining jurisdiction over a foreign state in United States courts"). Because jurisdiction over the foreign government must come solely from the FSIA, only where one of the FSIA's exceptions to sovereign immunity applies can the alien's ATS claim proceed. Now re-focus on the limitations in the two FSIA exceptions discussed in this Chapter. If the jurisdiction of an alien's suit against another foreign government is based on the tortious conduct exception, the tortious conduct must have occurred *in the United States*. Otherwise the court lacks jurisdiction to hear the claim, because the foreign government is immune from suit. See, e.g., *Abur v. Republic of Sudan*, 437 F.Supp.2d 166 (D.D.C. 2006) (Court lacked jurisdiction to hear Kenyans' suit against Sudan and Iran for injuries caused in the bombings of U.S. embassies in Tanzania and Kenya, since those torts did not take place in the U.S.). And an alien cannot use the state-sponsored terrorism exception at all, since it applies only to *U.S. nationals* who are suing foreign governments or their agents. *Id.* But these problems are not present where the defendant is not a foreign government, as the cases in the previous Chapter demonstrate.

3. Even where jurisdiction exists over a foreign sovereign, that sovereign may defend the case using the "act of state" doctrine. This is a "substantive defense on the merits." *Republic of Austria v. Altmann*, 541 U.S. 677, 124 S.Ct. 2240, 159 L.Ed.2d 1 (2004). The act of state doctrine "bars courts from adjudicating a case when the relief sought or the defense interposed would require a court in the United States to declare invalid the official act of a foreign sovereign performed within its boundaries." *Beaty v. Republic of Iraq*, 480 F.Supp.2d 60 (D.D.C. 2007) (quoting *World Wide Minerals, Ltd. v. Republic of Kazakhstan*, 296 F.3d 1154 (D.C. Cir. 2002)). This doctrine reflects the concern that the judicial branch, by undertaking such an inquiry, will interfere with the executive branch's conduct of foreign policy. See *W.S. Kirkpatrick & Co. v. Environmental Tectonics Corp.*, 493 U.S. 400,

110 S.Ct. 701, 107 L.Ed.2d 816 (1990). A court decides whether to invoke the act of state doctrine by assessing three factors: (1) the degree of consensus concerning a particular area of international law; (2) the implications of the issue for U.S. foreign relations; and (3) whether the government that perpetrated the act or acts at issue is still in existence. Courts have expressed "great skepticism about applying the act-of-state doctrine to suits brought under the FSIA's state-sponsored terrorism exception," a skepticism "rooted in the fact that the political branches enacted a statute whose text and structure expressly contemplate holding a foreign state liable for terrorist acts committed years earlier." *Beaty*, 480 F.Supp.2d at 89 (collecting cases).

4. A foreign nation may also invoke the "political question" doctrine in an FSIA case. This doctrine requires a court to dismiss any case that would require the court to adjudicate "questions, in their nature political, or which are, by the constitution and laws, submitted to the executive." *Alperin v. Vatican Bank*, 410 F.3d 532 (9th Cir. 2005) (quoting *Marbury v. Madison*, 5 U.S. (1 Cranch.) 137, 2 L.Ed. 60 (1803). As the Supreme Court has said, a court looks at six factors in deciding whether to dismiss on political question grounds;[2] the first, and most important of these, is whether there has been a "textually demonstrable constitutional commitment of the issues in the case to a coordinate political department." *Baker v. Carr*, 369 U.S. 186, 82 S.Ct. 691, 7 L.Ed.2d 663 (1962). Where the terrorism exception to the FSIA applies, however, the "political question" defense seems especially weak – since the other two branches of government by enacting that exception "stripped state sponsors of terrorism of sovereign immunity for conduct that was likewise clearly defined in a statute." *Beaty*, 480 F.Supp.2d at 74. That is, the very act of Congress in granting courts jurisdiction over particular kinds of foreign governmental acts, and of the President in signing the bill into law, may be the best evidence that adjudication of such claims does not interfere with the "political" branches of the U.S. government.

[2] See Chapter 3, sec. A.

Chapter 11

LIABILITY FOR DEFECTIVE PRODUCTS

The field of products liability is of great importance in a world that is increasingly inter-connected through trade and travel. It includes contractual responsibilities, or warranties in the U.S., as well as tort theories such as negligence and strict liability. Given the enormity of the topic, this chapter will focus on several problematic issues within the law of strict products liability, with an eye toward understanding how some other countries approach problems that have challenged U.S. courts.

Experts in the field of products liability agree that the substantive law of the U.S. is not radically different from the law in place in the rest of the world. However, what differs is the means by which other countries address product-related injuries and the way that the characteristics of their legal systems affect rates of litigation and recovery.

This section begins with a focus on substantive difference as it relates to what is perhaps the core issue in strict products liability: how does one determine whether a product is defective?

A. WHEN IS A PRODUCT DEFECTIVE?

1. *The U.S. Approach*

Strict products liability was first recognized in the United States in the 1960's. In a landmark case, *Greenman v. Yuba*

Power Products, Inc., 59 Cal. 2d 57 (1963), the Supreme Court of California found a power tool to be defective. The product did not grip a piece of wood in the way it should and the user was injured. The Court recognized a new tort theory, justified by public policy goals, and found the tool to be "defective." As is common in the emergence of new doctrines in a common law system, the Court did not attempt to definitively explain the boundaries of the new theory or to develop the concept of what makes a product "defective." Rather, the Court left the fine-tuning for future cases in the context of concrete issues.

Shortly after *Greenman*, the members of the American Law Institute relied heavily on the case in framing the requirements for this new tort theory in Restatement (Second) of Torts, §402A. They, too, expressed the standard for "defectiveness" in rather indefinite terms: whether the product failed to meet the ordinary consumer's expectations. They derived the consumer expectation test from the law of warranty and the concept of non-conforming goods. As applied to production (or manufacturing defects), it works well enough, but courts charged with applying the test in subsequent years have found the generality of this approach to be unworkable, particularly in cases involving design defects. In some instances it seems to shelter from liability products that should be found defective while in others the test invites the jury to speculate about technical matters about which a consumer would have no expectation. Courts decided that it was problematic to analyze all product defects in the same way and began to distinguish defects in manufacturing, design or information (warnings), and to develop alternative analyses, such as risk/utility balancing.

These analytical changes spurred some academics and judges to urge a re-examination of strict products liability as it had been articulated in the Restatement (Second). In 1998, the Restatement (Third) of Torts: Products Liability was finalized and urged a retreat from strict products liability except in cases involving manufacturing defects. The drafters would eliminate use of the consumer expectation test outside of that context.

2. *Overview of the Prevailing Approach in Europe and Elsewhere*

While the U.S. was developing strict products liability, other countries were dealing with product liability issues through their existing domestic laws. Some were quite strict and others lax. Germany, for example, has imposed very firm obligations on manufacturers of products within the fault-based structure of BGB §823. Under German law, design defects are treated more stringently than manufacturing defects, and the law imposes rigorous warning requirements in addition. Once a plaintiff establishes that a product is defective in design, various presumptions arise, including wrongfulness, fault, and causation between fault and the product defect. The manufacturer must then exonerate itself or be held liable, and it has only a very slim chance of rebutting these presumptions. WALTER VAN GERVEN, JEREMY LEVER & PIERRE LAROUCHE, CASES, MATERIALS AND TEXT ON NATIONAL, SUPRANATIONAL AND TRANSNATIONAL TORT LAW 612-616 (2000).

Notwithstanding the evolution of domestic laws dealing with injuries caused by manufactured goods, the Council of the European Community began work to address liability for defective products on a Community wide basis. After considerable wrangling among the Community institutions involved, the Product Liability Directive, Council Directive 85/374/EEC of 25 July 1985 was adopted. *See* John Culhane, *The Limits of Product Liability Reform Within A Consumer Expectation Model: A Comparison of Approaches Taken by the United States and the European Union,* 19 HASTINGS. INT'L & COMP. L. REV. 1, 28-33 (1995). Although some contend the Directive has had little impact in actual litigation, the EC's version of strict products liability has been copied or adapted in many parts of the world. Unlike RESTATEMENT 402A, the Directive is several pages long and quite detailed. It requires member states to harmonize their law in accordance with certain core provisions, but also permits them to opt out of liability in certain circumstances.

Mathias Reimann

Liability for Defective Products at the Beginning of the Twenty-First Century: Emergence of a Worldwide Standard?

51 Am. J. Comp. L. 751, 758-759, 765 (2003)

. . . Product liability made its first appearance in the form of caselaw, witness *MacPherson v. Buick Motor Co.,*[17] *Donoghue v.*

---

[17]111 NE 1050 (N.Y. 1916)[seminal U.S. negligence case where plaintiff was injured when the wheel on his car broke].

Stevenson,[18] the French jurisprudence expanding liability for vices cachés and garde de la structure[19] or the German chicken pest decision.[20] Yet, . . . the recent spread of product liability law throughout the world has largely manifested itself in special legislation.

Such legislation comes in three basic varieties. Perhaps the most common form is that of a specific and free-standing product liability act. Most European nations . . . as well as several Asian countries (Korea, Japan, Israel) and Louisiana now have such statutes. Another variety is the incorporation of special product liability rules into the torts chapter of a civil code (France, the Netherlands, Poland, Quebec, Russia). Finally, many jurisdictions have enacted special product liability rules as part and parcel of more comprehensive Consumer Protection Acts. Such acts seem to be the norm in Latin America (Argentina, Brazil, Chile, Peru) and fairly prevalent in Asia (China, India, Malaysia, Philippines, Taiwan) but even Australia, Greece, Russia and the United Kingdom have embedded their particular product liability legislation in more general consumer protection packages.

It would be wrong, however, to conclude that product liability has now by and large been completely codified in special acts. That is not the case by any means. Instead, the special legislation just mentioned is only one element in a much more complex picture. There are, in addition, myriad other rules which are actually often more relevant in practice. . . . Still a clear majority of the countries in which product liability is recognized as a special field have codified the core elements of the subject. . . . [J]urisdictions where the core of product liability is still a matter of caselaw, like the United States and Canada, have become exceptions to the rule. . . .

If the definition of a "product" is perhaps the easiest problem among the conditions of liability, the determination of what constitutes a "defect" is probably the most difficult. . . .

---

[18] [1932] AC 562 (H.L.) [a British case where a plaintiff was poisoned by ginger beer].

[19] French Report 1-2.

[20] Decision of the German supreme Court of Nov. 26, 1968, BGHZ 52, 91 (Hühnerpestfall) [involving an impure vaccine that prompted an outbreak of fowl-pest and resulted in the deaths of 4,000 chickens on the plaintiffs' farm].

First, there is a considerable diversity of definitions in the various product liability regimes. . . . Second, most systems ultimately tend to rely on one of two tests. The first of these tests looks to justified consumer expectations: roughly speaking, a product is defective if it is more dangerous than the average consumer has reason to anticipate. This test prevails in the majority of jurisdictions. It rules supreme in Europe where it is codified in art. 6(2) of the EC Directive and consequently applies in all EC member states as well as in most other European countries; it was also adopted in jurisdictions around the world, including Australia, Brazil, China, Japan, Korea, Malaysia, Peru, the Philippines, Quebec and Taiwan. The other major approach is the risk-utility analysis. It renders a product defective if its risks outweigh its utility. . . . This test tends to dominate in the United States. . . .

Third, there are three basic types of defects which may call for different treatment: manufacturing defects, design defects, and insufficient warnings. . . . The majority of specialized product liability schemes do not distinguish between them. . . .

---

3. *The EC Directive on Defective Products*

Directives are a unique feature of European Union law. They are passed by the European Commission and addressed to the Member States. Directives state an objective and bind the Member States to achieve a certain legal result, but they leave the Member States discretion as to how the legislation is implemented. The goal is to have laws that are harmonized, but not to force displacement of the Member States' own laws to the extent they are consistent with the Directive.

The EC Product Liability Directive (whose full name is Council Directive 85/374/EEC of 25 July 1985 on the Approximation of the Laws, Regulations, and Administrative Provisions of the Member States Concerning Liability for Defective Products) is the most prominent example of European harmonization in the area of tort law. It applies not only to the European Union Member States, but also to those in the European Economic Area. As Professor Reimann points out in the excerpt above, the Directive has proven extraordinarily influential in the law of other countries throughout the world. The impetus for the Product Liability Directive is explained in the excerpt below by one of its drafters.

Hans Claudius Taschner

Harmonization of Products Liability Law in the European Community

34 Tex. Int'l L. J. 21, 22-23, 25-26 (1999)

The Need for Harmonization

An essential element of the common market envisioned by the Treaty Establishing the European Community (EC Treaty) is undistorted competition. The legal differences between the laws of the European Community's (EC's) Member States impose different economic burdens on their competing industries. For example, prior to harmonization of product liability laws in Member States, if the economic loss caused by a defective product was borne by the producer, as was the case in France, the industry was in a much less favorable economic situation than in Italy where the damage caused had to be borne by the unfortunate victim. According to the fault liability principle in Italy, the victim could not secure compensation. This was true not only if actual damages paid were considered, but also in the context in which total insurance premiums were taken into account. In Germany, the total amount of insurance premiums paid by the pharmaceutical industry after the introduction of the Pharmaceutical Act in 1976 was 55 million DM at the value prevailing at the time. By contrast, the Italian industry had nothing to pay. Unequal economic burdens lead to distortions of competition.

Furthermore, variations in laws reflect major differences in approaches to consumer protection. Therefore a product user enjoys a much higher degree of protection if, in the event of damage, he can successfully bring an action against the producer, as was possible in France, but again he could not bring such an action in Italy.

One of the aims of the EC is consumer protection without discrimination in all Member States. Consequently, the EC should have uniform rules in such an important area as product liability. It must be borne in mind that the EC is much more than merely one international organization among others, such as the Council of Europe, European Free Trade Association (EFTA) or the United Nations. The EC has the power and authority to create directly applicable law under a legal procedure which is similar to that of sovereign states. The EC Treaty created the European Court of Justice with the power and authority to take and enforce decisions on legal disputes. Harmonized law promotes the economic and political integration of its member states, an example of which is the Product Liability Directive. . . .

Member States' Laws Before Approximation

The legal situation in the nine Member States greatly varied in 1977. Three groups of states can be distinguished. The first were the *Code Civil* countries—France, Belgium, and Luxembourg—where the courts had developed an extensive product liability law. Second were the countries where the law was based on the classical approach of fault as a precondition of liability, namely Italy and the three countries that joined the Community during either the Council deliberations or after adoption of the Directive-Greece in 1981 and Spain and Portugal in 1986. Finally, there were states in which courts had developed an intermediate solution reflecting industry and consumer interests by reversing the burden of proof and requiring the defendant producer to show that he did not act negligently during the manufacturing process. These states were the United Kingdom and Ireland, both common law countries, as well as Germany, The Netherlands, and Denmark. . . .

Notes

1. *Who is a proper defendant in a products liability suit?* The European Community reached different conclusions than U.S. courts about this issue. Under Article 3 of the Directive, liability extends to all persons who are "producers" of the product. Article 3 defines "producer" as the manufacturer of either the finished product, its component parts, or of any constituent raw material. Thus, unlike U.S. law, which imposes liability on the entire chain of distribution, designers of products and retailers are excluded. What are the arguments on either side of the debate over including designers and dealers as defendants?

One might wonder whether Article 3's coverage is sufficient to protect innocent consumers from products shipped by manufacturers outside of the EC, who may be difficult to find, much less to sue. The Directive addresses this issue with two exceptions. Article 3(2) provides that anyone importing products into the EC for commercial purposes is deemed a producer. The exception does not include imports within the EC. In addition, if a dealer supplies a product from an anonymous manufacturer, the dealer is treated as the producer unless he identifies the person who supplied the product. Article 3(3). How might an importer who is merely facilitating the sales of products made by others protect itself from liability?

2. *When is a product defective?* Article 6 of the Directive bears an uncanny similarity to what is known, under U.S. law, as the consumer expectation test. The EC's adoption of this surprised some in the U.S., as the excerpts below explain. Article 6 is a key provision, because it defines the concept of a defect. It provides that a product is defective:

> when it does not provide the safety which a person is entitled to expect, taking all circumstances into account, including: the presentation of the product; the use to which it could reasonably be expected that the product would be put; the time when the product was put into circulation. A product shall not be considered defective for the sole reason that a better product is subsequently put into circulation.

There are several nuances that distinguish Article 6 from the U.S. version of the same concept. As Professor Taschner explains, [t]he basic element of this concept is "safety." . . . It is up to the judge to decide what degree of safety may be expected. The term "entitle" relates to court decisions. The expectation is not that of the injured party, but that of the public at large. The concept is an objective one, not a subjective one. " Taschner, *supra* at 30.

Although Article 6 does not distinguish among types of defects, Professor Cees Van Dam suggests that these differences are in fact taken into account. For example, he argues consumers are entitled to expect that products will not be defective due to the manufacturing process, while they might well not be entitled to expect that a drug would be 100% safe if they had been warned about side effects. CEES VAN DAM, EUROPEAN TORT LAW 377 (2006).

3. *What defenses apply?* Defenses to liability include comparative negligence, as is now widely recognized in U.S. products cases, and various causation-related doctrines which, in the U.S., are allocated to the plaintiff's prima facie case. There is no liability when the defect was the result of mandatory regulation by the state or, in the case of a component part, when the defect is attributable to instructions of the manufacturer of the finished product.

4. *What damages are available?* Article 9 of the Directive addresses and resolves many damages issues that have percolated through the U.S. courts. It includes damage caused by death or by personal injuries. It does not provide for compensation for pure economic loss. It distinguishes between property in private and professional use, leaving damage to the latter to be covered by the national rules of each Member State. It excludes damages to the product itself and also imposes a threshold of 500 ECU for property damage, meaning that, in effect, any losses below that amount are allocated to the victim or must be collected under national law. In addition, the Directive leaves the amount of compensation, and in particular the question of whether non-pecuniary damages are available, to national law. Article 9 thus leaves a large and important area "un-harmonized."

5. *What about "unknowable risks" and other controversial issues?* Professor Taschner explains that:

> [s]ince the Member States could not agree on three highly contentious issues, but needed a unanimous decision in Council, the Directive provides for . . . options. This means that every state can benefit from certain derogations concerning the provisions of the Directive. . . .
>
> Two questions that were the subject of particularly intense discussion during the Council deliberations, namely a "state-of-the-art" defense and "development risk liability," require particular attention. The two concepts must be distinguished. "State-of-the-art" centers on the problem of whether a product which was manufactured according to technical standards prevailing at the time of its production is non-defective, even if it has caused damage. "Development risk liability" relates to whether the producer should be held liable for damage caused by his defective product, even if the damaging characteristic, designated a "defect" if known, could not have been identified during the manufacture because the necessary scientific and technical knowledge did not exist at that time. . . .
>
> The Council refused to provide for a "state-of-the-art" defense. It is up to the courts alone to decide whether a product which was manufactured in accordance with the technical standards of its time is defective. Obviously, the safety expectations of the general public may be

influenced by those standards and guide the courts' ruling. . . .

As has already been pointed out, the Directive excludes a "development risk liability" but allows Member states to introduce such a provision.

Taschner, *supra* at 31-32. Luxembourg and Finland availed themselves of the option of unconditionally imposing liability for unknowable risks. Spain struck out the defense with respect to food and medicines, as did France with regard to blood and blood products. Germany generally allows the development risk defense, but makes an exception for drug manufacturers. VAN DAM, *supra* at 386. Needless to say, the countries excluding the development risk defense go in exactly the opposite direction of most U.S. courts that have ruled on the issue.

6. *Do any provisions limit liability?* The Directive contains some provisions that could be viewed as very protective of defendants. There is a statute of repose in Article 11 which terminates any rights of an injured person on expiration of a period of ten years from the date on which the producer put the product causing the damage into circulation. There is also an option in Article 16 for Member States to impose a liability ceiling of 70 million ECU for damage resulting from death or personal injury caused by identical items with the same defect. Many U.S. manufacturers have urged such provisions as part of tort reform proposals. What is your evaluation of the provision that terminates liability ten years after the product is placed in circulation? This will eliminate liability in cases where side effects might not emerge except in the long term, or even in a subsequent generation. What about the liability ceiling? Can such a provision be relied upon to provide adequate compensation to victims in the event of a mass tort?

7. *What happened once the Directive was approved?* The Member States had three years after approval (until 1988) to transpose the Directive to their own laws, but most required more time. France was in no hurry at all because the Directive provided less protection than French national law. France tried to argue that the Act implementing the Directive was only applicable to products put in circulation after May 19, 1998 – a position widely viewed as untenable. The European Commission took France before the European Court of Justice, and it was only after a decision against France that the Directive was implemented in the Code Civil. VAN DAM, *supra* at 370-371.

8. Do you think an approach such as a Directive would be workable in a federal system like the United States, where product liability is characterized by an extreme diversity of legal rules? Would the United States benefit from a system of harmonized laws relating to products liability?

B. THE DEBATE OVER THE LIKELY IMPACT OF THE DIRECTIVE

Because of the influence of the Directive, both in the EC and in many other countries that have subsequently modeled their legislation on it, there has been much analysis of its likely effect. Its influence has surprised some U.S. scholars, many of whom view American products liability law as "out-of-control." The American Law Institute, in adopting the Restatement (Third): Products Liability, consciously chose to try to rein in the parts of U.S. law deemed most unmanageable. The drafters were surprised, to say the least, that the EC Directive seemed not to have benefitted from the lessons the U.S. learned as products liability developed through case law. The next series of excerpts captures the thinking of the drafters of the Restatement (Third): Products Liability and scholars outside the U.S.

James A. Henderson and Aaron D. Twerski

What Europe, Japan, and Other Countries Can Learn From the New American Restatement of Products Liability

34 Texas Int'l L.J. 1, 2-3, 11, 20 (1999)

[T]his article argues that the recent substantive law developments in Europe, Japan, and elsewhere, taken at face value, suggest that the lessons learned the hard way in the United States have in certain important aspects been lost on the international legal community. The products liability law being developed outside the United States appears too simplistic to these American observers to perform adequately in the long run.

. . . [N]on-American commentators have argued that differences in civil litigation procedures tend to dwarf differences in substance, thus implying that the substantive differences do not matter. The American civil litigation system, with its reliance on percentage contingent fees, extensive pretrial discovery, quixotic lay juries, and generous measures of recovery, is believed to explain the differences between the American products liability experience and any likely to occur in other countries. A legal system in which theses uniquely American institutions are conspicuous by their absence, by clear implication, can get by quite nicely with a much simpler version of the underlying substantive text. . . .

From the broader perspective, it seems clear that both Europe and Japan are, with respect to the core definitions of product defect, committing themselves to essentially the same position that this country committed itself to in 1965 in Section 402A of the Restatement (Second). If this assessment is accurate, and if one assumes that cases involving classic design claims are brought before European and Japanese courts, then many of the same conceptual problems that plagued American law from 1965 into the 1990s can be expected to plague products liability in those countries in the years to come. . . .

[D]rafters of the EC Directive and the Product Liability Act in Japan have made a rather substantial mistake. Apparently believing they were taking a page from the United States' book by following Comment *i* to 402A, . . . they have unfortunately adopted a page from American legal history that the new Restatement has properly relegated to the waste basket. . . . [T]he consumer expectations test for defect adopted recently in Europe and Japan has been thoroughly discredited in the United States as a way to decide "classic design cases."

Jane Stapleton

Products Liability in the United Kingdom: The Myths of Reform

34 Tex. Int'l L.J. 45, 46-7, 65 (1999)

Comparative products liability is a dangerous business. For example, it may appear to U.S. eyes that the special U.S.-developed rule in the field was simply exported first to Europe and then elsewhere but this would be misleading. Certainly when it comes to the European Community, the story of the modern creation of a special cause of action for those injured by products is fundamentally different from the corresponding story in the United States. . . .

[W]hereas the history of the United States rule reveals no single episode galvanising concern about civil remedies available to consumers, the Thalidomide* disaster in Europe was clearly the catalyst for the reform processes that culminated in the 1985 Council Directive "on the approximation of the laws, regulations and administrative provisions of the Member States concerning liability for defective products." It provides a telling benchmark by which to evaluate the impact of the latter. . . .

Even more broadly, the socio-legal context in which the European rule operates would be unrecognizable to the average practitioner in the United States. In the United Kingdom, for example, the loser pays not only his own but the winner's costs; neither punitive damages nor juries (save in Scotland) are available for products liability claims; and the operation of the National Health Service has in the past operated to relieve most tortfeasors from the costs of their victims' medical treatment. . . .

[T]he findings have been that there has been no perceptible, or at least no reported, impact on insurance premiums, research and development activity, product innovation in general or product-caused injury rates. . . .

The truth is that the revolution in the products field that manufacturers feared and consumer advocates hoped the Directive would produce has simply not happened. What is the reason for this lack of impact? It may be that there is still a lack of consumer and/or solicitor awareness of the new law, or that consumers or their legal advisers are fearful of litigating novel provisions which might trigger a costly series of appeals, or

---

* Thalidomide was developed by German pharmaceutical company Grünenthal. It was sold from 1957 to 1961 in almost 50 countries under at least 40 names. It was sold and prescribed primarily to pregnant women to combat morning sickness and help them sleep. Before its release, inadequate tests were performed to assess the drug's safety, with catastrophic results for the children of women who had taken Thalidomide during their pregnancies. From 1956 to 1962, approximately 10,000 children were born with severe malformations, including limbs that resemble flippers, a condition called phocomelia. In 1962, in reaction to the tragedy, the U.S. Congress enacted laws requiring tests for safety during pregnancy before a drug can receive approval for sale in the U.S. Other countries enacted similar legislation, and it was not prescribed or sold for decades. Germany was particularly devastated by the thalidomide problem. It had in place a Pharmaceutical Products Act of 1961, but that proved insufficient to ensure drug security or provide recovery for injured persons. The Pharmaceutical Act of 1976 sought to remedy the deficiencies and established a strict liability claim for pharmaceutical products. *See* Manfred Wandt, *German Approaches to Products Liability*, 34 TEX. INT'L L. J. 71, 89-92 (1995)

lawyers may be uncertain as to what a court will regard as a defect as opposed to unreasonable conduct and unsatisfactory quality. I find none of these convincing.

In my view, the most convincing explanation for this no-significant-impact phenomenon is simply that the new law scarcely advances the position of the consumer at all — no doubt one reason it has been such a popular import by non-European Community governments of quite varied political hue. Save in a few peripheral contexts, no greater liability is imposed by the Directive than already exists under the other two main causes of action available to victims of defective products. . . . One might be forgiven for asking, if this is the case, why (apart from Euro-window-dressing) was such energy wasted on such a "reform" as the Directive?

Mathias Reimann

Liability for Defective Products at the Beginning of the Twenty-First Century: Emergence of a Worldwide Standard?

51 Am. J. Comp. L. 751, 810-812, 833, 835-838 (2003)

. . . What explains the dramatically different practical impact of (strict) product liability rules, especially the higher litigation volume, in the United States versus the Rest of the World? There is no simple answer. . . .

A factual explanation might be that products in the Rest of the World are safer and cause fewer accidents. . . . This is a quick reject. American safety standards are very high, particularly when it comes to consumer goods (due, among other reasons, to fear of product liability litigation). And certainly in developing countries, products are usually much less safe and much more prone to cause injury than in America. . . .

A somewhat more plausible explanation relates to political choice: 'Europe has tried to create a product safety regime based on regulations administered by public authorities' while the United States has more recently been committed to deregulation. This explanation rings true but has severe limits. It is difficult to tell whether the lower density of regulatory norms in the United States really has an impact on product liability litigation. Moreover, the level of public regulation cannot account for the virtual absence of product liability litigation in many other, especially developing, countries where safety norms are weak, or at least weakly enforced.

A third explanation is cultural: people in other countries are simply not as litigious as in the United States. They may very well be injured by defective products but they simply don't rush to court as Americans do. This may well be true for certain Asian societies in which conciliation is preferred over conflict, as in Indonesia or Thailand. But it is doubtful already for Japan. Japanese victims are not as reluctant to vindicate their rights as is widely believed. Of course, they often settle their claims but so do Americans most of whom understand full well that a lawsuit involves enormous hassle for everyone involved. With regard to continental Europe, this cultural explanation is even more implausible. Germans, for example, sue all the time, in great numbers, and for lots of reasons; they just do not bring a lot of product liability claims.

Much more powerful than any of these . . . reasons is the explanation that Americans sue more because they expect to win more. This is undoubtedly true to a large extent. Yet, even this argument is not fully satisfactory. . . . European and Japanese plaintiffs can win substantial judgments, amounting to tens or even hundreds of thousands of dollars. More importantly, even if they sue less because they expect to win less, this just leads to the question of why awards in their respective countries are so much lower than in the United States. . . .

The story of product liability also illustrates how the function of law may change when it is imported from one system into another. In the United States, product liability is a vital element in the overall system of accident compensation on which many victims must rely to seek recovery; at the same time, it has a significant regulatory function since it promotes product safety by threatening many otherwise loosely regulated industries with enormous liability. In most other countries surveyed here, especially Europe, product liability has come to play a more modest role. It mainly supplements the compensation available under various social or employment insurance regimes; and it has a much weaker regulatory function than in the United States because in matters of safety, European and many other countries have greater trust in governmental norms than in the incentives provided by private liability regimes. In short, even though product liability rules are quite similar, their purpose varies in different environments. . . .

The example of product liability law also confirms the need to compare substantive law not in the abstract but within its institutional, procedural, and social context. Much of what makes liability for defective products harsh or lenient is not whether its rules are phrased in terms of strict liability or negligence. It is how its rules are employed by victims and their lawyers, and how they are enforced by the courts, especially how often they are invoked and what awards they can generate. Most defendants would much rather be sued in strict liability in Italy than in negligence in the United States. . . .

If one had to group product liability systems of the world, the most important distinction would be between the United States and all other jurisdictions. It is true that today, the United States shares the principle of liability without fault or contract with a huge and growing number of other countries. But it stands apart in almost all other regards, for better or worse. It is virtually the only country with a full-fledged product liability law that shows no signs of European influence whatsoever. It is the only country that does not follow any of the trends noted in this report: product liability is still a domain of caselaw, not of statutes; there is no special treatment of consumers or consumer goods; and liability standards have recently become less, not more, severe because curbing liability, not expanding consumer protection, is currently the primary agenda. The United States is the only country where juries routinely decide product liability cases, where discovery rules are merciless, where the plaintiffs' bar is as specialized as it is resourceful, and where product liability is a major issue of public debate. As a result, it is the only nation where victims sue in product liability by the tens of thousands every year, where million-dollar awards are becoming routine, and where punitive damages are a real threat to defendants. In short, the United States is still the only country where product liability really matters on a grand scale.

Notes

1. Henderson and Twerski place greater importance on the role of substantive law in controlling the scope of liability for defective products than does Reimann. Are you persuaded that as the substantive law of product liability develops, the countries that follow the Directive's approach will rue the day they adopted the consumer expectation test for defective products?

2. While Stapleton acknowledges the significant socio-legal differences between the European Community and the United States, she believes the entire endeavor of trying to "harmonize" laws while leaving in place most of a country's domestic law relating to the same subject, coupled with significant substantive limitations in the Product Directive, explain why it has had little impact. If she is correct, what lessons are to be learned about law reform in the product liability arena?

3. Walter van Gerven and his co-authors agree with Stapleton, stating:

> One important weakness of the Directive is the combination of a full harmonization approach with a harmonized regime that does not replace or exclude existing national laws. Indeed, only Articles 15 and 16 allow Member States to deviate from the provisions of the Directive on certain points. Otherwise, they are bound to implement it as it is, and cannot for instance (as is usual in EC environmental law directives) include in their implementation statutes any provision that would provide more consumer protection than the Directive. Against that, Article 13 leaves national rules concerning product liability untouched, so that the regime created by the Directive will run in parallel to existing national law. As a result, it would be expected that national law will be preferred to the regime created by the Directive whenever it remains on balance more favorable to the plaintiff.

WALTER VAN GERVEN, JEREMY LEVER & PIERRE LAROUCHE, CASES, MATERIALS AND TEXT ON NATIONAL, SUPRANATIONAL AND TRANSNATIONAL TORT LAW 679 (2000).

4. Consider some of the reasons Reimann provides for his conclusion that the United States "is the only country where product liability really matters on a grand scale." He mentions the civil jury system, financing of litigation through contingent fees, availability of discovery, the role of insurance, differences in regulatory regimes and the role of regulation in various countries, and politics and media attention. On the topic of the civil jury, he states,

> [T]he most important concern about juries is not what they do but what they might do. Their unpredictability threatens a losing defendant with a potentially catastrophic verdict. Rather than gamble, most

manufacturers or sellers prefer to avoid the risk and settle, even at high cost.

Reimann, *supra,* at 84. Nonetheless, he concludes that specialized tribunals set up in several countries, particularly Asia, are not terribly effective at handling cases, particularly those involving serious injury. On the procedural front, he notes that high filing fees in other countries serve as significant barriers to entry into the legal system. The absence of discovery, differences in financing of litigation — contingent fees versus loser pays, lack of specialization of the bar, and the lack of a culture of expert witnesses to assist lawyers (as opposed to judges) outside of the U.S also account for the relative lack of litigation in the rest of the world. The role of insurance also differs. In the U.S., victims have little insurance and businesses hold large policies, giving an incentive to suit. In other countries, consumers are heavily insured (through national health insurance or work-related benefits), while manufacturers and sellers are less apt to have large policies. Finally, he suggests that the media attention given to products liability is unheard of in the rest of the world. Although some countries have paid particular attention to injuries from certain products, such as contaminated colza oil in Spain, or Thalidomide in Germany, by and large, the matter of products liability is not on the public radar. *Id.* at 815-835.

Does it make sense to think that these factors play a role in the number of lawsuits for defective products? Which of these attributes of the civil justice system could and should be modified if we want to reduce the number of lawsuits and the amounts of the judgments? Or should we look at the number of lawsuits in the U.S. as evidence that, unlike the Directive, our law really has an impact?

C. EXPLORING DIFFERENCES IN THE ROLE OF REGULATION

Although the European Union and most of the rest of the world experience far less litigation than the United States, they address consumer safety through a heightened emphasis on government regulation. The United States, too, has regulations in place, but in the U.S., the regulatory agenda is much more likely to be set by the subjects of regulation, and the content of the regulations is not infrequently the subject of litigation. Why do these differences exist? Would the U.S. be better off with greater regulation and less litigation, or is litigation a particularly important aspect of ensuring product safety? The following excerpt reveals the European view, as expressed by scholars from Britain and Finland.

Geraint Howells and Thomas Wilhelmsson

EC and US Approaches to Consumer Protection—Should the Gap Be Bridged?

17 Yearbook of European Law 207, 209-210, 212-217, 227-228 (1997)

Americans do not trust their business nor their regulators. In Europe, on the other hand, people tend to believe that most businesses, or at least the big well-reputed ones, are ethical and that the State will offer protection against those that are not. . . . The European consumers have not yet become familiar with using private remedies and the consumer movement has not learned how to participate fully in the changing climate.

The expectations of consumers and citizens

The way a U.S. citizen fundamentally understands the State often appears as rather strange for a European. For an American the State is at least potentially an "evil" against which one needs to be protected, at least from its worst excesses (with excesses being given a very broad definition to include some activities Europeans would expect their State to perform.) . . .

In line with these different views of the nature and role of the State there are also different expectations concerning the creation and defence of solidarity in society. Whilst Americans tend to put the emphasis on voluntary measures and the activities of private organizations, the European concept of the Welfare State clearly designates the public sector as being primarily responsible for social welfare policy. . . .

European consumer protection has in many countries been developed from above, by the State. The supervision of consumer markets is entrusted, for example in the very State oriented Nordic countries, to State authorities as well. . . . In countries like Germany where consumer organizations do fulfill an important supervisory function they are heavily subsidized by the State. Similarly in France the Government subsidized the Institute National de Consommation and the corporatist involvement of the Government in the field is also reflected in the fact that consumer groups which want to act legally for consumers have to register with the State. . . .

Consumer safety

. . . It is well known that product liability damages in the United States often act as a surrogate for a Welfare State. For many people in the United States tort damages are an important means to meet health costs and replace lost income. . . . However, product liability actions also serve a regulatory function as a surrogate for the political process. . . . [T]he deterrent threat of product-liability is seen as important to compensate for any weaknesses in the regulatory regime. The use of punitive damages in product liability actions is a clear expression of Americans' distrust of corporations.

United States

(i) Regulation

It is somewhat ironic that US citizens are sceptical of the ability of their regulators to assure consumer safety, whilst US consumer safety regulation is at the same time held up as a model for others to emulate. . . . One of the undoubted strengths of the US system is its injury data collection systems of which the centre-piece is the National Electronic Injury Surveillance System (NEISS). This relies on data recorded in a representative sample of hospital emergency rooms and was the inspiration for national systems in the United Kingdom, The Netherlands, and Denmark and eventually for the EHLASS system at the European Level. The American NEISS system remains the largest and most sophisticated product-related accident collection system. The information collected is used to target information campaigns and regulatory activity.

It is in the area of regulatory activity that the Consumer Product Safety Commission has been least successful. The Consumer Product Safety Act (CPSA) of 1972 had included fairly strong and innovative powers permitting the Safety Commission to ban or issue mandatory standards governing consumer products. But these powers became emasculated by the over bureaucratic procedures which came with them and the naïve approach of the Safety Commission in its early years. . . . The rule-making procedures of the CPSC were in need of an overhaul, but the 1981 amendments went further than this and virtually disempowered the CPSC as a rule-making body. . . . Since 1981 the CPSC can only promulgate a rule if it is satisfied that a voluntary standard is not suitable as it is either unlikely to eliminate or adequately reduce the risk of injury or that there was unlikely to be substantial compliance with the standard. This central role differs significantly from the function we shall see voluntary standards play in Europe. . . .

US standards bodies are far more decentralized than their European counterparts. There are estimated to be 400 voluntary standards writing bodies in the United States. A major concern is the lack of consumer involvement in the development of standards. . . . By contrast European consumer groups are active participants in the standardization process.

Europe

Product Safety

Europe was as concerned as the United States that product regulation should not stifle innovation. It was also anxious that national regulations should not impede the development of the internal market. However, it realized that the answer could not be a purely deregulatory approach. . . . The new approach involved adopting directives which cover a particular sector rather than individual products. These avoid detailed regulation. Each directive includes a general clause stating that such products may only be marketed if they do not endanger safety. An annex contains 'essential safety requirements' which the product must comply with. Producers can benefit from a presumption of conformity by complying with harmonized standards adopted to implement the directive; alternatively they can meet the essential safety requirements by other means, but then third party assessment is usually required. By complying with the conformity assessment procedures specified in each directive, producers can attach the 'CE' marking to their product, which should be their passport to the entire internal market. However, due to a safeguard clause, Member States remain free to take action against products which pose a risk to safety.

This system is by no means perfect. Although the political decisions as to the appropriate level of safety appear to be made by the politicians when they fix the essential safety requirements, in practice the standards drafting process is far from being a simple technical exercise and many of the hard decisions are delegated to this level. Criticisms of the standards process can be made. It was never intended to have such a heavy workload and there have been problems in developing standards quickly enough. Also standards bodies can be viewed as closely associated with industry and some have been slow to involve social partners, like consumers. The conformity assessment procedures can also be criticized for too often relying on manufacturer's self-declaration of conformity and for inconsistent application of the standards. . . .

However, when the European position is compared to the United States, one can conclude that the Community has made a fairly good stab at reconciling the demands for free trade and deregulation with the needs of consumer protection. There has been a determined effort to place voluntary standards within a legal framework which both determines the objectives standardization is seeking to fulfil and provides States with the ability to step in when products nevertheless reach or threaten to reach the market in a condition that poses a threat to safety. . . .

Notes

1. Howells and Wilhelmsson offer a variety of explanations for the existence of a more robust regulatory environment in the European community. Do you believe they accurately capture the attitude toward regulation in the United States? Do you agree with them that the Europe has shown it is possible to utilize regulation for consumer protection without suppressing free trade and innovation?

2. The authors assert that in the United States, consumers actively defend their legal rights through litigation, and courts regulate, at least in a *de facto* manner, as they work their way through litigation. In contrast, consumer participation in the European Union is much more closely monitored but encouraged as part of the regulatory process, while litigation is discouraged by many of systemic constraints mentioned in the Reimann excerpt in the last section. Is one system better than the other, or have both evolved to suit the prevailing legal, economic and social climate?

3. Since the regulatory regime in any country ultimately relies principally on the State, issues arise as to what citizens can and should expect the State to do. Japanese attorney Harushi Sarumida suggests that government regulators in Japan are more likely to take action with regard to public risks because they can be sued for failure to do so. Haroshi Sarumida, *Comparative*

Institutional Analysis of Product Safety in the United States and Japan: Alternative Approaches to Create Incentives for Product Safety, 29 CORNELL INT'L L. J. 79, 96 (1996). Sumida also attributes vigorous and consistent enforcement of regulations to the existence of a dedicated bureaucratic core of individuals who have made the government agencies their careers. *Id* at 127.

4. Should government be required to regulate to protect safety? In 2004, the French *Conseil d'Etat* issued several decisions that tightened State liability by holding that the State is under an obligation to adopt regulation in the face of scientific knowledge of the serious health risks concerning asbestos. But generally, there is a tendency to view failure to regulate as a discretionary function. *See* Willem H. van Boom and Andrea Pinna, *Liability for Failure to Regulate Health and Safety Risks, in* EUROPEAN TORT LAW 2005 2, 7-11 (Helmut Koziol & Barbara C. Steininger eds., 2006). Governmental liability is covered in more detail in Chapter 9.

In the United States, we seem not to have the political ability or will to develop a regulatory system like that in the EC or Japan. However, there is continuing discussion over the role of litigation as a mechanism to ensure greater product safety. Some scholars argue that the United States should recognize a regulatory compliance defense, and place much greater reliance on experts to determine what is and is not safe. Others point out the weaknesses of that view and the contributions of tort law. The following excerpt captures the tenor of the debate.

Robert L. Rabin

Keynote Paper: Reassessing Regulatory Compliance

Symposium, Regulatory Compliance as a Defense to Product Liability
88 Geo. L. J. 2049, 2052-2053, 2068-2069, 2070, 2073 (2000)

. . . Trial judges are lumped with jurors as generalists in a post-New Deal regulatory environment in which special competence means technical and scientific expertise, not just experience in hearing a great many similar cases. In the world view of critics like Peter Huber, the tort system bears major responsibility for stifling innovation and impeding progressive public health and safety measures.[16] According to Huber, tort law may do a tolerable job of dealing with the "private risks" in slip-and-fall or auto accidents cases. But the "public risks" that are the inevitable by-products of later Twentieth Century progress are identified as social costs by the tort system, without any sensitivity to the corresponding widely shared benefits of these activities. It follows that the role of tort law should be sharply constrained:

> Vaccines, pesticides, aircraft, electric power plants and the like all entail potentially enormous mass-exposure hazards. Precisely because they can create public risks of this nature, these products and services are also subject to the most searching and complete state and federal safety regulation. Administrative agencies may find it politically convenient to disclaim final responsibility for the public risk choices that inhere in such licensing decisions. But the simple fact is that an agency cannot intelligently issue a license for such public-risk activities without comparing the licensee's risks to those of the competition and determining that the new offering represents some measure of progress or, at worst, no measure of regression in the risk market in question. Once the determination has been made by an expert licensing agency, the courts should respect it. Regulatory agencies are equipped to make the risk comparisons on which all progressive transformation of the risk environment is based. The courts are simply not qualified to second-guess such decisions; when they choose to do so they routinely make regressive risk choices. Requiring – or at least strongly encouraging – the courts to respect the comparative risk choices made by competent, expert agencies would inject a first, small measure of rationality into a judicial regulatory system that currently runs quite wild.[18] . . .

Eliciting Information About Risk and Aberrant Conduct

If the regulatory system retains a comparative advantage on risk assessment, one can ask: what would be lost without tort?

---

[16]See Peter Huber, *Safety and the Second Best: The Hazards of Public Risk Management in the Courts,* 85 COLUM. L. REV. 277, 334-35 (1985).

[18]*Id.* at 334-335.

Assume for the moment that the regulatory process is expressly directed to engage in risk-benefit analysis, not the establishment of minimum standards. Assume that it is neither captured nor moribund – two other commonly raised argument against creating immunity from tort liability. And assume, with regard to the preceding section, that whatever tentative moves the tort system is making to take account of the views of independent experts, agency processes involving risk assessment incorporate professional expertise as a matter of course. Under these circumstances, does the regulatory process touch all bases and make tort law superfluous?

Somewhat begrudgingly, Marcia Angell* departs briefly from her denigration of the tort system to indicate that breast implant manufacturers, even if their product has never been scientifically linked to major diseases, were anything but scrupulous in their concern for product safety or for marketing their product in an honest fashion. Their dubious business ethics – if not revealing a "smoking gun" on product risks – came out through pretrial discovery in the tort litigation:

> What the documents did indicate was how little was known, how inadequate the studies had been, and how relentlessly the company pursued its market goals [including instructions to sales representatives to wipe the oily film off the product in a washroom before meeting with potential physician/buyers.] Adding to Dow Corning's problems was the discovery in 1992 that employees falsified some of the data about the manufacturing process, a charge that Dow Corning admitted. Evidently, some of the employees doctored the the [sic] automatic recordings of failures in the heat-curing process for the implants. According to Dow Corning, they did it to avoid review they would undergo if the failures were faithfully recorded.

Other authors have made much of the singular role of the courts in educating the public about unscrupulous and socially dangerous business practices detrimental to the public health. . . . It is true, of course, that business conduct, however reprehensible, is no basis for tort liability in the absence of causation. But in an

---

*MARCIA ANGELL, SCIENCE ON TRIAL: THE CLASH OF MEDICAL EVIDENCE AND THE LAW IN THE BREAST IMPLANT CASE, 60 (1996) [former editor, New England Journal of Medicine].

important sense that is beside the point: if we are substantially dependent on the tort system to provide the educational function of revealing massive cover-ups of health information by industries like asbestos, or occasional efforts to conceal risk information from regulatory agencies like the FDA, then it is undeniably the case that tort law is serving a positive function of some consequence.

Structurally, there is reason to think that the tort system does play this role with some regularity. In cases like asbestos and tobacco, there simply was no regulatory agency charged with monitoring industry products from a health risk perspective. Even in the case of a comprehensive regulatory regime like FDA certification of new drugs, the agency process is noninvasive: the burden is on the company to produce evidence in support of its new drug application, and the agency does not conduct its own testing and experimentation. It is, of course, true that fraud on the agency is ground for criminal penalties and will invalidate the certification. But the question is how the fraudulent conduct is to be unearthed if tort law is disengaged. It may be through an internal leak, or congressional investigation, or media scrutiny, but it is hardly reassuring to rely exclusively on these sources. . . .

Compensation Concerns

As I have suggested, the case for a regulatory compliance defense to a considerable extent turns on the superiority of the regulatory process over the tort system in making risk-benefit determinations, and in some cases, in identifying causal responsibility. . . .

In the absence of preemption, a state could rationally decide that it has a legitimate interest in ensuring compensation to its citizens in accidental harm situations and promoting broad risk-spreading on the part of product manufacturers. If so, why should the state defer to a regulatory agency that had more narrowly constrained safety purposes in mind when it promulgated its "optimal safety" regulations?

Notes

1. Are you persuaded that the tort system plays an important role in ensuring product safety and protecting consumers? Rabin asserts that even if the agencies are not moribund or captured, tort law makes an important contribution. It is even more important if the agencies are flawed. If he is

correct, one might expect legal systems in other countries make it easier to obtain these benefits by easing the barriers to litigation.

2. It is entirely possible to put regulations in place but achieve little benefit in terms of product safety. Sometimes the regulations are valid, but their content is skewed due to the power of lobbyists and interested parties. For example, a Texas anti-pollution law that went into effect in 1999 contained restrictions that were purely voluntary and had been drafted by leaders in the gas, oil and chemical industries. Then Governor George W. Bush refused to implement mandatory restrictions that had been suggested by his own state regulatory agency. Jim Yardley, *Bush Approach to Pollution: Preference for Self-Policing*, N.Y. TIMES, Nov. 9, 1999, at A1.

3. What should be the role of criminal law in ensuring the safety of products? Consider the case of China, which has recently been in the news because of a flurry of defective products that have been exported throughout the world. Products as diverse as pet food, tooth paste, tires, and toys are reported to have been contaminated with foreign substances that are very toxic. Within China as well, dozens of people have died from defective products. Yet China has tort law and product regulations in place. China's General Principles of Civil Law include a law of obligations much like that found in many other countries. It is a fault-based standard. The Product Quality Law was promulgated in 1993 to deal specifically with product liability. There are administrative measures to standardize, supervise, and license a wide range of products. There are also criminal laws to further enforcement. The punishments include imprisonment or fines, as well as capital punishment in the case of manufacture or sale of counterfeit pharmaceuticals. Will W. Shen & Iris H.Y Chiu, *Comparative Analysis of Key Aspects of Product Liability Law in China and the United States, in* LIABILITY FOR PRODUCTS IN A GLOBAL ECONOMY 311, 318-323, 354 (Dennis Campbell & Susan Woodley eds., 2005). Recently, the world witnessed China's use of criminal law in the product arena. The former head of the State Food and Drug Administration was recently sentenced to death following conviction for taking bribes to approve hundreds of drugs. David Barboza, *China Steps Up Its Safety Efforts,* N.Y. TIMES, July 7, 2007, at B1. The death sentence was subsequently carried out in July 2007.

But criminal sanctions need not be aimed at a person. Recently, the Court of First Instance No. 56, in Madrid, ordered the pharmaceutical company Merck to pay 50,000 euros to a fifty-four year old man who suffered a cerebral stroke after taking the drug Vioxx for more than two years. The sentence was imposed because the judge believed the "merchandising of the drug without the proper guarantees of quality, as corroborated by the withdrawal of the drug, produced the possibility, however small it might be, that this injury would occur." The amount of the fine was reduced from what had been asked because the patient had taken Vioxx without a medical prescription. Joaquín Manso, *Primera Condena en España contra la Compañia Merck por su Fármaco Vioxx,* elmundo.es, http://www.elmundo.es/elmundosalud/2007/08/02/dolor/1186082128.html.

Chapter 12

PRIVACY

Both in the United States and internationally, laws and jurisprudence have developed to protect privacy. In the United States, the evolution of tort theories specifically recognizing privacy rights began when lawyers Samuel Warren and Louis Brandeis wrote a famous law review article arguing that the protection of privacy rights through other tort theories, such as trespass, was insufficient. Over time, courts accepted this idea and recognized privacy claims. William Prosser, a famous torts scholar and law professor, suggested in 1960 that the cases where courts had recognized privacy interests fell into four basic categories: intrusions into one's private sphere; representation of a person in a false light; public disclosure of private facts; and commercial appropriation of a person's face or image. These protections have developed over time. In addition, U.S. courts have realized that there are free speech implications in some cases, and have addressed these through reliance on the Constitution and Bill of Rights. This section explores parallel legal developments in other common law and civil law countries, with a focus on the impact of the European Convention on Human Rights.

As the following excerpt illustrates, the protection of privacy is deeply rooted in the legal and moral traditions of many countries around the world. However, the recent development of privacy tort law on the international stage is in large part a response to the events of the first half of the 20th Century.

A. HISTORICAL BACKGROUND

Privacy finds its roots in many legal traditions. Greek and Roman laws and social practices recognized that to participate fully in society, individuals must be permitted a distinction between their public and their private lives. There are Biblical references to the value of privacy, and Jewish law has a doctrine that protects individuals from unwanted surveillance. Many cultures give special protection for family life and view the home as inviolable. The saying that "a man's home is his castle" dates back to a series of controversial search and seizure cases in the United Kingdom in the 1760's.

Privacy is identified as a fundamental human right in Universal Declaration of Human Rights (1948), the International Covenant on Civil and Political Rights (1976), the American Convention on Human Rights (1978), and the European Convention for the Protection of Human Rights and Fundamental Freedoms (1953).*

The European willingness to enter into Conventions protecting privacy and to enshrine it in their own laws is at least in part attributable to their strong reaction to privacy abuses by the Nazis. Centralized registries were used to facilitate persecution of the Jews and there was no respect for personal data or confidentiality.

B. IMPACT OF THE EUROPEAN CONVENTION ON HUMAN RIGHTS

1. Introduction

The Convention for the Protection of Human Rights and Fundamental Freedoms, commonly known as the European Convention on Human Rights (ECHR), was adopted on November 4, 1950 under the auspices of the Council of Europe in order to protect human rights and fundamental freedoms. All Council of Europe Member States are party to the Convention and new members are expected to ratify the Convention at the earliest opportunity. This ratification has the effect of incorporating the

---

*Full citations for these may be found in Chapter 3, pp. 32-33.

Convention into the domestic law of the Member State. There are presently 47 members of the Council of Europe.

On September 18, 1959, the Council established the European Court of Human Rights. The Court was created largely as an enforcement mechanism to establish whether the Member States have violated an article of the Convention. Although rarely utilized at its inception, the Court now operates on a full time basis. The Court is comprised of 47 judges (one from each Member State) who are elected to six year terms by the Parliamentary Assembly of the Council. It can be used either for the resolution of interstate disputes or by individuals seeking redress against their state of citizenship. In 2006, the Court received approximately 50,500 petitions for review and handed down 1560 judgments. The decisions of the Court are legally binding and the Court has the power to award damages if the Contracting State under the Convention does not allow or allows only partial reparation for the breach. The greatest influence of the ECHR has been its influence on the domestic tort law of some of the ECHR Member States. When the ECHR finds that a Member State's legislation, administrative law or judicial decisions would violate an Article of the Convention, this may prompt the Member State to rethink the direction of its domestic law, as appears to be happening with England in the case of privacy interests. In this way, the ECHR may influence a convergence among European countries on certain issues, paving the way for a more uniform common European tort law. WALTER VAN GERVEN, JEREMY LEVER & PIERRE LAROUCHE, CASES, MATERIALS AND TEXT ON NATIONAL, SUPRANATIONAL AND INTERNATIONAL TORT LAW 931-933 (2000). The European Convention is still the only international human rights agreement providing such a high degree of individual protection.

CONVENTION FOR THE PROTECTION OF HUMAN RIGHTS AND FUNDAMENTAL FREEDOMS

213 U.N.T.S., Nov. 4, 1950

ARTICLE 8

Everyone has the right to respect for his private and family life, his home and his correspondence.

There shall be no interference by a public authority with the exercise of this right except such as is in accordance with the law and is necessary in a democratic society in the interests of national security, public safety or the economic well-being of the country, for the prevention of disorder or crime, for the protection of health or morals, or for the protection of the rights and freedoms of others.

ARTICLE 10

Everyone has the right to freedom of expression. This right shall include freedom to hold opinions and to receive and impart information and ideas without interference by public authority and regardless of frontiers. This article shall not prevent States from requiring the licensing of broadcasting, television or cinema enterprises.

The exercise of these freedoms, since it carries with it duties and responsibilities, may be subject to such formalities, conditions, restrictions or penalties as are prescribed by law and are necessary in a democratic society, in the interests of national security, territorial integrity or public safety, for the prevention of disorder or crime, for the protection of health or morals, for the protection of the reputation or the rights of others, for preventing the disclosure of information received in confidence, or for maintaining the authority and impartiality of the judiciary.

---

2. The Effect of the ECHR in the UK, France and Germany

The rulings and jurisprudence of the ECHR have affected privacy law in signatory states in diverse yet fundamental ways. The cases and notes in this section discuss those effects in three countries.

a. United Kingdom

Prior to the passage of its Human Rights Act in 1998, the United Kingdom did not recognize a specific right to privacy. Despite several efforts by Parliament over the years to craft privacy laws, the protection of privacy remained, at best, "a patchwork affair."[**] Without a written Constitution or Bill of Rights, British plaintiffs had to rely on common law torts to provide legal remedies for privacy breaches. However, the existing torts proved largely inadequate for this purpose, as they were created to address specific legal wrongs which are often only tangentially related to the protection of privacy. In addition, these existing tort theories were difficult to prove and often did not provide remedies adequate to merit the bringing of the suit in the first place.

One cause of action commonly used to protect privacy rights was the common law tort of "passing off." Originally conceived to apply in business and trade settings, passing off occurs when the reputation of a plaintiff is misappropriated by defendant, such that defendant misrepresents his goods or services as the goods and services of the plaintiff, damaging the goodwill of the plaintiff. Thus, it was extrapolated, the tort of passing off should also apply to situations where a newspaper or media outlet uses the name or likeness of a certain celebrity without permission in order to improve upon its business.

However, there were several problems with using this cause of action to forward privacy rights in this manner. Because the law of passing off prevents a defendant from misrepresenting his goods or services as being the goods or services of the plaintiff, courts required a showing that plaintiff and defendant were competitors in the same field of business. It was often very hard for celebrity plaintiffs to prove that they were competitors in the same field of trade as defendants; indeed, it was often hard for plaintiffs to prove that they were traders at all. In *Kaye v. Robertson* [1991] F.S.R. 62, for example, the plaintiff, a well known television actor, was forced to spend time in the hospital after suffering a head injury. During his hospital stay, a reporter and photographer from the Sunday Sport entered plaintiff's room and interviewed him while he was under heavy sedation, despite notices on plaintiff's door and on the entrance to the hospital that plaintiff was not to be disturbed.

The plaintiff sued defendant newspaper to enjoin publication; among other claims, plaintiff alleged that the newspaper had engaged in "passing off," trying to increase its own reputation by publishing the interview and photos to which he had not consented. However, the court held that he was not a trader, as

---

[**] Ronald J. Krotoszynski, *Autonomy, Community, and Traditions of Liberty: The Contrast of British and American Privacy Law*, 1990 DUKE L.J. 1398, 1401.

contemplated by the passing off tort, because he did not normally engage in the business of selling stories about himself and his recovery. In cases like this one, UK courts interpret the elements of passing off very narrowly, effectively foreclosing its use in breach of privacy cases.

Occasionally, public figure plaintiffs would bring actions for trespass to land, particularly in cases where photographs were taken through high powered camera lenses. However, courts generally held that plaintiffs' land had not technically been "trespassed" or damaged in such cases. Similarly, actions for private nuisances normally failed because courts normally required plaintiffs to show some interest in the property being invaded.

By contrast, celebrity plaintiffs had some measure of success protecting privacy interests through the tort of breach of confidence. A claim for a breach of confidence requires a showing of three elements: (1) the existence of confidential information, usually shown when the property is not public property or public knowledge; (2) the information was disclosed in a confidential relationship, or under circumstances implying such a relationship; and (3) the information was used by one member of the confidential relationship without authority. In *Duchess of Argyll v. Duke of Argyll*, 1967 Ch. 302, for example, the court enjoined the Duke from publishing certain confidential information about the Duchess obtained while the two were married on the ground that it would constitute a breach of confidence.

The question UK courts had to grapple with was whether they would expand breach of confidence to cover the situation where paparazzi photograph a celebrity from a distance. While the House of Lords stated that the tort could be committed even though the paparazzi lacked a relationship with the celebrity, by and large the courts have construed the tort narrowly, precluding liability for pictures taken in public places by parties with no relationship to the subject of the picture.

As a result of Princess Diana's fatal car accident and the resulting outrage at the role of the media in that tragedy, the Parliamentary Assembly of the Council of Europe passed a Resolution on the right to privacy. The Resolution called on the governments of Europe to legally enshrine Article 8 of the ECHR within the domestic laws of their respective countries. Great Britain responded by passing the Human Rights Act in 1998, which incorporated the entire Convention, including Article 8, into

UK domestic law. This was the first true declaration of a right to privacy in the UK. The following case discusses the effect of the European Convention and the Human Rights Act on British privacy jurisprudence.

CAMPBELL v. MGN LTD.

[2004] UKHL 22; [2004] W.L.R. 1232

[The Daily Mirror published a front-page article about supermodel Naomi Campbell under the headline "Naomi: I am a drug addict." There was a small picture of Campbell emerging from a Narcotics Anonymous (N.A.) meeting and a larger picture of her and others outside a building with a prominent café signboard in the foreground. The others' faces were pixilated. The article gave a full account of her history of difficult behavior but was sympathetic to her attempts to 'beat the demons that have been haunting her.' The original source of the story was either a fellow attendee of N.A. meetings or a member of Miss Campbell's staff or entourage. Campbell had previously denied any involvement with illegal drugs. At trial, defendant newspaper argued, and plaintiff conceded, that the Mirror was entitled to publish the fact that Campbell was a drug addict and was in therapy in order to set the record straight. But, it was argued, the paper was not entitled to disclose that she was attending N.A. meetings, nor was it entitled to use the covert photographs of Ms. Campbell with other N.A. participants. The trial court found in favor of Campbell, holding that the information 'giving details of her attendance at N.A. meetings' clearly bore the badge of confidentiality, as defined by Article 8 of the ECHR. The Court of Appeal reversed this decision. Given what it was accepted could be disclosed, the photos and 'peripheral details' about her attendance at N.A. were part of the 'journalistic package' adding color and credibility to the story without increasing the breach of confidence. By a 3-2 vote, the House of Lords reversed the Court of Appeal.]

THE BARONESS HALE OF RICHMOND [in the majority]

. . . 126. My Lords, this case raises some big questions. How is the balance to be struck between everyone's right to respect for their private and family life under Article 8 of the European Convention on Human Rights and everyone's right to freedom of expression, including the freedom to receive and impart information and ideas under Article 10? How do those rights come into play in a dispute between two private persons? But the parties are largely agreed about the answers to these. They disagree about where that balance is to be struck in the individual case. In particular, how far is a newspaper able to go in publishing what would otherwise be confidential information about a celebrity in order to set the record straight? And does it matter that the article was illustrated by a covertly taken photograph? . . .

132. Neither party to this appeal has challenged the basic principles which have emerged from the Court of Appeal in the wake of the Human Rights Act 1998. The 1998 Act does not create any new cause of action between private persons. But if there is a relevant cause of action applicable, the court as a public authority must act compatibly with both parties' Convention rights. In a case such as this, the relevant vehicle will usually be the action for breach of confidence. . . .

134. This begs the question of how far the Convention balancing exercise is premised on the scope of the existing cause of action. . . .How does the scope of the action for breach of confidence accommodate the Article 8 rights of individuals? . . . The position we have reached is that the exercise of balancing Article 8 and Article 10 may begin when the person publishing the information knows or ought to know that there is a reasonable expectation that the information in question will be kept confidential. . . .

137. It should be emphasised that the 'reasonable expectation of privacy' is a threshold test which brings the balancing exercise into play. It is not the end of the story. Once the information is identified as 'private' in this way, the court must balance the claimant's interest in keeping the information private against the countervailing interest of the recipient in publishing it. Very often, it can be expected that the countervailing rights of the recipient will prevail. . . .

139. Each right has the same structure. Article 8(1) states that "Everyone has the right to respect for his private and family life, his home and his correspondence". Article 10(1) states that "Everyone has the right to freedom of expression. This right shall include freedom to hold opinions and to receive and impart information and ideas without interference by public authorities and regardless of frontiers . . ." Unlike the Article 8 right, however, it is accepted in Article 10(2) that the exercise of this right 'carries with it duties and responsibilities.' Both rights are

qualified. They may respectively be interfered with or restricted provided that three conditions are fulfilled:

(a) The interference or restriction must be 'in accordance with the law'; it must have a basis in national law which conforms to the Convention standards of legality.
(b) It must pursue one of the legitimate aims set out in each article. Article 8(2) provides for "the protection of the rights and freedoms of others". Article 10(2) provides for "the protection of the reputation or rights of others" and for "preventing the disclosure of information received in confidence". The rights referred to may either be rights protected under the national law or, as in this case, other Convention rights.
(c) Above all, the interference or restriction must be "necessary in a democratic society"; it must meet a "pressing social need" and be no greater than is proportionate to the legitimate aim pursued; the reasons given for it must be both "relevant" and "sufficient" for this purpose.

140. The application of the proportionality test is more straightforward when only one Convention right is in play. . . . It is much less straightforward when two Convention rights are in play, and the proportionality of interfering with one has to be balanced against the proportionality of restricting the other. As each is a fundamental right, there is evidently a "pressing social need" to protect it. . . .

Striking the balance

144. Examined . . . closely . . . this case is far from trivial. . . . The information revealed by the article was information relating to Miss Campbell's health, both physical and mental. . . . Drug addiction needs treatment if it is to be overcome. . . .

145. It has always been accepted that information about a person's health and treatment for ill-health is both private and confidential. This stems not only from the confidentiality of the doctor-patient relationship but from the nature of the information itself. . . .

146. The Court of Appeal in this case held that the information revealed here was not in the same category as clinical medical records. That may be so, in the sense that it was not the notes made by a doctor when consulted by a patient. But the

information was of exactly the same kind as that which would be recorded by a doctor on those notes: the presenting problem was addiction to illegal drugs, the diagnosis was no doubt the same, and the prescription was therapy, including the self-help group therapy offered by regular attendance at Narcotics Anonymous.

147. I start, therefore, from the fact – indeed, it is common ground – that *all* of the information about Miss Campbell's addiction and attendance at NA which was revealed in the "Daily Mirror" article was both private and confidential, because it related to an important aspect of Miss Campbell's physical and mental health and the treatment she was receiving for it. It had also been received from an insider in breach of confidence. That simple fact has been obscured by the concession properly made on her behalf that the newspaper's countervailing freedom of expression did serve to justify the publication of some of this information. But the starting point must be that it was all private and its publication required specific justification.

148. What was the nature of the freedom of expression which was being asserted on the other side? There are undoubtedly different types of speech, just as there are different types of private information, some of which are more deserving of protection in a democratic society than others. Top of the list is political speech. The free exchange of information and ideas on matters relevant to the organisation of the economic, social and political life of the country is crucial to any democracy. Without this, it can scarcely be called a democracy at all. This includes revealing information about public figures, especially those in elective office, which would otherwise be private but is relevant to their participation in public life. Intellectual and educational speech and expression are also important in a democracy, not least because they enable the development of individuals' potential to play a full part in society and in our democratic life. Artistic speech and expression is important for similar reasons, in fostering both individual originality and creativity and the free-thinking and dynamic society we so much value. No doubt there are other kinds of speech and expression for which similar claims can be made.

149. But it is difficult to make such claims on behalf of the publication with which we are concerned here. The political and social life of the community, and the intellectual, artistic or personal development of individuals, are not obviously assisted by pouring over the intimate details of a fashion model's private life. .

. . What entitled [MGN] to reveal this private information about [Ms. Campbell] without her consent?

151. The answer which she herself accepts is that she had presented herself to the public as someone who was not involved in drugs. . . . [T]he possession and use of illegal drugs is a criminal offence and a matter of serious public concern. The press must be free to expose the truth and put the record straight.

152. That consideration justified the publication of the fact that, contrary to her previous statements, Miss Campbell had been involved with illegal drugs. It also justified publication of the fact that she was trying to do something about it by seeking treatment. It was not necessary for those purposes to publish any further information, especially if this might jeopardise the continued success of that treatment. . . .

157. The weight to be attached to these various considerations is a matter of fact and degree. Not every statement about a person's health will carry the badge of confidentiality or risk doing harm to that person's physical or moral integrity. . . . Sometimes there will be other justifications for publishing, especially where the information is relevant to the capacity of a public figure to do the job. . . .

158. The trial judge was well placed to assess these matters. He could tell whether the impact of the story on her was serious or trivial. The fact that the story had been published at all was bound to cause distress and possibly interfere with her progress. But he was best placed to judge whether the additional information and the photographs had added significantly both to the distress and the potential harm. He accepted her evidence that it had done so. He could also tell how serious an interference with press freedom it would have been to publish the essential parts of the story without the additional material and how difficult a decision this would have been for an editor who had been told that it was a medical matter and that it would be morally wrong to publish it. . . .

160. I would therefore allow this appeal and restore the order of the judge.

[Lord Hope of Craighead and Lord Carswell agreed that the appeal should be allowed.]

Notes

1. Reaction by the press to the *Campbell* decision was predictably negative. Piers Morgan, the editor for defendant Daily Mirror, stated: "this is a very good day for lying, drug-abusing prima donnas who want to have their cake with the media, and the right to then shamelessly guzzle it with their Cristal champagne." The London Times provided a somewhat less histrionic but no less critical editorial on the possible effects of the rule announced in *Campbell*:

> The ruling here is part of a broader and disturbing trend. . . . There are obviously moments when photographs in newspapers are intrusive, trivial and add nothing to a story. There should be a presumption, however . . . in their favour. Events in an infinitely more important theatre – the treatment of prisoners in Iraq – have illustrated both the power of photography and the burden on pictures to be what they claim. This outcome is part of an inconsistent and undesirable pattern in which the judiciary, or parts of it, attempt to mould the old notion of a "duty of confidence" into something close to a law of privacy. The House of Lords has thus produced a confused, even blurred, judgment. In doing so, it has invited further, possibly damaging, cases.

London Times, *Photo Finish: the Curious and Disturbing Outcome in the Campbell Case*, May 7, 2004.

Is the Times correct in its assessment as to the potential impact of this ruling? How might the House of Lords distinguish a case involving photos of Iraqi prisoner abuse from the photographs at issue in *Campbell*? How might the court treat a case involving photographs of a noted politician entering a hospital for undisclosed reasons?

2. The decision in *Campbell* was a close one, with three Law Lords ruling that Ms. Campbell's right to privacy had been infringed, and two ruling that it had not. In dissent, Lord Hoffman noted that "the difference of opinion relates to a very narrow point which arises on the unusual facts of this case . . . the importance of this case lies in the statements of general principle on the way in which the law should strike a balance between the right to privacy and the right to freedom of expression, on which the House is unanimous." He went on to state:

> That brings me to what seems to be the only point of principle which arises in this case. Where the main substance of the story is conceded to have been justified, should the newspaper be held liable whenever the judge considers that it was not necessary to have published some of the personal information? Or should the newspaper be allowed some margin of choice in the way it chooses to present the story? . . .
>
> In my opinion, it would be inconsistent with the approach which has been taken by the courts in a number of recent landmark cases for a newspaper to be held strictly liable for exceeding what a judge considers to have been necessary. The practical exigencies of journalism demand that some latitude must be given. Editorial decisions have to be made quickly and with less information than is available to a court which afterwards reviews the matter at leisure. And if any margin is to be allowed, it seems to me strange to hold the *Mirror* liable in damages for a decision which three experienced judges in the Court of Appeal have held to be perfectly justified.

Did the court strike the proper balance between privacy protection and freedom of the media in this case? Should there instead be a presumption in favor of editorial discretion in such cases, as suggested by Lord Hoffman and the London Times article?

3. Not every invasion of privacy case involves a celebrity or public figure plaintiff. In *Peck v. United Kingdom*, [2003] ECHR 44647/98, decided only a year before *Campbell*, the plaintiff claimed that his privacy rights had been violated when a local Town Council sold CCTV footage of him walking through a town square carrying a knife to the BBC, for use in its program Crimebeat. The plaintiff later used the knife in a suicide attempt. The European Court of Human Rights ruled that plaintiff's right to privacy had been violated by the airing of the footage. Although the Town Council had provided the footage in accordance with a local government act to pursue the legitimate aims of preventing crime and promoting public safety, the court found that these concerns failed to justify the serious violation of plaintiff's Article 8 right to privacy. In particular, the court noted that there were

other, less intrusive means by which to pursue the legitimate government aims, the plaintiff's consent was not obtained, and the BBC had not taken adequate steps to conceal the plaintiff's identity.

b. France and *La Vie Privée*

France has historically recognized a strong right to privacy, which it has been forced to soften as a result of the ratification of the European Convention. French law has recognized the right to privacy, or *la vie privée*, in statutory form since 1868 and in case law going back even further. Although France is a civil law country, its first privacy protections were fashioned in court decisions interpreting duty based tort principles of Article 1382 of the French Civil Code (a general tort statute). See *The Rachel Affair*, T.P.I. [ordinary courts of original jurisdiction] Seine, June 16, 1858, D.P. III 1858, 52 (holding that "no one may, without explicit consent of the family, reproduce and bring to the public eye the image of an individual on her deathbed, whatever the celebrity of the person involved.") France considers the right to privacy to fall within a bundle of rights known collectively as "personality rights," which include the right to protection of honor and reputation, and the right to one's own image. Statutory law provides for stiff penalties for any violation of the right. See Jeanne M. Hauch, *Protecting Private Facts in France: The Warren & Brandeis Tort is Alive and Flourishing in Paris*, 68 TUL. L. REV. 1219, 1222-1224 (1994).

In 1970, France formally recognized privacy by adding a new Section 9 to the Code Civil. Article 9(1) states that "Each person has the right to respect for his private life" and 9 (2) provides that a judge may employ "all measures such as sequester, seizure and others, capable of avoiding or ending a violation of the intimacy of private life [and] these measures can given urgency, be ordered by one judge sitting in chambers.") Code Penal art. 226(1) supplements civil remedies by punishing any invasion of privacy by "fixing, recording, or transmitting, through any device, the image of a person in a private place, without their consent" and providing for penalties of one year in prison plus a fine. Although technically fault is required, a delictual fault is committed as soon as a person's privacy has not been respected. Thus, as a practical matter, liability is strict. Usually the damages recoverable are *dommage moral* and are often presumed. As in other areas of French law, the case law tends to stand in rather stark contrast to that of the U.S. For example, an actress was awarded damages against a newspaper that revealed that she was going to have a baby, on the ground that even "artists have a right to the respect of their private life." JOHN BELL, SOPHIE BOYRON & SIMON WHITTAKER, PRINCIPLES OF FRENCH LAW 369-370 (1998).

Not surprisingly, French journalists have challenged applications of French law as violations of European Convention Article 10 with a large degree of success. See *Fressoz & Roire v. France*, 31 Eur. H.R. Rep. 2 (2001) (conviction of journalists for publishing extracts of tax assessment forms violated Article 10); *Lehideux & Isomi v. France*, 30 Eur. H.R. Rep. 665 (2000) (conviction of journalists for publishing an advertisement about French Vichy leader Marshal Petain violated Article 10); *Du Roy & Malaurie v. France*, (2000), [2000] ECHR 34000/96 (conviction of journalists for publishing information about joinder of parties in a civil case violated Article 10). For an in depth discussion of French privacy law and its similarities and differences from British privacy law, *see* Kathryn F. Deringer, *Privacy and the Press: The Convergence of British and French Law in Accordance With the European Convention of Human Rights*, 22 PENN ST. INT'L L. REV. 191 (2003).

c. Germany

Klaus Vieweg

The Law of Torts

_in_ INTRODUCTION TO GERMAN LAW

Werner F. Ebke & Matthew W. Finkin, eds., 1996

pp. 203-205

I. Liability for Violation of an Absolute Right, § 823 I BGB

§ 823 I BGB provides: "A person who, intentionally or negligently, and unlawfully injures the life, body, health, liberty, ownership or any other right of another person is bound to compensate him for any damage arising therefrom." Hence, for an action to be based on § 823 I BGB the following *requirements* have to be met. There must be an interference with one of the enumerated rights or interests or any other right. Since a tort claim requires the defendant's responsibility, either an action or a nonfeasance is necessary. A causal connection between the tortfeasor's action or nonfeasance and the violation of the right or interest is required as well. The absolute right must have been injured unlawfully and culpably. Lastly, a restitutionable detriment and a causal connection between the interference with the absolute right and the damage suffered are required. . . .

Courts and scholars have developed the so-called "general right of personality" (right to privacy or *allgemeines Persönlichkeitrecht*) as a further "other right" within the meaning of § 823 I BGB. This right was recognized for the first time by the Federal Supreme Court in 1954 in the *Schacht* case.* The plaintiff was the attorney of Dr. Schacht, who had been Economics Minister under Hitler. The defendant was a weekly journal which had published an article objecting to Dr. Schacht's founding a bank. The attorney had been instructed by Dr. Schacht to send to the defendant in his capacity as Dr. Schacht's attorney a letter demanding that certain corrections be made. The defendant left out parts of the letter and published the rest under the heading 'Letters to the Editors,' thereby creating the incorrect impression that it was a mere expression of opinion by a reader on the previous article about Dr. Schacht and that the plaintiff was supporting Dr. Schacht as a private individual. The court held that this publication had to be corrected. The reasons given by the Federal Supreme Court were that the defendant had violated plaintiff's general right of personality by publishing the letter in that manner and presenting a false picture of the author's personality.

The creation of this new right had been possible mainly because of the lack of effective protection of human dignity and personal freedom during the Nazi regime and because Articles 1 and 2 of the Basic Law (*Grundgesetz* – GG) gave these values a more important position than any previous German constitution. . . .

Notes

1. Scholars describe *Schacht* as the most important case in German tort law during the 20th century. It stems from a "somewhat strained" interpretation of the Constitution of Bonn of 1949. It is significant because it linked the civil law with the Constitution. In the United States, the linkage to the Constitution has led to diminished privacy protection due to free speech interests, while in Germany it has led to the enhancement of the protection of privacy. In addition, the linkage between private and public law has led to privacy cases being resolved before the Constitutional Court. BASIL MARKESINIS & HANNES UNBERATH,

---

*BGHZ 13, 334.

THE GERMAN LAW OF TORTS: A COMPARTIVE TREATISE 472 (4th ed. 2002).

2. Echoing the link mentioned above between Germany's experience with the Nazis and the recognition of privacy rights, Markesinis and Unberath note the irony that Schacht was a former Nazi. Prior to the rise of Hitler, he had served as President of the Reichsbank and became a supporter of the Nazi party. When Hitler came to power, Schacht played a leading role in the rearmament program, but in 1938-39, he began to oppose arms expenditures as the only way to balance the budget and reduce inflation. He was confined to a concentration camp in 1944 and was one of the first to be tried at Nuremberg. He was acquitted at trial, and then retried before the German People's Court in Stuttgart where he was sentenced to eight years in a labor camp. Ultimately, he successfully appealed his conviction and returned to a career as a financier. *Id.* at 473.

VON HANNOVER v. GERMANY

European Court of Human Rights
(2005) 40 EHHR1; [2004] E.M.L.R. 21; 16 B.H.R.C. 545,
24 JUNE 2004

The Facts

I. The circumstances of the case

8. The applicant, [Princess Caroline Von Hannover] who is the eldest daughter of Prince Rainier III of Monaco, was born in 1957. Her official residence is in Monaco but she lives in the Paris area most of the time.

As a member of Prince Rainier's family, the applicant is the president of certain humanitarian or cultural foundations, such as the Princess Grace foundation or the Prince Pierre de Monaco foundation, and also represents the ruling family at events such as the Red Cross Ball or the opening of the International Circus Festival. She does not, however, perform any function within or on behalf of the State of Monaco or one of its institutions.

A. Background to the case

9. Since the early 1990s the applicant has been trying-often through the courts-in a number of European countries to prevent the publication of photos about her private life in the tabloid press.

10. The photos that were the subject of the proceedings described below were published by the publishing company Burda in the German magazines *Bunte* and *Freizeit Revue,* and by the Heinrich Bauer publishing company in the German magazine *Neue Post.* [The photos depicted Von Hannover in a variety of everyday and recreational situations, accompanied in some by her children, her one time boyfriend, French actor Vincent Lindon, and her later husband Prince Ernst August von Hannover.]

B. The proceedings in the German courts

18. On 13 August 1993 the applicant sought an injunction in the Hamburg Regional Court against any further publication by the Burda publishing company of the first series of photos on the ground that they infringed her right to protection of her personality rights. . . .

[The Hamburg Regional Court granted relief insofar as the magazines were distributed in France, citing Article 9 of the Civil Code. It denied injunctive relief against further publication in Germany because the plaintiff was a public figure; "where figures of contemporary society "*par excellence*" were concerned, the right to protection of private life stopped at their front door."

The Hamburg Court of Appeals dismissed the appeal and set aside the injunction against subsequent publication in France.

Von Hannover appealed to the Federal Court of Justice. It granted a judgment against publication of the photos of her in a restaurant where she and her boyfriend were seated in the back with the deliberate goal of being out of the public eye. The Court stated, however, that the Princess had to tolerate other photos of herself in public places, even if unrelated to public functions, because she was a figure of contemporary society "*par excellence.*"

Next came an appeal to the Federal Constitutional Court, which allowed the appeal in part, as to photos of the applicant with her children, on the ground that they violated her personality rights and her right to family protection under the Basic Law. The appeal regarding the other photos was dismissed.]

The Law

I. Alleged violation of art 8 of the convention

43. The applicant submitted that the German court decisions had infringed her right to respect for her private and family life guaranteed by Article 8 of the Convention, which is worded as follows:

> (1) Everyone has the right to respect for his private and family life, his home and his correspondence. (2) There shall be no interference by a public authority with the exercise of this right except such as is in accordance with the law and is necessary in a democratic society in the interests of national security, public safety or the economic well-being of the country, for the prevention of disorder or crime, for the protection of health or morals, or for the protection of the rights and freedoms of others.

B. The Court's Assessment

1. As regards the subject of the application

49. [T]he court considers it important to specify that the present application concerns the following photos, which were published as part of a series of articles about the applicant:

(i) the photo published in *Bunte* magazine (issue no 32 of 5 August 1993) showing the applicant on horseback. . . .

(ii) the photos published in *Bunte* magazine (issue no 34 of 19 August 1993) showing the applicant shopping on her own; with Mr Vincent Lindon in a restaurant; alone on a bicycle; and with her bodyguard at a market. . . .

(iii) the photos published in *Bunte* magazine (issue no 10 of 27 February 1997) showing the applicant on a skiing holiday in Austria. . . .

(iv) the photos published in *Bunte* magazine (issue no 12 of 13 March 1997) showing the applicant with Prince Ernst August von Hannover or alone leaving her Parisian residence. . . .

(v) the photos published in *Bunte* magazine (issue no 16 of 10 April 1997 showing the applicant playing tennis with Prince Ernst August von Hannover or both of them putting their bicycles down. . . .

(vi) the photos published in *Neue Post* magazine (issue no 35/97) showing the applicant tripping over an obstacle at the Monte Carlo Beach Club. . . .

53. In the present case there is no doubt that the publication by various German magazines of photos of the applicant in her daily life either on her own or with other people falls within the scope of her private life.

3. Compliance with Art. 8

a. The domestic courts' position

54. The Court notes that, in its landmark judgment of 15 December 1999 [[1999] 10 BHRC 131], the Federal Constitutional Court interpreted §§ 22 and 23 of the Copyright (Arts Domain) Act by balancing the requirements of the freedom of the press against those of the protection of private life, that is, the public interest in being informed against the legitimate interests of the applicant. . . . It considered that the applicant, as a figure of contemporary society *'par excellence'*, enjoyed the protection of her private life even outside her home but only if she was in a secluded place out of the public eye to which persons concerned retire with the objectively recognisable aim of being alone and where, confident of being alone, they behave in a manner in which they would not behave in public.' . . . The court attached decisive weight to the freedom of the press, even the entertainment press, and to the public interest in knowing how the applicant behaved outside her representative functions.

b. The general principles governing the protection of private life and the freedom of expression

57. The Court reiterates that although the object of Art. 8 is essentially that of protecting the individual against arbitrary interference by the public authorities, it does not merely compel the State to abstain from such interference: in addition to this primarily negative undertaking, there may be positive obligations inherent in an effective respect for private or family life. These obligations may involve the adoption of measures designed to

secure respect for private life even in the sphere of the relations of individuals between themselves. . . .

The boundary between the State's positive and negative obligations under this provision does not lend itself to precise definition. The applicable principles are, none the less, similar. In both contexts regard must be had to the fair balance that has to be struck between the competing interests of the individual and of the community as a whole; and in both contexts the State enjoys a certain margin of appreciation. . . .

58. That protection of private life has to be balanced against the freedom of expression guaranteed by Article 10 of the Convention. In that context the Court reiterates that the freedom of expression constitutes one of the essential foundations of a democratic society. Subject to paragraph 2 of Article 10, it is applicable not only to 'information' or 'ideas' that are favourably received or regarded as inoffensive or as a matter of indifference, but also to those that offend, shock or disturb. Such are the demands of that pluralism, tolerance and broadmindedness without which there is no 'democratic society.'. . .

In that connection the press plays an essential role in a democratic society. Although it must not overstep certain bounds, in particular in respect of the reputation and rights of others, its duty is nevertheless to impart—in a manner consistent with its obligations and responsibilities—information and ideas on all matters of public interest. . .

59. Although freedom of expression also extends to the publication of photos, this is an area in which the protection of the rights and reputation of others takes on particular importance. The present case does not concern the dissemination of 'ideas', but of images containing very personal or even intimate 'information' about an individual. Furthermore, photos appearing in the tabloid press are often taken in a climate of continual harassment which induces in the person concerned a very strong sense of intrusion into their private life or even of persecution.

60. In the cases in which the court has had to balance the protection of private life against the freedom of expression it has always stressed the contribution made by photos or articles in the press to a debate of general interest. . . .

c. Application of these general principles by the Court

61. The Court notes at the outset that in the present case the photos of the applicant in the various German magazines show

her in scenes from her daily life, thus engaged in activities of a purely private nature such as engaging in sport, out walking, leaving a restaurant or on holiday. . . .

63. The Court considers that a fundamental distinction needs to be made between reporting facts – even controversial ones – capable of contributing to a debate in a democratic society relating to politicians in the exercise of their functions, for example, and reporting details of the private life of an individual who, moreover, as in this case, does not exercise official functions. While in the former case the press exercises its vital role of 'watchdog' in a democracy by contributing to 'impart[ing] information and ideas on matters of public interest' . . . it does not do so in the latter case.

65. As in other similar cases it has examined, the Court considers that the publication of the photos and articles in question, the sole purpose of which was to satisfy the curiosity of a particular readership regarding the details of the applicant's private life, cannot be deemed to contribute to any debate of general interest to society despite the applicant being known to the public. . . .

66. In these conditions freedom of expression calls for a narrower interpretation. . . .

68. The Court finds another point to be of importance: even though, strictly speaking, the present application concerns only the publication of the photos and articles by various German magazines, the context in which these photos were taken – without the applicant's knowledge or consent – and the harassment endured by many public figures in their daily lives cannot be fully disregarded. . . .

69. The Court reiterates the fundamental importance of protecting private life from the point of view of the development of every human being's personality. That protection – as stated above – extends beyond the private family circle and also includes a social dimension. The court considers that anyone, even if they are known to the general public, must be able to enjoy a 'legitimate expectation' of protection of and respect for their private life. . . .

70. Furthermore, increased vigilance in protecting private life is necessary to contend with new communication technologies which make it possible to store and reproduce personal data. . . . This also applies to the systematic taking of specific photos and their dissemination to a broad section of the public.

71. Lastly, the Court reiterates that the Convention is intended to guarantee not rights that are theoretical or illusory but rights that are practical and effective.

72. The Court finds it hard to agree with the domestic courts' interpretation of §23(1) of the Copyright (Arts Domain) Act, which consists in describing a person as such as a figure of contemporary society '*par excellence*.' Since that definition affords the person very limited protection of their private life or the right to control the use of their image, it could conceivably be appropriate for politicians exercising official functions. However, it cannot be justified for a 'private' individual, such as the applicant, in whom the interest of the general public and the press is based solely on her membership of a reigning family whereas she herself does not exercise any official functions.

74. The Court therefore considers that the criteria on which the domestic courts based their decisions were not sufficient to protect the applicant's private life effectively. . . .

d. Conclusion

76. As the Court has stated above, it considers that the decisive factor in balancing the protection of private life against freedom of expression should lie in the contribution that the published photos and articles make to a debate of general interest. It is clear in the instant case that they made no such contribution since the applicant exercises no official function and the photos and articles related exclusively to details of her private life.

77. Furthermore, the Court considers that the public does not have a legitimate interest in knowing where the applicant is and how she behaves generally in her private life even if she appears in places that cannot always be described as secluded and despite the fact that she is well known to the public.

Even if such a public interest exists, as does a commercial interest of the magazines in publishing these photos and these articles, in the instant case those interests must, in the Court's view, yield to the applicant's right to the effective protection of her private life.

78. Lastly, in the Court's opinion the criteria established by the domestic courts were not sufficient to ensure the effective protection of the applicant's private life and she should, in the circumstances of the case, have had a 'legitimate expectation' of protection of her private life.

79. Having regard to all the foregoing factors, and despite the margin of appreciation afforded to the state in this area, the court considers that the German courts did not strike a fair balance between the competing interests.

FOR THESE REASONS, THE COURT UNANIMOUSLY

Holds that there has been a violation of art 8 of the Convention. . . .

Notes

1. The ECHR describes the judgment of the German Constitutional Court as a "landmark" decision. And yet, groundbreaking though it was, the German court did not go far enough in protecting Von Hannover's privacy. Do you agree with the court's more restrictive definition of public figures?

2. Judge Cabral Barreto concurred in the opinion but disagreed somewhat with the reasoning of the majority. He concluded that regardless of the fact that the appellant was not performing official functions, she was a public figure and the public does have a right to be informed about her life. In his view, the balancing test between the right to privacy and freedom of expression should depend upon whether a public figure has a "legitimate expectation" of privacy from the media. Judge Barreto believed that Von Hannover could not have a legitimate expectation of privacy at the Monte Carlo beach club or while shopping, because these were places frequented by the general public and clearly visible from neighboring buildings. Thus, the photos did not intrude upon her right to privacy, regardless of the fact that they were taken secretly from long distances away. However, pictures taken in places and under circumstances suggesting the expectation of privacy (such as playing tennis or horseback riding) did in fact violate Von Hannover's Article 8 rights.

With whom do you agree?

3. Can Princess Caroline enforce the ECHR decision in her favor? The decision has only such force as Germany opts to give it. However, if Germany gives it no effect, Germany is subject to sanctions.

4. One commentator critiques the Court's reasoning as follows:

> While the Court arguably made the correct determination in the case before it, its reasoning is not fully convincing because it oscillates between two yardsticks: a substantive and a personal one. On the one hand, the judges look to the contents of the information disseminated. On the other hand, they draw a distinction between "politicians exercising official functions" and "private individuals." The latter differentiation may suffice in such cases as this. However, this distinction cannot serve as a general rule because it fails to address (a) the case of nonpoliticians who are nonetheless persons of social or economic influence, or the case of well-known people who seek publicity in the interests of a political or social cause, and (b) persons who choose to make their private lives public by virtue of political or personal objectives. An example of the first instance is that of a high clergyman arguing for criminalizing abortion. The public could have a legitimate interest in knowing that, in his past, this person wanted a girlfriend to have an abortion. Examples of the second type would be politicians featuring their families in election campaigns or celebrities using their fame in support of a good cause, such as a foundation for abused children. Surely, in all these situations, the public would be entitled to know, for example, whether such persons beat their own children and, hence, to receive information about their private lives.

Beate Rudolph, *Council of Europe: Von Hannover v. Germany*, 4 INT'L J. CONST. L. 533, 537 (2006).

5. The Court suggests that it would attach a higher value to freedom of expression in relation to the freedom of privacy in cases where the information relates to matters of legitimate public concern. Indeed, the Court has repeatedly held that the limits of freedom of the press are wider with respect to politicians. See, e.g., *Oberschlick v. Austria* (No. 2) (1998) 25 EHRR 357; *Nilsen and Johnsen v. Norway*, (2000) 30 EHRR 878 [1999], ECHR 23118/93; and *Krone Verlag GmbH & Co. KG v. Austria*, (2003) 36 EHRR 57. In one recent case, it even applied the same analysis to a politician's spouse, *Karhuvaara and Iltalehti v. Finland*, [2004] ECHR 53678/00. In a case decided shortly before *Von Hannover*, *Editions Plon v. France*, (2006) 42 EHRR 36, [2004] ECHR 58148/00 the court upheld the publication of confidential medical information about late French President Francois Mitterand

because the French public had a legitimate interest in knowing whether a former president had lied about his health. Is this similar to the publication of plaintiff's drug addiction in *Campbell*? How are the cases distinguishable?

Chapter 13

DEFAMATION

The law of defamation protects one's reputation. This is done largely through damages. Although American defamation law descends directly from that of England, U.S. law now diverges in significant ways. This Chapter focuses on that divergence, and then turns briefly to some important features of defamation in civil law systems.

As the following historical excerpt reveals, civil and common law approaches to defamation share common roots. Protection of one's reputation from false statements is a value reflected in many legal systems throughout the world. Early laws redressing defamation were harsh, to say the least. The following selection sheds light on the history of this tort.

A. HISTORY

Van Vechten Veeder

The History and Theory of the Law of Defamation

3 Colum. L. Rev. 546, 548-51 (1903).

The beginnings of the law of defamation among the Germanic people take us back to the first stages in the development of organized society. The blood feud had supplanted indiscriminate vengeance, but the substitution of the *wer*, or money payment, as compensation for injury, was not very old when the early *Leges Barbarorum* were compiled. The process is very clearly marked in the case of defamation. . . . If one calls a man "wolf" or "hare" he must pay three shillings; for a false imputation of unchastity against a woman the penalty is forty-five shillings. By the terms of the Norman Costumal, if one falsely calls another "thief" or "manslayer" he must pay damages, and, holding his nose with his fingers, must publicly confess himself a liar.[3] It is a mistaken idea, therefore, to suppose that the primitive Teuton could feel only blows, and treated hard words of no account. . . .

More than a thousand years ago King Alfred provided that the slanderer should have his tongue cut out, unless he could redeem it with the price of his head. . . . If the defendant had beaten the plaintiff, this was done to the plaintiff's damage to the amount of so many shillings, and to his dishonor . . . to the amount of so many shillings more.

Actions for defamation were common in the seigniorial courts in the thirteenth and fourteenth centuries. Many would doubtless resort to the duel, but for the mass of humble folk these courts probably did substantial justice. . . .

Meanwhile the Church punished defamation as a sin. Throughout Europe in the Middle Ages a great government existed, independent of the separate states; the temporal government was local, but there was a spiritual jurisdiction that was universal. . . . The demarcation of the real province of this ecclesiastical jurisdiction was a difficult task. . . . But its broadest claim was the correction of the sinner for his soul's health. Under this head, along with the whole province of sexual morality, usury and perjury came defamation. Contumelious words were among the various matters which had been embraced in Roman law under the title *"injuria." "Injuria,"* in its legal acceptation, meant insult; but it was more comprehensive than the modern significance of the word. . . . Reproachful language which lessened one's good fame was . . . an injury; and this class of injuries grew in ecclesiastical law into the distinct title "diffimation.". . . The usual ecclesiastical penance for the offence was an acknowledgment of the baselessness of the imputation, in the vestry room in the presence of the clergymen and church wardens of the parish, and an apology to the person defamed.

---

[3]. . . [A]s these penalties were regarded as compensation to the wronged individual, in exchange for his older right of private vengeance, there is a tendency to make the penalty correspond to the degree of irritation which the wrong would naturally excite. Thus in early Icelandic law, the man accused of cowardice had the right of slaying his accuser. . . .

Notes

1. In England a statute was passed in 1275 for the benefit of the aristocracy. Called the *De Scandalis Magnatum,* the statute made it a crime to defame the "great men of the realm." The statute was directed at political scandal and administered by the infamous Star Chamber. Eventually all defamation cases were heard in the Star Chamber. By the time of Henry VII, the Chamber's authority was practically unlimited; it followed no rules of evidence and appointed and heard only its own counsel. Eventually, as the power of the printed word became apparent, its focus was printing and writing and libel became identified with treason and sedition. Ultimately, the Star Chamber's jurisdiction passed to the common law courts, and the Star Chamber was abolished.

2. The lengthy traditions of different legal systems, their differing purposes and authority, and their interpretations and indeed, perversions, of earlier law in the development of their own doctrine all contributed to make the common law of defamation in England complicated and convoluted. Much of this confusion passed to the common law as applied in the United States.

B. COMPARISON OF ENGLISH AND AMERICAN LAW

Several features of English law are important for purposes of comparison with American common law. At common law, defamation was a strict liability tort and it remains so in Britain. Thus, in the famous *Cassidy v. Daily Mirror Newspapers, Ltd.*, [1929] 2 K.B. 331, 69 A.L.R. 720, the Court upheld a wife's action for damages when the newspaper published a picture of her husband with another woman and described them as engaged. The newspaper apparently had no reason to know the man was married, but the court accepted the wife's argument that the innuendo of the caption was that she was not lawfully married to the man and thus was a person of bad morals. It was irrelevant that the newspaper had no intent to make any such statement about the plaintiff. Other features that made defamation law extraordinarily favorable for plaintiffs included the presumption of the falsity of the defamatory statement and the availability of presumed damages in certain types of cases.

This was the law in the United States until the 1960's, when the U.S. Supreme Court "constitutionalized" the tort in *New York Times Co. v. Sullivan*, 376 U.S. 254, 84 S.Ct. 710, 11 L.Ed.2d 686 (1964). Prior to that time, U.S. and English law relied on truth as a defense and absolute and qualified privileges that protected certain narrow categories of speech. After *New York Times*, public officials alleging defamation were required to prove "actual malice" by clear and convincing evidence, thus converting the tort into one requiring a high level of intent and culpability with regard to the truth or falsity of the speech. This process of constitutionalization expanded through a series of cases to include public figures and many private individuals, thus making it very difficult for a plaintiff suing in the United States to establish liability. British law did not follow suit. The importance of this divergence between English common law and defamation law as applied in the United States cannot be overstated. It has made England a "libel capital" and led some U.S. courts to refuse to enforce English defamation judgments. *See e.g., Bachchan v. India Abroad Publications, Inc.*, 154 Misc. 228, 585 N.Y.S.2d 661 (Sup. Ct. 1992); *Matusevitch v. Telnikoff*, 877 F.Supp. 1 (D.D.C. 1995).

C. THE *REYNOLDS* PRIVILEGE

Although the prima facie case for defamation in Britain remains heavily pro-plaintiff, there have been changes that provide greater protection for free speech. England recently adopted a new qualified privilege which provides a fascinating contrast with the approach followed in the U.S.

REYNOLDS v. TIMES NEWSPAPERS LTD.

[2001] 2 A.C. 127 (H.L.)(appeal taken from N.Ir.)(U.K.)

[An article about Mr. Reynolds' resignation as Taoiseach (prime minister) of Ireland and leader of the Fianna Fail party was entitled "Goodbye gombeen man" and subtitled, "Why a fib too far proved fatal for the political career of Ireland's peacemaker and Mr. Fixit." Mr. Reynolds pleaded that the innuendo of the statement was that he had deliberately and dishonestly misled the Irish Parliament and his coalition cabinet colleagues by withholding vital information and lying to them about when the information had come into his possession. Among the other issues in the case, the Times argued for a qualified privilege for political speech, which the trial judge rejected. Eventually, the issue was presented to the House of Lords, which recognized a new privilege of comment in the public interest that extended beyond the fair comment privilege and included factual inaccuracies. Lord Nicholls stated:]

As highlighted by the Court of Appeal judgment in the present case, the common law solution is for the court to have regard to all the circumstances when deciding whether the publication of particular material was privileged because of its value to the public. Its value to the public depends upon its quality as well as its subject matter. . . . As observed by the Court of Appeal, this principle can be applied appropriately to the particular circumstances of individual cases in their infinite variety. It can be applied appropriately to all information published by a newspaper, whatever its source or origin.

Hand in hand with this advantage goes the disadvantage of an element of unpredictability and uncertainty. The outcome of a court decision, it was suggested, cannot always be predicted with certainty when the newspaper is deciding whether to publish a story. To an extent this is a valid criticism. . . . However, the extent of this uncertainty should not be exaggerated. With the enunciation of some guidelines by the court, any practical problems should be manageable. . . .

My conclusion is that the established common law approach to misstatements of fact remains essentially sound. The common law should not develop 'political information' as a new 'subject-matter' category of qualified privilege, whereby the publication of all such information would attract qualified privilege, whatever the circumstances. That would not provide adequate protection for reputation. Moreover, it would be unsound in principle to distinguish political discussion from discussion of other matters of serious public concern. The elasticity of the common law principle enables interference with freedom of speech to be confined to what is necessary in the circumstances of the case. This elasticity enables the court to give appropriate weight, in today's conditions, to the importance of freedom of expression by the media on all matters of public concern.

Depending on the circumstances, the matters to be taken into account include the following. The comments are illustrative only.

> 1) The seriousness of the allegation. The more serious the charge, the more the public is misinformed and the individual harmed, if the allegation is not true.
> 2) The nature of the information, and the extent to which the subject- matter is a matter of public concern.
> 3) The source of the information. Some informants have no direct knowledge of the events. Some have their own axes to grind, or are being paid for their stories.
> 4) The steps taken to verify the information.
> 5) The status of the information. The allegation may have already been the subject of an investigation which commands respect.
> 6) The urgency of the matter. News is often a perishable commodity.
> 7) Whether comment was sought from the plaintiff. He may have information others do not possess or have not disclosed. An approach to the plaintiff will not always be necessary.
> 8) Whether the article contained the gist of the plaintiff's side of the story.
> 9) The tone of the article. A newspaper can raise queries or call for an investigation. It need not adopt allegations as statements of fact.
> 10) The circumstances of the publication, including the timing.

. . . The press discharges vital functions as a bloodhound as well as a watchdog. The court should be slow to conclude that a publication was not in the public interest and, therefore, the public had no right to know, especially when the information is in the field of political discussion. Any lingering doubts should be resolved in favour of publication. . . .

[Applying the above criteria, the House of Lords upheld the Court of Appeal ruling, finding that although the subject matter was of undoubtedly of public concern, the allegations, "presented as statements of fact but shorn of Mr. Reynolds' explanation," were not information the public had the right to know, and would not be protected by the privilege.]

Guy Vassall-Adams, Barrister at Law

A Resounding Victory for Newspapers

Times Online, October 11, 2006

www.timesonline.CO.UK/td/comment/article668356.ece

[In *Reynolds*], Lord Nicholls developed the common law defence of qualified privilege in libel cases to establish a public interest defence for newspaper articles that were the product of responsible journalism. The aim was to strike a better balance between the protection of reputation and freedom of expression, affording greater protection to free speech in cases where a newspaper or broadcaster was unable or unwilling to prove the truth of a defamatory allegation. . . .

Although there is relatively little evidence about the effect of the *Reynolds* judgment, what evidence does exist suggests it had a beneficial effect on free speech, enabling journalists to anticipate how to protect themselves when making defamatory allegations whose truth they might be unable to prove and deterring claimants from bringing defamation claims in respect of allegations framed in suitably responsible terms.

When it came to the crunch and a case did actually reach trial, however, newspapers were dismayed and bewildered to find that *Reynolds* was applied in such a way that they almost always lost the case. It was not enough that the article, taken as a whole, was a piece of responsible journalism on a matter of public interest. Instead, Lord Nicholls' ten relevant factors were elevated into a judicial obstacle course, where every single defamatory allegation was treated in isolation and tested against the ten-point checklist, with any adverse finding potentially fatal to the defense. As a result, *Reynolds* only succeeded at trial on two occasions.

The *Jameel* case [excerpt follows below] graphically illustrates the problem [with *Reynolds*.] Mr. Jameel and a company of his sued the Wall Street Journal Europe after it published an article asserting that his company was one of a number of named Saudi Arabian companies being secretly monitored by SAMA, the Saudi Arabian central bank, at the request of the American Government, to establish whether their bank accounts were being used, wittingly or unwittingly, as sources of terrorist funding. Five months after 9/11, it was hard to think of a topic of greater public interest for the readership of a serious international newspaper. But the defence failed in both the High Court and the Court of Appeal, in the latter on the very narrow basis that the paper had failed to wait to get a comment from Mr. Jameel before publication.

JAMEEL & OTHERS v. WALL STREET JOURNAL EUROPE SPRL

[2006] UKHL 44, [2007] 1 A.C. 359
(appeal taken from Eng.)(U.K.)

LORD HOFFMAN:

[40] The article was written by Mr. James Dorsey, the paper's special correspondent in Riyadh and checked by Mr. Glenn Simpson, a journalist based in Washington who was concentrating almost exclusively on terrorist funding and had daily contact with sources at the United States Treasury. It was published in the New York edition but the claimants have brought their proceedings in this country against the publishers of the European edition, the Wall Street Journal Europe, in which it also appeared. . . .

[42] The jury found that the article was defamatory of both claimants. The newspaper did not attempt to justify any defamatory meaning and there is no appeal against the finding that it was defamatory. The absence of a plea of justification is not surprising. In the nature of things, the existence of covert surveillance by the highly secretive Saudi authorities would be impossible to prove by evidence in open court. That does not necessarily mean that it did not happen. Nor, on the other hand, does it follow that even if it did happen, the Jameel group had any connection with terrorism. The U.S. intelligence agencies sometimes get things badly wrong.

[43] The newspaper's principal defence was based on *Reynolds v. Times Newspapers Ltd.*, [2001] 2 AC 127. It is called in the trade 'Reynolds privilege', but the use of the term privilege, although historically accurate, may be misleading. A defence of privilege in the usual sense is available when the defamatory statement was published on a privileged occasion and can be defeated only by showing that the privilege was abused. . . .

[46] Although [in *Reynolds*] Lord Nicholls uses the word "privilege," it is clearly not being used in the old sense. It is the material which is privileged, not the occasion on which it is

published. There is no question of the privilege being defeated by proof of malice because the propriety of the conduct of the defendant is built into the conditions under which the material is privileged. The burden is upon the defendant to prove that those conditions are satisfied. It might more appropriately be called the Reynolds public interest defence rather than privilege. . . .

[56] In Reynolds . . . Lord Nicholls gave his well-known non-exhaustive list of ten matters which should in suitable cases be taken into account. They are not tests which the publication has to pass. In the hands of a judge hostile to the spirit of Reynolds, they can become ten hurdles at any of which the defence may fail. . . . But that, in my opinion, is not what Lord Nicholls meant . . . The standard of conduct required of the newspaper must be applied in a practical and flexible manner. It must have regard to practical realities.

APPLYING *REYNOLDS*

[48] . . . The first question is whether the subject matter of the article was a matter of public interest. In answering this question, I think that one should consider the article as a whole and not isolate the defamatory statement. . . .

[49] . . .The question of whether the material concerned a matter of public interest is decided by the judge. As has often been said, the public tends to be interested in many things which are not of the slightest public interest and the newspapers are not often the best judges of where the line should be drawn. . . . But this publication easily passes that test. The thrust of the article as a whole was to inform the public that the Saudis were co-operating with the United States Treasury in monitoring accounts. It was a serious contribution in measured tone to a subject of very considerable importance. . . .

[52] In the present case, the inclusion of the names of large and respectable Saudi businesses was an important part of the story. It showed that co-operation with the United States Treasury's requests was not confined to a few companies on the fringe of Saudi society, but extended to companies which were by any test within the heartland of the Saudi business world. . . .

[53] If the publication, including the defamatory statement, passes the public interest test, the inquiry then shifts to whether the steps taken to gather and publish the information were responsible and fair. . . .

[58] This may be divided into three topics: the steps taken to verify the story, the opportunity given to the Jameel group to comment and the propriety of publication in light of United States diplomatic policy at the time. [Lord Hoffman then reviewed the evidence in light of these factors, concluded the evidence at trial supported the defence, and that the action should be dismissed.]

Notes

1. Do you agree with the House of Lords' position that there should be no qualified privilege for political speech that can be lost only by proof of malice? Why? Is it because speech in the public interest is broader than political speech and therefore, such a qualified privilege would be too narrow? Or would a qualified privilege for political speech protect too much? Does the availability of a defamation action for someone like Reynolds help ensure that the political process is not polluted by false misstatements?

2. Lord Nicholls was confident that the factors enumerated would not generate an undue amount of uncertainty as to whether speech was privileged. Do you agree? Has the *Jameel* case clarified the use of the factors enough to reduce that uncertainty?

3. The *Reynolds* privilege is narrow, even as restored to vitality by the decision in *Jameel*. Do you think journalists will feel confident that their stories about current events pass the "public interest" test? Do you agree with the Court that members of the public would tend to view "public interest" more broadly than judges?

D. PUBLIC VERSUS PRIVATE FIGURES

Students of U.S. defamation law are aware that the *New York Times v. Sullivan* ruling was in a libel case brought by a public official, but, in the intervening years, the requirement of proof of actual malice expanded to cases brought by public figures and even by private individuals seeking presumed and punitive damages in cases of public concern. Although the Supreme Court justified the expansion to public figures with the rationale that these individuals assume the risk of false statements by injecting themselves into the public eye, and that they have access to the media to rebut falsehoods, it is not self-evident that stardom or leadership on matters of public importance ought to limit legal recourse to redress of defamation.

The United Kingdom's law places no barrier to actions by public figures.

Heather Maly

Publish at Your Own Risk or Don't Publish At All: Forum Shopping Trends in Libel Litigation Leave the First Amendment Un-Guaranteed

14 J. L.& Pol'y 883, 905-906 (2006).

The United Kingdom has notoriously plaintiff-friendly laws for defamation that attract "libel tourists" who try to take advantage of the pro-plaintiff laws. For example, film director Roman Polanski recently succeeded in a libel suit in the UK against American magazine Vanity Fair, for defamatory statements contained in the magazine. Polanski is a resident and citizen of France, and a fugitive from justice in the United States. At trial he had to testify via video because his fears of extradition prevented him from entering the UK, his chosen venue. He won a verdict of £50,000. The lawsuit arose from an article in which *Vanity Fair* recounted a story of the sexual advances Polanski allegedly made toward a woman just after the death of his wife. It is generally agreed that the story is true, but that the date of the incident was incorrectly reported. He further contests some statements he allegedly made that appeared in the article and portray him as insensitive in the wake of his wife's murder.

Polanski had no real ties to the UK, and Vanity Fair's circulation there was minimal compared with its larger American audience. If Polanski's predominant concern was vindicating his reputation, the action would have more of an impact in the US where the article was more widely read, or in France where Polanski lived. But, since the UK is the "libel capital of the Western world," it provided the more plaintiff-friendly forum. In the US, Polanski would be considered a public figure, and thus, subject to the more press protective principles first defined in New York Times and extended in Curtis Publishing. Under British law, the qualified privilege would not apply since this is not a matter of public concern and so, Vanity Fair had to establish truth to defeat the suit. This case demonstrates how the British libel laws are used to circumvent the stricter American laws.

Note

Although from the standpoint of Vanity Fair the loss of the suit based on small factual inaccuracies seems harsh, the larger question is why any privilege *ought* to be afforded for reporting about Polanski or others stars. Baroness Hale, in *Jameel*, explained the UK's position as she delineated the limits of the public interest privilege: "First, there must be a real public interest in communicating and receiving the information. That is, as we all know, very different from saying that it is interest which interests the public – the most vapid tittle-tattle about the activities of footballers' wives and girlfriends interests large sections of the public but no one could claim any real public interest in our being told about it."

E. THE IMPACT OF THE EUROPEAN CONVENTION ON HUMAN RIGHTS

1. Defamation laws in Europe

Most countries within Europe retain criminal defamation laws and they are actively used. In contrast, while criminal defamation laws exist in the U.S. in nineteen states, they are rarely applied. Usually, the sanction for violation of European laws is imprisonment or hefty fines. Although some countries, such as France, the Netherlands and Norway, require that public officials meet a higher standard of proof, in other jurisdictions no distinction is made between the public and private status of the plaintiff. Many countries, such as Spain, Austria, Greece and Turkey, retain and enforce laws that make it a crime to insult the government, public officials, the army, members of the royal family and government institutions. The European Court of Human Rights has overturned decisions from Austria, Spain and Turkey. Other countries, such as Italy, have similar provisions but rarely enforce them.

Another controversial type of defamation law makes it illegal to deny the Holocaust. While such laws would be unthinkable in the United States, many European countries have statutes that make it a criminal offense to trivialize or deny the historical facts of the Holocaust or to justify National Socialist genocide. The penalties range from fines to prison terms; in Austria, a maximum of twenty years in prison is possible. These statutes were enacted in response to public denials of the Holocaust that began immediately after World War II but gained strength in the 1970's. Some of the denials are published in journals that appear neutral and academic. The French statute was passed in 1990 following a surge in anti-Semitism and the desecration of Jewish cemeteries. It is a broad statute that outlaws all racist, anti-Semitic or xenophobic acts. Although the possibility that such laws may be abused has been considered by these countries, they retain them. As one Irish professor and human rights attorney explains:

> [H]ate speech was once mainstream speech. It was central to European culture. There were no 'hate groups' espousing racism and white superiority when it was in fact the official ideology or mainstream idea. Today's racists wear our castoffs, and we have a responsibility for what is done with those castoffs. Anti-Semitism has a similar history. The prejudice and hatred against Jews came to its apotheosis in the Holocaust but these crimes came out of centuries of prejudice built into mainstream Christianity—Catholic and Protestant."

Kevin Boyle, *Hate Speech—The United States Versus the Rest of the World*, 53 ME. L. REV. 487, 493 (2001).

The furor over publication of cartoons depicting the Prophet Mohammed in a Danish newspaper, in defiance of religious objection to any depiction of the Prophet, brought Europe's laws relating to defamation into controversy. Many Muslims, knowing that hate speech and Holocaust denial are criminalized throughout Europe, found it hypocritical to defend publication of the Danish cartoons on freedom of speech grounds. What is your evaluation?

2. International Treaties and Conventions

Even if countries lack formal protection of free speech as part of their own defamation law, if they are signatories to the European Convention on Human Rights, they have felt the influence of the European Commission of Human Rights and the European Court of Human Rights. These international bodies have developed a jurisprudence that is strongly protective of free speech.

CONVENTION FOR THE PROTECTION OF HUMAN RIGHTS AND FUNDAMENTAL FREEDOMS

213 U.N.T.S., Nov. 4, 1950

ARTICLE 10

(1) Everyone has the right to freedom of expression. The right shall include freedom to hold opinions and to receive and impart information and ideas without interference by public authority and regardless of frontiers. . . .

(2) The exercise of these freedoms, since it carries with it duties and responsibilities, may be subject to such formalities, conditions, restrictions or penalties as are prescribed by law and are necessary in a democratic society, in the interests of national security, territorial integrity or public safety, for the prevention of disorder or crime, for the protection of health or morals, for the protection of the reputation or rights of others, for preventing the disclosure of information received in confidence, or for maintaining the authority and impartiality of the judiciary.

Note

The Court's analysis of alleged violations of the freedom of expression guaranteed by Article 10 generally consists of three steps. It asks (1) whether the "interference" by a public authority was "prescribed by law;" (2) if the interference has an aim that is legitimate under Article 10, paragraph 2, and (3) whether the interference was "necessary in a democratic society." Cases tend to be won or lost based on the third factor. The Court scrutinizes the nature of the interference with freedom of expression and its relationship to the aims sought to be achieved, but gives a "margin of appreciation" to the national courts whose prior resolution of the cases is being challenged.

LINGENS v. AUSTRIA

European Court of Human Rights
(1986) 8 E.H.R.R. 407, [1986] ECHR 9815/82

[The applicant, Mr. Lingens, was the publisher of a magazine in Vienna which printed two articles criticizing the Austrian Chancellor and accusing him of protecting former members of the Nazi SS for political reasons and of promoting their participation in Austrian politics. The Chancellor, Kreisky, brought private prosecutions for violation of Article 111 of the Austrian Criminal Code, which provides:

> 1. Anyone who in such a way that it may be perceived by a third person accuses another of possessing a contemptible character or attitude or of behavior contrary to honor or morality and of such a nature as to make him contemptible or otherwise lower him in public esteem shall be liable to imprisonment not exceeding six months or a fine.
>
> 2. Anyone who commits this offence in a printed document, by broadcasting or otherwise in such a way as to make the defamation accessible to a broad section of the public shall be liable to imprisonment not exceeding one year or a fine.
>
> 3. The person making the statement shall not be punished if it is proved to be true. As regards the offence defined in paragraph 1, he shall also not be liable if circumstances are established which gave him sufficient reason to assume that the statement was true.

The Vienna Regional Court found Lingens guilty of defamation for having used the expressions "basest opportunism," "immoral," and "undignified." The court considered these comments directly or indirectly aimed at Mr. Kreisky personally. The court held that Lingens had not provided evidence to justify his expressions nor proven truth. Lingens was convicted of criminal defamation, fined, and issues of his magazine were confiscated. He was also ordered to publish the text of the judgment against him in the magazine. An appeal was taken to the European Commission on Human Rights, which ruled the conviction violated Article 10, and the matter then was presented to the European Court of Human Rights.]

2. . . . Mr. Lingens claimed that the impugned court decisions infringed his freedom of expression to a degree incompatible with the fundamental principles of a democratic society. . . . In the Government's submission, on the other hand, the disputed penalty was necessary in order to protect Mr. Kreisky's reputation. . . .

35. . . . It was not disputed that there was "interference by public authority" with the exercise of the applicant's freedom of

expression. . . . Such interference contravenes the Convention if it does not satisfy the requirements of paragraph 2 of Article 10. It therefore falls to be determined whether the interference was "prescribed by law," had an aim or aims that is or are legitimate under Article 10(2) and was "necessary in a democratic society" for the aforesaid aim or aims.

36. As regards the first two points, the Court agrees with the Commission and the Government that the conviction in question was "indisputably based on Article 111 of the Austrian Criminal Code"; it was moreover designed to protect "the reputation or rights of others" and there is no reason to suppose that it had any other purpose. . . . The conviction was accordingly "prescribed by law" and had a legitimate aim under Article 10(2). . . .

37. In their respective submissions the Commission, the Government and the applicant concentrated on the question whether the interference was "necessary in a democratic society" for achieving the above-mentioned aim. . . .

39. The adjective "necessary," within the meaning of Article 10(2), implies the existence of a "pressing social need." The Contracting States have a certain margin of appreciation in assessing whether such a need exists, but it goes hand in hand with a European supervision, embracing both the legislation and the decisions applying it, even those given by an independent court. The Court is therefore empowered to give the final ruling on whether a "restriction" or a "penalty" is reconcilable with freedom of expression as protected by Article 10. . . .

41. In this connection, the Court has to recall that freedom of expression, as secured in paragraph 1 of Article 10, constitutes one of the essential foundations of a democratic society and one of the basic conditions for its progress and for each individual's self-fulfillment. Subject to paragraph 2, it is applicable not only to "information" or "ideas" that are favourably received or regarded as inoffensive or as a matter of indifference, but also to those that offend, shock or disturb. Such are the demands of that pluralism, tolerance and broadmindedness without which there is no "democratic society."

These principles are of particular importance as far as the press is concerned. Whilst the press must not overstep the bounds set, *inter alia*, for the "protection of the reputation of others," it is nevertheless incumbent on it to impart information and ideas on political issues just as on those in other areas of public interest.

Not only does the press have the task of imparting such information and ideas: the public also has a right to receive them. . . .

42. Freedom of the press furthermore affords the public one of the best means of discovering and forming an opinion of the ideas and attitudes of political leaders. More generally, freedom of political debate is at the very core of the concept of a democratic society which prevails throughout the Convention.

The limits of acceptable criticism are accordingly wider as regards a politician as such than as regards a private individual. Unlike the latter, the former inevitably and knowingly lays himself open to close scrutiny of his every word and deed by both journalists and the public at large, and he must consequently display a greater degree of tolerance. No doubt Article 10(2) enables the reputation of others – that is to say, of all individuals – to be protected, and this protection extends to politicians too, even when they are not acting in their private capacity; but in such cases the requirements of such protection have to be weighed in relation to the interests of open discussion of political issues.

43. . . . The articles dealt with political issues of public interest in Austria which had given rise to many heated discussions concerning the attitude of Austrians in general - and the Chancellor in particular – to National Socialism and to the participation of former Nazis in the governance of the country. The content and tone of the articles were on the whole fairly balanced but the use of the aforementioned expressions in particular appeared likely to harm Mr Kreisky's reputation. . . .

45. . . . The defendant had submitted that the observations in question were value-judgments made by him in the exercise of his freedom of expression. . . . The Court, like the Commission, shares this view. The applicant's criticisms were in fact directed against the attitude adopted by Mr Kreisky, who was Federal Chancellor at the time. . . .

46. . . . In the Court's view, a careful distinction needs to be made between facts and value-judgments. The existence of facts can be demonstrated, whereas the truth of value-judgments is not susceptible of proof. The Court notes in this connection that the facts on which Mr Lingens founded his value-judgment were undisputed, as was also his good faith. . . .

Under paragraph 3 of Article 111 of the Criminal Code, read in conjunction with paragraph. 2, journalists in a case such as this cannot escape conviction for the matters specified in paragraph 1 unless they can prove the truth of their statements. . . .

As regards value judgments this requirement is impossible of fulfilment and it infringes freedom of opinion itself, which is a fundamental part of the right secured by Article 10 of the Convention. . . .

47. From the various foregoing considerations it appears that the interference with Mr Lingens' exercise of the freedom of expression was not "necessary in a democratic society . . . for the protection of the reputation . . . of others"; it was disproportionate to the legitimate aim pursued. There was accordingly a breach of Article 10 of the Convention. . . .

FOR THESE REASONS, THE COURT UNANIMOUSLY

1. *Holds* that there has been a breach of Article 10 of the Convention;

2. *Holds* that the Republic of Austria is to pay to the applicant 284,538.60 Schillings (two hundred and eighty-four thousand five hundred and thirty-eight Schillings sixty Groschen) as "just satisfaction."

Notes

1. While the European Court of Human Rights acknowledges that there should be wider latitude for speech about public officials, it also acknowledges that their reputations may be protected consistent with Article 10 of the Convention. The Court's balancing test does not provide very clear guidance as to when protection of a public official's reputation will trump freedom of speech. This may be a plus if you agree with some critics of *New York Times v. Sullivan* that the actual malice standard of the case is too protective of false speech. On the other hand, the actual malice standard does provide a fairly clear rule that has proven to be effective at protecting the values the European Court of Human Rights discusses. What is your evaluation of the two approaches? Are they equally protective?

2. Another international standard worth knowing about is the United Nations International Covenant on Civil and Political

Rights, Mar. 23, 1976, 1988 U.S.T. LEXIS 202, 999 U.N.T.S. 171. It has been ratified and binds over 140 countries. Article 19, sections (1) and (2) set out principles protecting the freedom to hold opinions and the right to freedom of expression. Section (3) recognizes these rights are subject to restriction for respect of the rights or reputations of others, or for protection of national security, public order, or public health or morals. Article 20 prohibits advocacy of "national, racial or religious hatred that constitutes incitement to discrimination, hostility or violence." An independent committee established under the Covenant monitors how states implement commitments under the treaty. The United States ratified the treaty in 1992, some 23 years after it came into force, and made a reservation providing that Article 20 would not require any action on its part. The U.S. viewed Article 20 as violative of the First Amendment. What do you think?

3. The ECHR, though not bound by *stare decisis*, has been mindful that the influence and credibility of its decisions is increased by continuity and internal consistency. Although at first the court was reluctant to upset the expectations of member states, it has found a violation of Article 10 in 75% of the cases that have come before it. The ECHR has developed a hierarchy of protected expression that takes into account the status of the individual injured and the nature of the speech. Political speech and criticism is given broad protection, while less protection is given to speech about public servants such as judges. Private persons' reputations merit more protection from infringement, although the court is less protective when they have involved themselves in matters of public concern. There is virtually no protection for speech in a commercial context. The court's case law thus mirrors principles of U.S. First Amendment law. See Dan Koslowski, *"For the Protection of the Reuputation or Rights of Others": The European Court of Human Rights' Interpretation of the Defamation Exception in Article 10(2)*, 11 COMM.L & POL'Y 133, 139-140 (2006).

F. COUNTRIES NOT PARTY TO THE EUROPEAN CONVENTION ON HUMAN RIGHTS

Turning now to countries outside of Europe, one finds a wide variation in the strictness of defamation laws and the protection, if any, given to speech. For example, Latin America's experience parallels that of Europe in some respects, but the law of certain countries is more harsh. In Colombia, the Supreme Court recognized a special type of strict tort liability for journalists for conveying inaccurate or libelous information. The Colombian Constitutional Court construed Article 20 of the Colombian Constitution to establish liability based on negligence for inaccurate communication of information. As in Austria's *Lingens* case, media defendants may be forced to publish the entire text of a court decision on defamation. Many of the criminal defamation laws in the Codes are not routinely enforced, though they certainly could be since they remain valid law.

The American Convention on Human Rights, like the European Convention, guarantees freedom of expression. The Organization of American States Commission on Human Rights issued a report in 1994, in a case involving an Argentine journalist who had been convicted of violating insult laws, concluding that insult laws were incompatible with freedom of expression. As a result, Argentina and several other countries repealed their insult provisions and Argentina actually adopted the *New York Times* standard. *See* Jairo E. Lanao, *Legal Challenges to Freedom of the Press in the Americas*, 56 U. MIAMI L. REV. 347 (2002).

The experiences of countries formerly within the communist bloc are a study in evolution of greater protection of free speech. Under the communist government in the Soviet Union, defamation against a Soviet authority was a criminal offense punishable by seven years imprisonment. The author of one article notes that after the end of the communist era, it was expected that the communist bloc countries would follow either Europe or the United States in protecting freedom of expression. This has not uniformly been the case. The author notes that the countries that have joined the Council of Europe and ratified the European Convention on Human Rights are considered to have more freedom of the press. Entry into the Council is by application and some countries, like Belarus, have found themselves suspended for failure to show solidarity with the political values of the Council. *See* Elena Yanchukova, *Comment, Criminal Defamation and Insult Laws: An Infringement on the Freedom of Expression in European and Post-Communist Jurisdictions*, 41 COLUM. J. TRANSNAT'L L. 861, 884 -91 (2003).

Finally, there are countries that do not share the values of freedom of the press embodied by the *Times* privilege, the *Reynolds* privilege or international accords. Singapore is one of the countries that is least protective of speech criticizing public officials. The International Herald Tribune (IHT), a paper published jointly by the New York Times and The Washington Post, is a highly-regarded international publication. About 4000 copies go to Singapore each day. After the IHT article used the term "dynastic politics" in reference to Singapore, it was ordered to pay damages of over $670,000 to Lee Kuan Yew (Senior Minister and former Prime Minister), Lee Ksien Loong (Lee Kuan Yew's son and the Deputy Prime Minister), and Goh Chok Tong (Prime Minister). The plaintiffs objected to the implication that the younger Lee's rapid rise to political leadership in Singapore may have had something to do with his father's influence. The IHT issued what one writer called "the most debasing apology in the history of American journalism", but that was not enough to head off liability. Don Kirk, *Singapore "Justice" Claims a New Victim*, NEWSDAY, August 11, 1995, at A39. Senior Minister Lee Kuan Yew subsequently described his policy as, "when you put up an idea which I know is wrong and believe profoundly to be wrong and will do us harm, I must crush it." *If You Were My Granddaughter . . .* (S.M. Lee's TV Forum with Youths), STRAITS TIMES, August 2, 1996. More recently, a Singapore bank was fined $2 million for accidentally publishing a mildly libelous statement during heated discussion of a takeover bid. Despite the fact that the mistake was corrected quickly, that there was no intent to do harm and that no harm was done, the offended parties were awarded $1 million each. The *Business Times* declined to report on the matter because one of the libeled parties objected.

G. REMEDIES

In the United States, the remedy for defamation is damages. Sometimes a plaintiff succeeds in obtaining a retraction of the defamatory statement from a newspaper or a broadcaster, but usually this is because the law protects certain media defendants by limiting damage exposure if they retract. Prior restraints in the form of injunctions of allegedly defamatory materials are highly disfavored in this area. Given the high fault standards required by the cases construing the Constitution, and the resulting constitutional constraints on presumed and punitive damages, certain defamation plaintiffs believe there is virtually no point in bringing suit. This caused some Supreme Court justices to complain that American law is insufficiently protective of reputation, to the detriment of individuals, and to the detriment of society, which is polluted by falsehoods. See, e.g., *Gertz v. Robert Welch, Inc.*, 418 U.S. 323, 370(1974)(Justice White, dissenting).

The law in other countries offers defamation plaintiffs a broader array of remedies. In England, the structure of common law monetary damages is not unlike that in the United States. However, by statute, a defendant may give the plaintiff notice of her intention to apologize. This "Offer to Make Amends" must contain a written commitment to make and publish a suitable correction and apology and to pay any compensation or costs as determined applicable. The effect of the offer depends on whether it is accepted or rejected by the recipient and on whether the person making the offer is relying on the offer as a defense or merely in mitigation of damages. See generally 28 HALSBURY'S LAWS OF ENGLAND 84-87 (Lord Hailsham of St. Marylebone ed., 4th Ed. 1997). Although imprisonment on charges of criminal libel remains possible in England, prosecutions are not common. Injunctive relief is possible if granted by the High Court, even on an interlocutory basis, although the standards for relief are high.

In China, reputation is protected under Article 38 of the Constitution and in the General Principles of Civil Law, Article 101.[4] Unlike common law systems that sometimes require proof of pecuniary loss in certain types of cases, China's law provides for emotional damages regardless of whether any economic loss is sustained.[5] A defaming party may be ordered to eliminate the influence of a defamatory statement and extend a formal apology in addition to paying damages.[6] Chinese law also gives near relatives standing to sue for the reputation of a deceased family member.[7] In the U.S., the general rule is that interest in reputation terminates upon death, so that relatives have no cause of action unless the words independently reflect upon the survivors. One interesting Chinese case involved a mother who brought suit in the 1980's to protect the reputation of her daughter, who had died in 1944. The daughter was the subject of a fictionalized novel. The mother recovered damages and the author and a newspaper were required to print apology statements for three days in succession. The court also ordered

---

[4]GENERAL PRINCIPLES OF THE CIVIL LAW (P.R.C.) (LEXIS, through Chinalawinfo)(promulgated by the Standing Comm. Nat'l People's Con., April 12, 1986, effective Jan 1, 1987.)

[5] *Id. at* Article 120.

[6]*Id.*

[7]Reply of the Supreme People's Court to the Questions in the Trial of the Cases Concerning the Right of Reputation, Fa Fa (1993) no. 15.

that the novel as written could not be published until modifications were made and that the novelist must consult with the relatives prior to publication.[8]

Defamation law in China is of much current interest because of a perception that the law is yet another means of state control over a Chinese media that is increasingly eager to demonstrate its autonomy. A recent study of defamation litigation in China reveals more nuance than has been reported.[9] Professor Benjamin Liebman's study of 223 cases led him to perceive two major groupings of plaintiffs. He noted that there were sixty two cases brought by local public officials or Party-state entities seeking to punish and control the media. There were fifty-two suits by businesses and corporations for the same purpose. However, there were fifty-seven cases brought by ordinary persons and fifty-two by famous persons or those related to them. *Id.* at 71-79. Professor Liebman finds the litigation goals to be as diverse as the plaintiffs. They include: "monetary damages, cessation of tortious activity, and an apology. Yet their goals also include stopping critical media coverage, retaliating against the media, restoring personal honor, and seeking an official decision different from one already rendered." Chinese and Western scholars link strong protection of reputation to Chinese culture and history, including a desire to avoid returning to the personal attacks that occurred during the cultural revolution. Liebman's study finds that most plaintiffs demand an apology and that it is ordered by the courts, but media often refuse to apologize and courts rarely enforce the judgment.

---

[8]Zhang Jing v. Yu Lingfeng, First Instance Court: The Intermediate People's Court of TianJin Municipality, 06/1989; Second Instance Court: The Higher People's Court of TianJin Municipality, 04/1990.

[9]Benjamin L. Liebman, *Innovation Through Intimidation: An Empirical Account of Defamation Litigation in China,* 47 HARV. INT'L. L. J. 33, 60-92 (2006).

Chapter 14

GLOBAL TORT LITIGATION: A CASE STUDY

This book has introduced you to many substantive theories that may apply on a given set of facts. In addition, you have become acquainted with numerous features that distinguish civil law systems from the common law system used in the United States: different types of courts and judicial opinions, different legislative instruments, and the absence of juries, to name only a few. Even common law systems such as England differ markedly from the U.S. system with regard to use of juries, financing of litigation, and availability of punitive damages. You have, in addition, encountered alternative ways to think about fundamental concepts like precedent or judicial independence.

One aspect we have not explored is the interplay between substance and procedure. The procedural rules, whether in the U.S. or in the courts of another country, profoundly affect one's ability to use the substantive theories we have examined here. Although a full exposition of the role of procedure in global litigation must be left to the volume of this series dealing with procedure,* your study of the substantive law will be more meaningful if you understand some basic principles.

The attributes of the U.S. civil justice system discussed in Chapter 1 – juries, the ability to hire a lawyer on a contingent fee basis, the absence of a "loser pays" system of fee shifting and higher damages awards than elsewhere in the world – are a

---

*THOMAS O. MAIN, GLOBAL ISSUES IN CIVIL PROCEDURE (2006).

powerful draw to litigants. Thus, even if a foreign litigant injured by a defective product made in the United States could sue the distributor in her own country, she may choose to come to the United States to sue if the case is worth enough. We know that this is not always true (recall that defamation plaintiffs gravitate towards England), but it is often true, particularly if the claim can be litigated together with those of similarly situated plaintiffs. Likewise, residents of the U.S. will usually pick this forum even if it would be possible to bring suit in another country. For them, the convenience and benefits of suing here are unlikely to be outweighed by a substantive advantage elsewhere.

There are certain features of U.S. substantive law that are particularly attractive to plaintiffs. For example, recall that in the products liability arena, U.S. law is still more inclusive of the potential defendants (the entire production line) than the European Community Products Directive. However, despite some substantive advantages and the favorable characteristics of the U.S. civil justice system, bringing a lawsuit and winning presents formidable procedural obstacles. This becomes clear in the following case study of a piece of litigation that has been hard-fought in the United States and is now pending in Nigeria. If you read John Le Carre's *The Constant Gardener*, or saw the movie, you are already familiar with the topic.

A. CASE STUDY BACKGROUND

1. Introduction: Clinical Trials Using Foreign Citizens

U.S. pharmaceutical companies often seek to conduct clinical trials outside of the United States. The participants in those trials must agree to participate in the research. There are both international and domestic regulatory norms that govern this research. Given that clinical trials can involve administration of placebos or less effective treatment to some participants, or that the drug under review may prove to have health risks, there are potentially serious ramifications to participation. There are a number of cases in which participants in clinical studies in other countries have sought to pursue claims arising from those clinical studies here in the United States.

What motivates U.S. companies to conduct experimentation outside of the United States? There are a number of considerations, as the following excerpt explains.

Esther Chang

Fitting a Square Peg Into a Round Hole? Imposing Informed Consent and Post-Trial Obligations on United States Sponsored Clinical Trials in Developing Countries

11 S.Cal. Interdisc. L.J., 339, 342-43 (2001-2002).

The increase in U.S.-sponsored clinical trials in developing countries is attributable to a number of factors. First, clinical trials are more effective when scientists can successfully recruit a statistically significant sample size. This task is easier to accomplish in areas with a higher prevalence of the researched disease, infection or condition. For example, the World Health Organization ("WHO") estimates that sixty-five percent of the world's HIV-infected population resides in sub-Saharan Africa. Accordingly, an increasing number of HIV/AIDS clinical trials have been conducted in Africa over the past decade. Second, testing in developing countries can be cheaper and more efficient. For example, U.S. medical standards dictate that tuberculosis ("TB") patients should be treated with prophylaxis regimens. In contrast, local standards in developing countries leave TB patients with few treatment options. Thus, overseas placebo-controlled studies of TB infections may avoid the expense of costlier baseline treatments (e.g., prophylaxis) that would otherwise be required for U.S. domestic trials. These studies may also cut down on costs by providing statistically significant outcomes in a shorter time period. Furthermore, investigators may avoid some of the pre-trial bureaucracy found in countries like the United States that substantially delay the commencement of clinical studies. Third, researching abroad may be necessary in countries that require domestic testing prior to drug approval. Fourth, a host country may actively seek out U.S. collaboration on interventions for indigenous health problems. Some countries cannot afford the standard medical treatments of wealthier nations and seek to discover cheaper, effective alternatives that can be practically initiated under their own economic and cultural circumstances.

---

2. *International Declarations, Guidelines and Conventions*

Much of the international legal structure relating to experimentation arose after the end of World War II. The Nazis had engaged in a systematic program of human experimentation that came to light during the Nuremberg trials of German medical officers. The world was horrified to learn of experiments on Jews and other prisoners and the Nuremberg Military Tribunal presented ten principles consisting of moral, ethical and legal limits on experimentation that have become known as the Code of Nuremberg (1947).*

In response to the promulgation of the Nuremberg Code and heightened awareness of the responsibility of medical personnel to make sure that these atrocities did not reoccur, the World Medical Association adopted the Declaration of Helsinki in 1964. The Declaration, which has been amended several times, is a non-binding effort at self-regulation. There is a debate among commentators about how useful the Helsinki Declaration is, and the truth is, it appears to be a mixed bag. Arguably, it relaxes standards for informed consent in some ways, but it heightens accountability by providing that the research protocols are subject to review by an independent committee, as opposed to one convened by the sponsor of the research. The independent review component was bolstered in 1982 through guidelines by the Council of the International Organization of Medical Societies and the World Health Organization. However, these guidelines are not legally binding or enforceable. See Benjamin Mason Meier, *International Protection of Persons Undergoing Medical Experimentation: Protecting the Right of Informed Consent,* 20 BERKELEY J.INT'L L. 513, 525-26 (2002).

The Council of Europe drafted a Convention on Human Rights and Biomedicine which, in 1997, became the first binding international agreement to address consent in vulnerable populations. While it severely curtailed non-therapeutic research on vulnerable populations, it contained a huge exception which allowed a physician to avoid informed consent where the subjects are incapable of giving consent and the research has the aim of benefitting the broader population with the patient's condition and involves only minimal risk for the individual concerned. Article 17(2). The Convention is comprised of broad guidelines which are effectuated through regulations of individual countries.

---

* The Code was printed in the Judgment issued by the court in the case of *United States v. Karl Brandt and Others* (147-48), in Trials of War Criminals Before the Nuremberg Military Tribunals ... vols I/II, The Medical Case, Washington DC: United States Government Printing Office 1948/49.

The United Nations and organizations within it have issued statements about human experimentation, though there is no international treaty governing it. The International Covenant on Civil and Political Rights contains the strongest statement about the need for informed consent as a fundamental principle. A continuing issue is what weight should be given to these statements, both in a litigation context and as a guide to pharmaceutical companies conducting trials. See Dawn Joyce Miller, Comment, *Research and Accountability: The Need for Uniform Regulation of International Pharmaceutical Drug Testing,* 13 PACE INT'L L. REV. 197, 206-211 (2001).

3. U.S. Regulatory Law

In Chapter 11, Products Liability, we saw that the United States, as a country, seems much more hostile to regulation than countries in Europe or elsewhere. This antipathy to government regulation is manifested not by an absence of regulation so much as a system that places much of the onus of developing standards and testing protocols on industry. With regard to the issue of testing pharmaceutical products abroad, there are several different standards. The regulations of the Food and Drug Administration (FDA) contain highly detailed rules regarding informed consent, but they do not apply outside the United States' borders unless the research is conducted or funded by the United States. The FDA states that it will accept clinical studies conduct outside the United States only if the study conforms to the ethical principles of the 1989 version of the Declaration of Helsinki or the laws and regulations of the country in which the research was conducted.*

The problem is that the countries in which the research is conducted may lack the ethical guidelines for informed consent or have guidelines that are far less strict than those for trials within the U.S. Researchers must then make their own decisions about how to discharge their ethical obligations. Some countries may fail to exert much oversight on research because they see it as a way to obtain beneficial drugs for their populations or they may feel pressure to cooperate with drug companies so as to obtain benefits. There have also been instances where researchers try to use the highest ethical standards, but are forced into less

---

*21 CFR 312.120(c)(1). and FDA Information Sheet at http://www.fda.gov/oc/ohrt/irbstoc4.html (last viewed August 24, 2007). *See also* Finnuala Kelleher, *The Pharmaceutical Industry's Responsibility for Protecting Human Subjects of Clinical Trials in Developing Nations,* 38 COLUM. J. L. & SOC. PROBS. 67, 84-85 (2004).

demanding research designs due to officials in the host country. Miller, *supra,* at 224-226.

4. The Pfizer Meningitis Study in Nigeria

The case that follows arises out of litigation against Pfizer, Inc., a huge drug manufacturer, in connection with a study of an antibiotic drug called Trovan.* The parties to the litigation disagree as to some of the facts, but it is undisputed that Pfizer brought Trovan to Nigeria in response to Nigeria's call for international aid during a meningitis epidemic in 1996. The drug had promise, in part because it could be administered as a tablet, which would make it easier to use with children than the standard method of an injection of a different drug. Because its use in children was not approved in the U.S., Pfizer offered the drug in Nigeria as part of a clinical trial. Pfizer contends that parents of children who took the drug were fully informed of the nature of the clinical trial by staff who spoke Hausa, one of Nigeria's main languages. The plaintiffs claim they were not informed that Trovan had not been approved for children. They also allege in their complaint that the study divided children into two groups and low-dosed those not receiving Trovan with Ceftriaxone, administering one-third of the recommended dosage. The plaintiffs also allege that had they been informed of the trial nature of the treatment, they could have availed themselves of treatment by another medical group, *Medicins Sans Frontieres* (Doctors Without Borders), which was in the area and was providing children with a safe and effective treatment for meningitis.

Trovan was approved in the United States in 1997 for treatment of a number of infections, but not meningitis. It was later pulled from the market because it caused liver disease. The Nigerian plaintiffs allege that the children who participated in the study suffered paralysis, deafness, and blindness.

The litigation over Trovan is still pending, as you will see, but the effects of the drug trial continue to ripple. In 2003, the residents of Kano, Nigeria boycotted a polio vaccine, believing it was part of a plot to make Africans infertile. When asked about their refusal to vaccinate their children, they cited the experience with Trovan. As a result of the refusal to vaccinate, a polio

---

*The factual basis for the lawsuit is set forth in an unpublished opinion, Abullahi v. Pfizer, Inc., 2002 WL 31082956 (S.D. N.Y. 2002).

epidemic resulted and spread to 25 polio-free countries. *See* Heidi Vogt, *Ethical Questions Raised by Pfizer Test*, SACRAMENTO BEE, Aug. 12, 2007, at D1.

B. THE SUBSTANTIVE AND PROCEDURAL HURDLES TO LITIGATING AGAINST PFIZER IN THE UNITED STATES

As a result of the episode described above, a group of plaintiffs brought a class-action lawsuit against Pfizer in the United States. That suit entailed much litigation, and, as you will see, it was eventually dismissed.

AJUDU ISMAILA ADAMU v. PFIZER, INC.

399 F. Supp.2d 495 (S.D.N.Y. 2005).

MEMORANDUM AND ORDER

PAULEY, District Judge.

Plaintiffs bring this putative class action seeking redress for injuries arising from the experimental administration of an antibiotic in Nigeria by defendant Pfizer, Inc. ("Pfizer" or "Defendant").* Plaintiffs bring their action under 28 U.S.C. § 1350, the Alien Tort Statute (the "ATS"), claiming that Pfizer violated the Nuremberg Code, the Declaration of Helsinki, the guidelines promulgated by the Council for International Organizations of Medical Services ("CIOMS"), article 7 of the International Covenant on Civil and Political Rights ("ICCPR"), Article 5 of the Universal Declaration of Human Rights and other customary international law as well as the FDA regulations. Plaintiffs also allege that Pfizer violated the Connecticut Unfair Trade Practices Act ("CUTPA") and the Connecticut Products Liability Act ("CPLA").

Defendants move to dismiss for failure to state a claim, lack of subject matter jurisdiction, and *forum non conveniens*. For the reasons discussed below, Pfizer's motion is granted. . . .

---

*This case was originally filed in 2001, and is the subject of several U.S. District Court opinions and one Second Circuit opinion. All of the litigation has centered on the same sorts of issues raised in this opinion.

II. *Claims Under the ATS*

Plaintiffs rely on the Nuremberg Code, the Declaration of Helsinki, the guidelines authored by the CIOMS, article 7 of the ICCPR, Article 5 of the Universal Declaration of Human Rights and the FDA regulations to frame their ATS claim. Pfizer moves to dismiss for failure to state a claim and lack of subject matter jurisdiction under the ATS. While this action could be dismissed solely on *forum non conveniens* grounds, this Court also considers the question of subject matter jurisdiction under the ATS for the sake of judicial efficiency.

[The court referred to and incorporated its analysis of the ATS in *Abullahi III,* 2005 WL 1870811. There, it applied *Sosa v. Alvarez-Machain, supra* Chapter 3, and found that the Abullahi plaintiffs could not state a claim under the ATS. The alleged violations of the Nuremberg Code, the Declaration of Helsinki and the Universal Declaration of Human Rights were insufficient to constitute violations of treaties or customary international law, as these are non-binding aspirational guidelines not universally adopted by the international community. The court reiterated that formal lawmaking and official actions of States are the primary source of international law, with works of scholars, or aspirational guidelines having only secondary value as evidence of an established practice. As to the claim under article 7 of the ICCPR, the court referred to the *Sosa* Court's opinion that it was not self-executing and did not create obligations enforceable in federal courts. Accordingly, jurisdiction could not be properly based on the ATS.]

III. *Claims Under the Connecticut Statutes*

Plaintiffs also bring Connecticut statutory claims under the CUTPA [Connecticut Unfair Trade Practices Act] and the CPLA [Connecticut Products Liability Act.] Pfizer moves to dismiss these claims, arguing that under Connecticut choice of law principles, this action is governed by Nigerian law – not Connecticut statutes. Here, there is no dispute that Nigerian law affords redress for Plaintiffs' claims. *See Abdullahi III,* 2005 WL 1870811, at 3-5.

Because this action originated in the District of Connecticut, this Court as "the transferee district court [is] . . . obligated to apply the state law that would have been applied if there had been no change of venue." Thus, Connecticut choice of law principles apply to this action.

Connecticut adheres to the doctrine of *lex loci delicti,* under which the "substantive rights and obligations arising out of a tort controversy are determined by the law of the place of injury." However, where strict application of *lex loci delicti* would frustrate "the legitimate expectations of the parties" or undermine "an important policy of this state," Connecticut courts refuse to apply the doctrine. . . .

Section 145 of the Restatement (Second) of Conflict of Laws provides that "[t]he rights and liabilities of the parties with respect to an issue in tort are determined by the local law of the state which, with respect to that issue, has the most significant relationship to the occurrence and the parties under the principles stated in § 6." Restatement (Second), Conflict of Laws § 145(1). Section 6, in turn, provides:

> (1) A court, subject to constitutional restrictions, will follow a statutory directive of its own state on choice of law.
> (2) When there is no such directive, the factors relevant to the choice of the applicable rule of law include:
> (a) the needs of the interstate and international systems,
> (b) the relevant policies of the forum,
> (c) the relevant policies of other interested states and the relative interests of those states in the determination of the particular issue,
> (d) the protection of justified expectations,
> (e) the basic policies underlying the particular field of law,
> (f) certainty, predictability and uniformity of result, and
> (g) ease in the determination and application of the law to be applied.

For assistance in evaluating the "policy choices set out in §§ 145(1) and 6(2) [of the Restatement]," a court should consider § 145(2) "which establishes black-letter rules of priority to facilitate the application of the principles of § 6 to tort cases." That subsection provides:

> (2) Contacts to be taken into account in applying the principles of § 6 to determine the law applicable to an issue include:
>
> (a) the place where the injury occurred,
> (b) the place where the conduct causing the injury occurred,
> (c) the domicile, residence, nationality, place of incorporation and place of business of the parties, and

(d) the place where the relationship, if any, between the parties is centered.

These contacts are to be evaluated according to their relative importance with respect to the particular issue. Restatement (Second), Conflict of Laws § 145(2).

The alleged improper conduct is Pfizer's failure to inform the children or their parents about the potential problems with Trovan, and the administration of Trovan and low dosage of Ceftriaxone. Application of the § 145(2) factors suggests a strong case for applying Nigerian law because the Nigerian contacts to this litigation are stronger than Connecticut's. . . . First, Plaintiffs' injuries occurred in Nigeria. Second, Pfizer's alleged improper actions occurred in Nigeria. Third, Plaintiffs are Nigerian nationals and reside there; Pfizer, on the other hand, is a Delaware corporation with its headquarters in New York. Finally, Nigeria is the place where the parties' relationship is centered. Thus, factors (a), (b) and (d) point toward applying Nigerian law, while factor (c) is in equipoise.

Plaintiffs' sole basis for arguing that Connecticut law should govern is that Pfizer performed research and development with respect to Trovan and planned the Nigerian experiment in Connecticut. However, this sole contact with Connecticut is insufficient to defeat the Nigerian interest in applying its own laws. . . . Therefore, Nigerian—not Connecticut—substantive law governs, and Plaintiffs' claims under the CUTPA and the CPLA are dismissed.

IV. *Forum Non Conveniens*

"[F]orum non conveniens is a discretionary device permitting a court in rare instances to 'dismiss a claim even if the court is a permissible venue with proper jurisdiction over the claim.'" Dismissal is appropriate where "the balance of convenience tilts strongly in favor of trial in the foreign forum." First, the defendant must demonstrate the existence of an adequate alternative forum. If an adequate forum is available, the court then considers the public and private interest factors set forth in *Gulf Oil Corp. v. Gilbert,* 330 U.S. 501, 508-09, 67 S.Ct. 839, 91 L.Ed. 1055 (1947), and its progeny. Based on those factors, a court examines whether a trial in the plaintiff's chosen forum would create "oppressiveness and vexation to a defendant . . . out of all proportion to plaintiff's convenience," or whether the "chosen forum [is] inappropriate because of considerations affecting the court's own administrative and legal problems." After considering the "private interest factors" concerning the convenience of the litigants and "public interest factors" affecting the convenience of

the forum, a "court may, in the exercise of its sound discretion, dismiss the case."

A. *Adequate Alternative Forum*

[The court reaffirmed its earlier finding that Nigeria is an adequate forum. Referring to U.S. Supreme Court decisions, the court stated that if a defendant is subject to service of process and if the forum permits litigation of the disputed subject matter, the forum is deemed adequate. The absence of an identical cause of action or law that differs from U.S. law is not given substantial weight. The Abullahi plaintiffs did not dispute the existence of a cause of action for negligence with money damages in Nigeria, but instead argued the courts were not independent or impartial. They claimed the judiciary was subject to influence from a corrupt government that continues to hunt down political opponents or anyone perceived to be working against the government. They introduced U.N. and Department of State Reports stating that Nigeria's judiciary was plagued by understaffing, inefficiency and corruption, and that it remained subject to political pressure. The court reiterated its view that it is not the role of the U.S. courts to assume responsibility for supervising the judiciary of a sovereign country. It also found the allegations of corruption and bias to be too conclusory.]

B. Gilbert *Factors*

Because Nigeria provides an adequate alternative forum, this Court must weigh the *Gilbert* public and private interest factors to determine which forum "will be most convenient and will best serve the ends of justice." The *Gilbert* public interest factors include: (1) administrative difficulties associated with court congestion; (2) the unfairness of imposing jury duty on a community with no relation to the litigation; (3) the local interest in having localized controversies decided at home; and (4) avoiding problems in conflict of laws and the application of foreign law. The *Gilbert* private interest factors include (1) the ease of access to evidence; (2) the cost for witnesses to attend trial; (3) the availability of compulsory process; and (4) other factors that might shorten trial or make it less expensive.

Plaintiffs have demonstrated no meaningful ties to this district, the District of Connecticut or the United States. Instead, Plaintiffs argue that this Court should defer to their choice of forum because Pfizer performed research and development with respect to Trovan and made plans for the Nigerian experiment in Connecticut. However, such allegations do not affect Plaintiffs' ties to the state.

Because Plaintiffs assert claims under international law, any concerns regarding the difficulty in applying foreign law are not present here. Moreover, it is undeniable that Nigeria has a very strong interest in this litigation. The Trovan testing occurred in Nigeria and all the alleged victims are Nigerian. Further, Plaintiffs allege that Pfizer's experiment was made possible with the aid of several of Nigeria's own government officials. On the other hand, citizens of this district as well as the District of Connecticut share an interest in this litigation because Pfizer developed, produced and performed preliminary testing of Trovan and designed the Kano treatment protocol within the United States as part of its plan to obtain FDA approval to sell and distribute Trovan domestically. *See Carlenstolpe v. Merck & Co., Inc.,* 819 F.2d 33, 35 (2d Cir.1987) (affirming a finding that there was a strong United States public interest in a products liability action concerning a vaccine that was developed in the United States but approved for distribution in Sweden). Thus, the *Gilbert* public interest factors do not strongly support either forum over the other. . . .

With regard to the *Gilbert* private interest factors, while discovery related to Pfizer's alleged tortious conduct must occur within the United States, Plaintiffs must establish proof of causation, injury and damages. Witnesses crucial to those factual inquiries-including the local hospital personnel who communicated with the Plaintiffs during the Trovan treatment, the Nigerian government officials who approved the study, the Kano IDH Ethics Committee and other Nigerian individuals with knowledge of the relevant events-are all located in Nigeria. Thus, evidence of numerous elements essential to Plaintiffs' claims is beyond Plaintiffs' control and, therefore, not amenable to discovery in this forum.

Further, most of the documents and witnesses located in the United States are within Pfizer's control. Pfizer has stipulated that it will facilitate any Nigerian action by providing Plaintiffs with relevant records; making past or present Pfizer employees available for depositions pursuant to 28 U.S.C. § 1782; and using its "best efforts" to make past and present employees of Pfizer who would be subject to subpoena in the Southern District of New York available to testify at trial in Kano at Pfizer's cost. Thus, the balance of the *Gilbert* private interest factors clearly weighs in favor of granting Pfizer's motion to dismiss for *forum non conveniens.*

CONCLUSION

For the foregoing reasons, this Court grants Pfizer's motion to dismiss the Complaint for lack of subject matter jurisdiction under the Alien Tort Statute, Connecticut Unfair Trade Practices Act and the Connecticut Products Liability Act. Even if this Court had subject matter jurisdiction, it would dismiss the action on *forum non conveniens* grounds for the reasons stated in Part IV. This Court would condition dismissal on *forum non conveniens* grounds on the following grounds:

1. Defendant Pfizer consents to suit and acceptance of process in any suit Plaintiffs file in Nigeria on the claims that are the subject of the instant suit;

2. Defendant Pfizer waives any statute of limitations defense that may be available to it in Nigeria;

3. Defendant Pfizer makes available for discovery and for trial, at its own expense, any documents, or witnesses, including retired employees, within Pfizer's control that are needed for a fair adjudication of Plaintiffs' claims; and

4. Defendant Pfizer will not act to prevent Plaintiffs from returning to this Court if the Federal High Court in Nigeria declines to accept jurisdiction of this action, if it is filed in Nigeria within 60 days of the entry of this Order.

The Clerk of the Court is directed to mark this case closed.

SO ORDERED.

Notes

1. Currently, the Attorney General of Nigeria is suing Pfizer in Nigeria seeking $7 billion in damages; the State is suing for $2 billion dollars. Ali Ahmad, one of the plaintiffs in the U.S. class action, claims that the government of Nigeria is now taking advantage of the plaintiffs' situation to enrich itself as they will receive none of any monies these governmental entities might ultimately recover.

2. Would the court have dismissed the case on grounds of *forum non conveniens* if the plaintiff had stated a claim under Connecticut law? Under New York law? Under federal law?

3. Do you agree with the court that it is inappropriate for a U.S. court to sit in judgment on the adequacy of a foreign judicial system? How would Nigeria have reacted if the American court had found their courts too corrupt to handle the case? What if the

court viewed the litigation as too complex for the Nigerian courts? On the other hand, isn't it incumbent on the U.S. court to ensure some basic standards of fairness in adjudication? But what are those standards? Those the court cites are so general as to be almost toothless. In support of its decision, the court cited numerous instances where the U.S. courts had found other forums adequate, and some of the examples are suprising. For example, Ecuador was found adequate despite the courts' lack of financial resources, the almost complete absence of technology such as computers, congestion resulting in a case load of 1000 cases per judge, and delays so severe that at least one commercial case had been pending for twelve years. Indonesia was found adequate despite the extensive discussion and documentation of the corruption of its judiciary in newspaper articles, statements by Indonesian politicians, a survey conducted by a government reform committee, a World Bank Report and statements by the U.S. government.

4. Class certification, not dealt with here, is a huge and complicated issue in many U.S. products cases. However, it may be the only cost effective way to litigate a complex products case. Because of recent legislative action, class action litigation on tort claims can nearly always be heard in a federal forum, a result that displeases some tort lawyers. Many countries do not have procedures for collective litigation, so if plaintiffs return to their home country to sue, they have to proceed individually. Some countries may provide the plaintiffs with legal aid, but others do not, and contingent fees are normally out of the question outside of the United States. Are these practical barriers proper for a court to consider when ruling on a *forum non conveniens* motion?

5. The Restatement (Second) of Conflicts approach to the choice of law issue is the dominant approach in the United States. Are you convinced of Nigeria's interest in applying its own law to this dispute? Should factors such as political instability of a forum matter?

6. The doctrine of *forum non conveniens* is an increasingly potent reason for dismissal. Over time, *forum non conveniens* has evolved from a rigid doctrine that was rarely invoked to justify a dismissal to a fluid form that courts use more frequently. Should courts be allowed to exercise this discretion only in exceptional cases?

7. A dismissal on *forum non conveniens* grounds is a matter within the discretion of the court. Another aspect of that discretion, visible in this case, is that dismissal is conditional. Notice the four conditions at the end of the order. Should the authority to dismiss include the authority to require consent to

discovery if Nigeria has much more restrictive discovery procedures than the U.S.?

8. For the view that a *forum non conveniens* dismissal worked an injustice to the victims of the toxic gas leak from Union Carbide's plant in Bhopal in 1984, *see Bhopal Victims, Again*, INT'L HERALD TRIBUNE, Jan. 16, 1997, p. 8, col. 1. The Second Circuit dismissed that case on *forum non conveniens* grounds in *In re Union Carbide Corp Gas Plant Disaster*, 809 F.2d. 195 (2d Cir. 1987).

9. This case study has dealt with the situation in which foreign plaintiffs seek to utilize a U.S. forum to sue a U.S. company, but equally complex questions may arise when U.S. plaintiffs seek to sue a foreign defendant here. Personal jurisdiction questions, in particular, may pose significant obstacles to litigation in the United States.

C. CONCLUDING THOUGHTS

The Second Circuit's reference to the various Abdullahi opinions reveal how much litigation has occurred over the course of years, and of course, it all ends in dismissal of the action without ever reaching the merits.

As human interactions become increasingly global, it is realistic to think that the next generation of tort lawyers will encounter many of the issues we have covered in this book. Your knowledge and appreciation for other legal systems and your awareness that sometimes they approach a question from an entirely different perspective will help you navigate the issues you confront. It will no doubt also lead you to re-examine various attributes of U.S. tort law and our civil justice system, and hopefully, to assist in solving problems in an insightful and creative way.

*

Index

References are to Pages

†